Also available at all good book stores

9781785316470

9781785313929

9781785315466

9781785317576

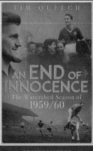

9781785317583

9781785317613

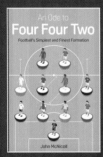

9781785318382

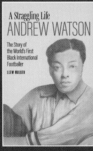

9781785318207

9781785318450

PROGRAMMES!
PROGRAMMES!

PROGRAMMES! PROGRAMMES!

FOOTBALL AND LIFE
FROM WARTIME TO LOCKDOWN

CLIFF HAGUE

First published by Pitch Publishing, 2021

Pitch Publishing
A2 Yeoman Gate
Yeoman Way
Worthing
Sussex
BN13 3QZ
www.pitchpublishing.co.uk
info@pitchpublishing.co.uk

ISBN 978 1 78531 856 6

Typesetting and origination by Pitch Publishing

Printed and bound in India by Replika Press Pvt. Ltd.

Contents

Programme Spotlights

Dedication

To the memory of my parents, Kathleen Hague (nee Sedgwick) (1917–2004) and Bertram Hague (1916–1979), who gave me a loving start in life.

Acknowledgements

THANKS ARE due to family members who, in their different ways, made this book possible. The main debt is to our son, Euan, who as a teenager bought many of the programmes that I have drawn upon. In addition he provided insightful comments on the first draft of the book, and good suggestions on how to improve it. Similarly, daughter Sophie also read and commented on the first draft, while my other two daughters, Alice and Celia, were supportive of my endeavours throughout the long period that I was preparing the book. I also owe much to my wife, Irene: firstly, for not acting on her instinct to throw out the programmes; secondly, for tolerating the boxes crammed with programmes that take up so much of the floor of the study; and, last but not least, for being such a loving and wonderful companion since our teenage years.

I also want to thank my friend the poet and author Steve Harvey for his support, and in particular for suggesting the title, *Programmes! Programmes!* Thanks are also due to Roland Láposi for his translation of a page of a programme from Hungarian into English, and explanation of what it was all about (see Chapter 12). Thanks are also due to people who gave me programmes; while early donors have faded from memory, from more recent times Ian Paterson, Robin Paice and Michael Lee deserve special mention.

The willingness of clubs and associations to allow the use of images of programmes in the book is also much appreciated. Thanks are therefore due to: Aberdeen; Accrington Stanley; AFC Wimbledon; Arsenal; Blackburn Rovers; Bolton Wanderers; Bourne Town; Brentford; Brønshøj; Cambridge City; Cambridge United; Carlisle United; Chester; Clyde; the Commission for History and Statistics of the Football Association of the Czech Republic; the Dansk Boldspil Union; Derby County; Dukla Praha; Grimsby Town; FC United of Manchester; Heart of Midlothian; Hibernian; Hull City; the Irish Football Association; ISI Photos (for J. Brett Whitesell); Manchester City; Manchester United; Millwall; Peterborough United; Preston North End; the Scottish Football Association; Sheffield Wednesday; South China Athletic Association; Sparta Rotterdam; Tottenham Hotspur; UEFA; West Ham United; and Wolverhampton Wanderers. Copyright owners for some other programmes could not be traced, or in a few cases did not respond to my several efforts to contact them; no doubt lockdowns caused by the Covid-19 pandemic played a part. I apologise to anyone who believes their rights have been infringed.

Finally, I must thank the team at Pitch Publishing who oversaw the editing and publication process, and Duncan Olner for his cover design.

'Let the man of letters who, as such, is aware of being a fool, in virtue of this self-awareness which knows it cannot fulfil itself, therefore be allowed to cultivate his passion for the written word, which helps him to keep going, to feed… on old prefaces, programmes, playbills, obituaries and posters; and to write what comes, catching at images and sentences as best he can.'

Claudio Maris, *Danube*

Chapter 1

Junk, Historical Objects and Magical Memories

SOME BOOKS inspired by football memorabilia tell the story of men undergoing a mid-life crisis, steeped in nostalgia for the 1980s. They chart the journey from naive nerd, standing on the terraces with laddish mates, and then with a succession of girlfriends who, with varying degrees of disinterest, observed the on-field displays of their temporarily beloved's heroes. Punk rock provides the mood music to the occasional brush with the National Front or opposition casuals. Marriage, divorce and contentment with a second wife follow, as our protagonist takes his seat in the stands with a nostalgic sigh for a youth now lost forever.

This book is different. Yes, it intertwines my own life as one of the now grey-haired 'baby boomer' generation with the changes within the game, but – spoiler alert – that life, while not uneventful, has not been punctuated by multiple liaisons. More than 50 years of marriage to the same woman, while cherished, is a thin basis for dramatic shifts of plot. The sum total of my wife's engagement with all things football amounts to little more than a polite but perfunctory 'Did they win?' before returning to her knitting. My response, giving a concise explication of the decisive moments behind the score – the flying header, the hapless own goal – remains a monologue: insightful certainly, yet still strangely failing to ignite interest. Lest it be thought that, as long-married pensioners, our days are spent over cups of tea in silence, we do talk to each other; just not about football. But then again, while this book is inspired by a lifelong love of football, it is not only about football. It is about the changing times through which I, my generation, and subsequent generations have lived, and the forces that have shaped our destiny, from the days when a brass band provided the pre-match entertainment to the 21st century where taking a selfie and posting it on social media is an indispensable part of the matchday experience.

Football programmes carry personal memories but are also historical objects, laden with stories about their place and time. So this book aims to tease out some of those memories and stories, and share them with readers who have experienced the excitement of hearing the programme sellers' cries of 'Programmes! Programmes!', the clank of the turnstile, and then getting that awe-inspiring first view of the pitch. Any match is an occasion, rooted in a particular place and time; some are unforgettable, others quickly fade from the mind, having served their purpose as fleeting entertainment, just an afternoon out and a chance to meet up with a few friends, leaving only the match programme as an ephemeral yet tangible record that you were there that day.

The book is built around the many programmes in my collection. Some are presented as 'Programme Spotlights', and accompanied by images in the photographs section, to give a bit more detail, and so enrich the narrative and close the gap with the past. That past represents the collective leisure experience of generations of ordinary people, and the programmes sketch in some other aspects of their lives. Football programmes tell history from the bottom up, a history not of kings and queens (though occasionally they show up to present a trophy) but rather about everyday life – the new TV, the local brewery, a holiday, unemployment, the fate of places where we live.

How did I become the custodian and curator of a collection of almost 2,000 football programmes? Why would anybody collect football programmes, especially retrospectively from matches they had not actually attended, in places they had never visited? No doubt there are papers in peer-reviewed psychology journals that provide possible answers, at least to collecting in general, and perhaps to the sub-species of football programmes in particular. In my case it all began when I was still a child, and by the place and times in which I grew up.

I lived with my parents and my mother's widowed mother and her cocker spaniel in a 'two-up, two-down' terraced house with no bathroom and an outside toilet in the Harpurhey area of Manchester. As a seven-year old, I had learned to read, and unlike many of my classmates at Alfred Street Elementary School, I was lucky enough to avoid the beatings with a leather strap that were regularly meted out to other boys by our teachers. I had quit my career in the muscular environment of the local Cub Scouts, never progressing beyond Tenderfoot status. We had no TV at home, and there were no video games to stream online, but there were trips to local cinemas, not least for the children's matinees which provided first-hand experience of anarchy, though the word was not part of my vocabulary at that age. At Christmas there was occasionally a trip to the pantomime, a short walk from home at the Queen's Park Hippodrome. The name had been appropriated to impart classical grandeur during the already faded era of music hall. Likewise the cinemas in the Harpurhey area proclaimed affinity with a world that bore ludicrously little relation to their actual locale – The Palladium, The Coliseum, The Princess, The Adelphi, The Empire, and The Moston Imperial Palace (less impressively, but more commonly, referred to as

'The Mip'). Within these parameters of culture and everyday childhood, as part of a gang of other scruffy kids, I played cowboys and indians, hide and seek, but especially football. We played in the streets, where the handcart of the rag and bone man or a horse-drawn milk cart was as common a sight as a car; in the back alleys; in the school playground and in the local rec'. So the football came first, then the programmes followed.

While this childhood world was intensely local, I can remember listening to the commentary of the 1952 FA Cup Final on the BBC Light Programme, though the match programme is a gap in the collection. As the name of the station implied, the Light Programme was for those who found the agenda of the BBC's Home Service too serious or taxing, while the Third Programme, with its classical music, emphatically was not for the likes of us – we had no gramophone or instruments in the house. Arsenal played most of that final with ten men after full-back Wally Barnes suffered a serious knee injury, and there were no substitutes in those days. I remember that the only goal was scored by George Robledo, meaning that Newcastle United became the first club in the 20th century to retain the cup. There is an evocative five-minute Movietone Newsreel of the match on YouTube, complete with Winston Churchill, and the crowd singing 'Blaydon Races'. It includes an intriguing flashback to the 1932 final meeting of the same sides, which shows how Newcastle's equaliser came from a cross after the ball had been run out of play; controversial refereeing decisions and the case for the Video Assistant Referee go back at least that far.

When my eighth birthday came along, at the start of the 1952/53 season, my present was to go to watch the league champions Manchester United play Arsenal. I already supported United. Growing up in Manchester meant you were either United or City. I don't think my father had ever been to a match: his own father had died in 1916 when my dad was only a few weeks old, and he was brought up by his elder sisters, while his mother worked in a textile mill to support her four surviving children. So I sought advice on which team to follow from Uncle Arthur, my mother's younger brother. Having been captured in North Africa and spent time as a prisoner of war, he now worked as a ticket seller/'conductor' on the Manchester Corporation buses, a description that does not do justice to his talents or the way he went about his job. He was a performer and the bus was his auditorium. He did not just take the coppers and threepenny bits and dispense the tickets, he provided his passengers with a stream of information and quips, a cross between a bingo caller and a stand-up comedian. He also loved his football and cricket. As he lived in another terraced street nearby, and was a frequent visitor to our house, he was the obvious oracle to approach for guidance on what would be a life-defining decision for me as a seven-year-old. I asked a sensible, cautionary question: which was the better team, City or United? The answer was truthful, 'United', so that was that.

So, on a balmy Wednesday evening in early September 1952, my mother took me to see United host the famous north London club who had run them close for the title the previous season. Walking down Warwick Road to the stadium, I was amid the greatest and most excited throng of people I had ever experienced. Enterprising residents in the streets near the ground were renting their back yards out for those cycling from work to park their bikes. Along the length of the bridge over the railway line was painted 'BAN THE A-BOMB UNITED WE WIN'. Even at that early age I knew about atomic bombs, but decoding the intent of this message puzzled me for a long time. Was it a triumphant response to a United victory – but why should United ban the bomb? Or, with an emphasis on the 'we', was it the taunt of a set of visiting supporters, so carried away by their success that they felt able to prevent a nuclear holocaust? It took me years to realise that 'united' was not United.

Mum and I watched the match from the Stretford Paddock, the area of standing in front of the main stand. To reach the turnstiles we had passed outside the dressing rooms, where the smell of liniment hung in the air, mingling with the smoke from the adjacent railway and the Woodbines of the crowd. It must have been the first 'proper' game my mother had been to. I recollect that admission to the paddock cost an adult three shillings, and half that, 1/6d, for me. Once inside the ground, my mum was disappointed to find that this expensive investment had not purchased us seats. So I stood at the front, eye-level to the pitch, not far from the tunnel from which the players emerged for the 6.30pm kick-off, and watched a goalless draw play out. My one clear mental image from those 90 minutes so long ago is that United's Stan Pearson took a through pass in an inside-left position and put the ball in the Arsenal net. Mum got excited and cheered, but I, with the know-all nonchalance of an eight-year-old boy, explained that he was offside and it wouldn't count. Yet let nothing take away from my gratitude to my mother: I don't think that she ever got a proper grasp of the offside law, and was regularly confused when TV began to show replays of goals ('Is that another one?'), but there were not many women going to football in those days, especially without the company of a man. She may have been naïve about what to expect, but I admire her courage and devotion to introducing her little boy to the wonders of a professional football match staged before a crowd in a stadium.

Inexperience or thrift might explain why I do not have a programme from that first big game, or I may simply have lost it. It is one of those that got away, and later chapters will touch on others that would have enhanced the collection, but for one reason or another are not part of it. Their absence is a kind of reminder that while the clock ticks down to 90 minutes there is always a chance of a winning goal coming in injury time. Who knows what might still turn up? Meanwhile, for the sake of clarity, programmes that are in the collection and referred to in the text will be listed in chronological order at the end of each chapter. They are not all of classic matches by any means; some merit mention because they are definitively of their time, but others simply show the quirky side, if not of football, then at least of the programme editors and their readers. How else to explain the jokes, poems and misprints?

So the programme collection really began with my second visit to Old Trafford, for Manchester United v. Blackpool, a 2.15pm kick-off on Boxing Day 1952, a day after the sides had drawn 0-0 at Bloomfield Road; yes, they played back to back on Christmas Day then Boxing Day at the time! Indeed, Christmas Day football continued in England until 1959 and in Scotland until 1976, when 7,500 turned out to watch Alex Ferguson's St Mirren draw 2-2 with Clydebank, and Alloa v. Cowdenbeath drew a crowd of 750. Blackpool's 1952 team was their best-ever side, with their superstar right-winger Stanley Matthews, the powerful Stan Mortensen leading the line, little Ernie Taylor providing the tricks and the passes and Harry Johnson the rock around which their defensive game was built. These men would provide the dramatic climax to that season in the 'Matthews' Final a few months later, in which the seaside club came from behind to beat Bolton Wanderers 4-3. That final, in which Bolton led 2-0 and 3-1 helped by catastrophic goalkeeping from Scottish international George Farm (whose career had begun with Armadale Thistle, then Hibernian), was the first game I watched on our new TV with its 12in screen, but again, alas, the match programme has eluded me.

I did not actually see Blackpool play that Boxing Day game, though I do have the programme. We did not have a car, so

Mum, Dad and I travelled across Manchester from our home in the north of the city by public transport, changing from a trolley bus to a petrol bus in the city centre. However, as we alighted and began to walk down Warwick Road, there were streams of people coming in the opposite direction: the gates were already closed on a capacity holiday crowd of 48,000. Maybe the programme was purchased to compensate for my disappointment at missing my Christmas treat, I don't know. But, crucially, I kept the programme. It must have meant a lot to me. We had no books in the house, and the only personal possessions I can recall are a bicycle, some tin cowboys and indians, a cap pistol, a cheap cricket bat, and a tennis ball that was used for cricket and football on the croft – a small triangle of vacant land – behind our house. So saving a programme of a game which I had not seen was a conscious and significant act for a young boy.

The evidence that I was a collector before my ninth birthday is confirmed by the fact that I also have in my collection the programmes from the two other games I went to during that 1952/53 season. Another 'uncle', the short-term husband of my mother's niece, took me to see United beat Aston Villa 3-1 on Saturday, 7 February; then I was taken by my mum when United beat Liverpool by the same score on 20 April 1953 in a 6.30pm Wednesday match (no floodlights in those days). These first steps in programme collecting were uncultured, unstructured, and maybe even accidental. I used to cut out football and cricket pictures from newspapers and stick them in a scrapbook, and that is where these first programmes also went, secured by sellotape. My curating skills were undeveloped.

The next stage of collecting – acquiring programmes not as a by-product of going to a game, but as an end in itself – began a year or two later. The intoning of the football results on *Sports Report* on the Light Programme at 5pm on a Saturday was an introduction to the geography of Great Britain. In my Harpurhey-centric world view, there seemed to be something exotic about places like West Bromwich (yes, I know) or Brighton and Hove that prompted me to write off to those clubs requesting a copy of their programme and enclosing a stamped addressed envelope. The boyfriend of the elder sister of a girl I knew from a later seaside holiday gave me some programmes of London clubs from the 1940s and early 1950s, including Chelsea, Arsenal, Queens Park Rangers and Tottenham Hotspur. Other programmes found their way to me in similar fashion, given to me by people who probably wanted rid of them.

My burgeoning collection was kept in an old shoe box under my bed. Then, as a teenager I was going to matches each week and always getting a programme. Also I was able to swap programmes at school or with pen pals. *Charles Buchan's Football Monthly* magazine was a bit like what would now be called a platform; it included listings of people wanting to swap programmes. So it was that I acquired a significant number of Wolverhampton Wanderers home programmes for example, some of which are discussed in Chapter 4. Out there, somewhere, hopefully still alive and well, there is a pensioner who supported Wolves as a boy, and has a collection of 1950s Manchester United programmes that I provided. Also I remember a kind of 'bring and buy' sale at school from which I was able to add some programmes.

Going to university in Cambridge in 1963 interrupted my match-going apart from occasional trips down to London and vacations back in Manchester. Though I would still buy and keep the programme when I did get to a game, I was no longer an active collector of other programmes. This state of affairs continued after I moved back to Manchester to do a post-graduate Diploma in Town and Country Planning. Married in 1966, we lived in a small, damp terraced house built 140 years earlier, with a cellar that had an earth floor where water accumulated. Thus for two years the programmes were kept protected in a trunk that had been used to shuttle my clothes and books between home and university while I was an undergraduate. When we moved to Scotland in 1968, the programmes came with us, and programmes from the Glasgow clubs, and then after a move in 1971, the Edinburgh clubs began to be added, along with Manchester area programmes from matches during holiday periods.

That would have been the end of the story, had our son, Euan, not succumbed to the same fascination with programmes. As a teenager in the 1980s he followed Hearts, and so every week or two another programme was added to the collection. More significantly, he invested money earned from newspaper delivery rounds into building the whole collection. He was informed by a couple of books, Phil Shaw's *Collecting Football Programmes* (1980) and Julian Earwaker's *The Definitive Guide to Football Programmes* (1987). Euan's collecting was much more strategic than mine had been. He bought FA Cup Finals, adding to the few I had, and also programmes of games that were in ways (sometimes weird ways) significant or unusual, such as the 1964 match between a Scandinavian select and the Rest of Europe (see Programme Spotlights 1). Suffice to say that our collection includes an otherwise inexplicably high number of Torquay United programmes as they struggled in the lower reaches of the Fourth Division around the end of the 1980s. No spoilers – the full story comes in a later chapter.

Reading a draft manuscript of this book, he explained, 'I think that some of the really obscure programmes may have been freebies – many dealers sent a free programme with your first order, etc. Or I think you could buy "mixed bags" of, say, five programmes chosen by the seller for a pound. I did try to buy programmes for record scores, though I'm not sure how robust the market is these days for Stoke City's record win programme. Also cup finals, United Europeans (home and away) and as many of the United 1957/58 season (home and away) that we were missing as I could. And the fastest own goal which for a while had been scored by Pat Krause of Torquay. Obviously.'

In 1990, Euan spent part of a gap year in London, where, before the days of GPS-enabled phones, he was wont to tear the relevant pages out of the *A to Z* so as to navigate his way to all the major London grounds – and add the programmes to the collection.

As parents of young adults might appreciate, when in 1994 Euan headed off to Syracuse University in New York State to do a PhD, his programmes did not travel with him; rather they remained behind in our house. In 1998 he returned to the UK for a couple of post-doctoral years at Staffordshire University, living in Stoke, during which time he added programmes from venues comfortably reachable from the Potteries. When he returned to the USA and settled in Chicago, by some oversight, the boxes and boxes of programmes that he had accumulated and originally catalogued as a boy on a BBC 'B' computer, never accompanied him across the Atlantic. 'My' collection had become 'our' collection, but I had become, and remain, the sole curator.

As well as purchases, including from a short-lived programme shop that was close both to my place of work and to Euan's school, donations swelled the collection. While still at secondary school, Euan had displayed some of his collection in the church that my wife took him and his three sisters to, and an elderly congregant who was a Heart of Midlothian fan gave him some Hearts programmes from the 1950s and 1960s, which get a mention in Chapter 9. A colleague with whom I played cricket for Heriot-Watt University Staff was pleased to offload some of his Charlton Athletic programmes to us. Such serendipity continued even as I was writing this book, when an exchange of Christmas e-mails with a work colleague from 50 years before resulted in his contributing three Portsmouth programmes from his own boyhood years.

- -

Programme Spotlights 1: A star-studded line-up showcased by Danish design

Scandinavia 2 Rest of Europe 4, 20 May 1964, friendly

A crowd of 45,600 watched this game, which was staged to celebrate the 75th anniversary of the Danish Football Union. The Rest of Europe was a star-studded selection with British players prominent. They lined up with Lev Yashin (USSR) in goal; Ray Wilson (England) and Jozef Bomba (Czechoslovakia) as full-backs; Ján Popluhár (Czechoslovakia) as centre-half with Valerie Voronin (USSR) and Jim Baxter (Scotland) as the wing-halves; then a forward line of José Augusto (Portugal), Jimmy Greaves (England), Paul van Himst (Belgium), Denis Law (Scotland) and Bobby Charlton (England). The best known Scandinavian was probably right-winger Roald Jensen (Norway) who would go on to play for Heart of Midlothian between 1965 and 1971.

Greaves opened the scoring after four minutes and added another before half-time. Eusébio replaced van Himst for the second half, when Hans Tilkowski (Germany) took over in goal. Law stretched the lead after 48 minutes, then Juhanni Peltonen (who joined Hamburg that summer, becoming the first Finnish player to play in the German Bundesliga) pulled one back, only for Eusébio to restore the three-goal advantage minutes later. Swede Harry Bild got a late consolation goal.

The programme cost one kroner, and is all in Danish. It is rare for an image of a sculpture to dominate the front page of a programme (reproduced by permission of the DBU), and even rarer to have the name of the sculptor printed there. Knud Nellemose (1908–'97) sculpted boxers and athletes as well as footballers. The work featured on this front cover captures the muscular dynamic of a tackle, though nowadays the defender would probably get a yellow card, and the attacker should be depicted falling over and grasping his shin. The dramatic colliding shapes show football as an art form. The white background, and sparse, clean font draw the eye to the excitement and drama captured by the sculpture. This cover exemplifies how good design has been central to all aspects of Danish life for more than 50 years. I have not found an equivalent image fronting a British programme.

- -

So why wait until now to mine this seam? Well, it was a long time since I had looked at the collection. It was packed in bags and cardboard boxes, on dusty shelves in cupboards rarely opened, the sort of places where you keep life insurance policies and old birthday cards, life's unsorted and unconscious accumulation of 'stuff' that you never get the time to sort out, until it's too late and grieving family members have to do it for you. Could you really trust them to appreciate the riches that lie there, among what my wife is prone to refer to as 'junk'? Aye, there's the rub. Could it all end in a charity shop, or worse still simply be consigned to the paper recycling bin, an ecologically correct solution, but an act of cultural and historical vandalism? You bet it could!

So, action not words, deeds not dither! Or at least action with words and just enough dither over each programme to distil its uniqueness; that is what I resolved. What I had not anticipated was just how massive the collection was, and in particular how many programmes Euan had acquired. I still retained a clear mental image of the front covers of many of the programmes that I had collected as a boy – the *United Review*, of course, with its drawing of a player and a fan shaking hands above a black and white photo from the previous match at Old Trafford, or the squarish *Hatters* programme of Luton Town, or the image of the crenelated stand at Molineux across the

Wolverhampton Wanderers programmes. As I began to re-catalogue the collection on 21st-century software, I became aware of the way programmes are valued by dealers and auction rooms. A cup final fetches more than a run-of-the-mill Fourth Division match, and pre-1960 programmes have more of a premium than later equivalents. The Scandinavia v. Rest of Europe programme could be worth a few pounds, but I have not been able to put even a minimal value on the likes of Airdrieonians v. Hibernian on 13 November 1971, or the eight-page York City v. Tranmere Rovers programme from 23 January 1982, despite it being in mint condition.

Yet even seemingly mundane programmes can contain something to catch the eye, be it a player, a match report from a previous game, or some quirk. For example, by the 1980/81 season some programmes had become syndicated, so the Cambridge United v. Coventry City on 4 November (see Programme Spotlights 2) and Middlesbrough v. Wolves on 22 November programmes shared several features and advertisers. These included a feature on rock music of the day, and a full-page advertisement for a pre-internet computer dating service. A page headed 'Humour' included a couple of jokes stereotyping Irish people. Sportopia Promotions' 'Poem on Soccer' competition was also there in both programmes as a double-page feature. It offered £250 for the winner and two £50 prizes for the runners-up, and £5 for each poem published. The invitation to submit entries well conveys the expectations:

> *If you're into fame,*
> *A few lines on the game,*
> *May win you the prize of the year,*
> *So now is the time*
> *For stories and rhyme*
> *So come on let's hear, let's hear!*

The published entries in the Cambridge United v. Coventry City and Middlesbrough v. Wolves programmes fall some way short of the works of Shakespeare and Keats. My Team by Mr P. Cooper reads:

Southampton are great,
They could beat all the rest,
But they must be playing
At there [sic] very best.
As on runs Wells,
Who looks very small,
But there's nobody better,
To look after the goal.

And here comes the team,
In there [sic] red and white vest,
Now is the time,
To be put to the test.

The ball leaves the spot
And up comes a cheer,
As we make a run,
And Keegan is clear.

A nice early goal,
Just what we need,
To put us on top,
And one in the lead.

Now were [sic] one up,
Were [sic] have to defend,
But who better to do it,
Than McMenemy's men.

Well what a match,
I knew were [sic] do well,
But there's no better team,
Than the saints at the Dell.

Programme Spotlights 2: Time for a rhyme: Sportopia 1980

Cambridge United 0 Coventry City 1, League Cup fourth round replay, 4 November 1980

Cambridge had managed a creditable 1-1 draw in the first meeting. The 1-0 replay win, secured by a Steve Hunt goal in front of a crowd of over 10,000, was a stepping stone on Coventry's path to the semi-final where they lost 4-3 on aggregate to West Ham United, who in turn lost the League Cup Final replay 2-1 to Liverpool. Coventry had put out Manchester United in the first round, winning both legs 1-0. Coventry were then a First Division team (i.e. in England's top division), while Cambridge United were in the Second Division, but had eliminated two other top level cubs, Wolverhampton Wanderers and Aston Villa, to reach the last 16. They had achieved successive promotions in 1977 (managed by Ron Atkinson) and 1978, and in 1980 had finished eighth in the Second Division, which was the highest placing in their history at the time and has only been beaten once since.

The front cover emphasises the club's colours both through the action photo and the black and yellow stripes either side of it. It also gives prominence to a black player, Cambridge winger Derrick Christie. At that time relatively few black players were appearing in the Football League. The picture shows that shirt sponsorship was still quite discrete at this time (see Chapter 10 for more on sponsorship).

This programme includes the same double-page spread on the Sportopia poetry competition, with the same poems that appeared in the Sportopia-produced Middlesbrough v. Wolves programme on 22 November 1980. Both programmes have 40 pages, and also share articles by leading football journalists of the day, while also including some features relevant to the home team and the particular match: for example, pen portraits of the opposition. The 'Reel to Reel' feature in both programmes was about rock stars of the day, Sting, Phil Lynott of Thin Lizzie, and the American Southern rock band Blackfoot.

The Sportopia programmes also shared the same corporate advertisers: presumably, the ability of the company to sell space in the programmes of several clubs, rather than just one, achieved some economies of scale and enhanced appeal to larger companies. One such advertisement catches the eye. 'We'll make you believe in computer dating,' proclaimed Dateline, offering a 'Free Matching Test'. This was still in the pre-internet age. By completing the form on the bottom half of the page and mailing it (enclosing two first-class stamps) to their London address, your details would be put through 'our amazing computer' and possible matches identified. Who knows what marriages might have been made not in Heaven, but by somebody clipping out a page from their programme at the Abbey Stadium that chilly November night?

- -

What can I say? Presumably the confusions between 'there' and 'their', and 'were' and 'we're' and even 'we'd' were in the original and tolerated by Sportopia editors as poetic licence, and Mr Cooper received his £5. Any further deconstruction of his verse can be limited to noting that Kevin Keegan had joined in the summer of 1980 from Hamburg where he had twice been named European Footballer of the Year and reached a European Cup Final, and manager Lawrie McMenemy was at the peak of his career, while The Dell was the club's home ground in those days. Were readers from Middlesbrough to Cambridge entranced by such odes? Are they too flimsy a basis on which to infer snobbish comparisons between the cultural norms of English fans and those of Danish football followers who imbibed the artistic merits of the cover of the 1964 programme from the game with the Rest of Europe (Programme Spotlights 1)?

Checking online to get an idea of the market value of our programmes, not surprisingly I found that there can be a large differential in price for the same programme depending on the condition it is in. Write in the team changes, substitutes, score, scorers and half-time scores and the value of your asset plummets. Cut out the token to get priority for buying tickets for a big game, and you reduce the eventual resale value. Fold up the programme to stuff it in your inside pocket as you stand on a rain-drenched 1950s open terrace, and half a century or more later that same fold makes you worse off. In other words, all that makes a programme an authentic document, everything that adds particularity and a human stamp, is a devaluation in the eyes of traders, and presumably their clients. Before the age of bland consumerism, programmes were functional. They told you who was playing, so if there were changes you needed to write them in. You were told the half-time scores, and like you did with information given to you by your school teachers, you wrote them down, 'ours not to reason why'.

In general, older programmes command a higher price. However, the earliest dated programmes in our collection are actually reprints, not originals, so they are not worth much. That said, like so many others, they provide fascinating insights into the game and the times. One is a full-colour reproduction, issued in 1974, of the first programme that Aston Villa produced, which was for their First Division meeting with Blackburn Rovers on 1 September 1906, a game the Villa won 4-2. The original price for Volume 1 Number 1 of *The Villa News and Record* was one penny. The front cover is dominated by an advert for Rover Cycles which 'never wear out', 'When you see a cyclist on a "ROVER" you can be sure that he or she have [sic] paid for their bicycle. We do not "touch" the penny or twopence a day business.' The advertisement rates shown inside suggest that Rover would have paid £2 for this splendidly disdainful front cover advert. On the inside of the back cover was an advert for the ferocious-looking McGregor Football Boot, as worn, the text assures potential purchasers, by players at a long list of professional clubs. The illustration accompanying the 'lace to toe' boot shows it as having 12 pairs of eyes for the laces, and extending not just over the ankle, but midway up the shin. The toe cap was no mere decoration, but rather a statement of intent that would strike fear into any opponent who did not fancy facing a future with a permanent limp.

A message from the Villa directors indicated that they hoped the new publication would contribute to the 'delectation of our readers', and that they were following the lead of 'other important clubs', while also noting that club journals and programmes could be an important source of revenue. Page three devoted two paragraphs to 'The Players' Comforts', explaining how a gymnasium had been created beneath the grandstand, and a reading room and 'well equipped' library, 'containing all that could reasonably be required for the well being and edification of the players'. 'Edification' is not a word likely to appear in 21st-century programmes, though lockdown has forced recognition that wellbeing really does matter.

That inaugural Villa programme reported that Newcastle were the most financially successful club the previous season, recording a profit of £4,399, quite a lot of money in those times. In contrast, 'Chelsea's loss [was] little less than stupendous. Had the club, however, attained the height of its ambitions and gained a place in the First Division of the League, the £5,000 deficit would have given no cause for anxiety.' Apart from the figure of £5,000, this sounds a familiar story, though, despite the 1905 Russian revolution, there were no Tsarist oligarchs looking to buy an overspending club to launder their fortunes to countries where they would be safer.

Our other reprint from a pre-war programme is the famous 1923 FA Cup Final, the first to be held at The Empire Stadium, Wembley, in which Bolton Wanderers beat West

Ham United 2-0. As archive clips on YouTube show, the game was played with spectators standing around all the touchlines, and only after mounted police, one very visible because of his 'white' horse (it was actually grey, but showed up as white in the newsreels), had cleared the playing area. Like most FA Cup Final programmes, the one for 1923 was actually rather bland. The most interesting pages were about the new stadium and the forthcoming Empire Exhibition. There was no hint of the slavery and oppression on which the empire had been built, rather the pomp of empire was flaunted, 'This vast stadium, the largest in the world, the most comfortable, the best equipped, holds more than 125,000.' Indeed, the crowd for that final was estimated to be double that figure, as people scaled perimeter walls to get access to the stadium. While the area of the stadium would equal that of 'the Biblical city, Jericho', it was a small part of the 216-acre site being developed for the 1924 exhibition, where 'will be displayed all the wealth, the manufactures, raw materials and resources of the greatest Empire the world has ever known'. Readers were encouraged to visit the exhibition, which was to be 'the most wonderful, the most romantic enterprise in history. After a hideous and crippling war, we are going to build a new and greater trade, find new prosperity, make stronger still the bonds that link us and our fellow-citizens overseas together in one ideal of friendship.' Just three years later, in May 1926, there were tanks on the streets of London as the General Strike began, when a million coal miners had been locked out of their workplaces after a dispute with the coal owners who wanted them to work longer hours for less money.

The oldest original programmes in the collection are both single sheets on pink paper, with a fold creating four pages. They were produced by Hertford Town. Their reserves hosted Wood Green Reserves in a Spartan League Second Division game on the evening of Thursday, 16 September 1926, while the second programme is for their first team's encounter in the Spartan League First Division with ex-champions G.E. Romford on Saturday, 27 August 1927. The price of each programme was one penny. Even that far back, and at non-league level, the three basic features of the programmes were much the same as today. There were advertisements, the team line-ups and club notes.

At the top of the front cover, Ibbot and Co. advertised their 'Rich clean milk – We often please where others fail', a claim that makes one wonder just how stringent were environmental health controls all those years ago? 'The Club Outfitters', Drury Bros., promoted their 'Tip-Top Topcoat', and Dye and Sons offered two 14-seater motor coaches for hire, while on the back page, the Hertford Candy Company tempted readers to their 'large selection' of 'high class' confectionary and chocolates, with delights such as Swiss rolls, cream sandwiches and Dundee cakes. On the inside pages, around the team line-ups, along with various local businesses, and at diagonally opposite corners to each other were the Castle Cinema and the Premier Theatre. The former claimed to screen a continuous programme of 'the finest pictures' every day from 6pm to 10.30pm and all 'at popular prices'. In contrast, the theatre assumed a cultural superiority: in small print that would have challenged the eyesight of those unable to afford reading glasses, it described itself as, 'The popular little Theatre for High Class and refined Entertainments where the leading Musical Comedy Concert Parties appear in all the latest productions.' Lest there be any doubt about the sort of people it aimed to attract, it listed prices from the most expensive (1/6d) to the cheapest (sixpence). Collectively, though the adverts were few in number, they show an acute appropriation and endorsement of middle class norms and expectations.

The display of the players dominates the centre pages. They are lined up in the traditional 2-3-5 formation, with the home players wearing numbers from one (goalkeeper) to 11(outside-left), while the visitors were numbered from 12 (outside-left) to 22 (goalkeeper). This is the same system as used in that 1905 Aston Villa programme, and now looks distinctly odd, though it had a logic in its day. For the Wood Green Reserves match, there seems to have been a problem with a clash of strips. Hertford Town were down to play in red and green, and their visitors in red and black. Had nobody noticed?

Among the Club Notes section, two comments catch the eye. Those at the reserves game were given the distressing information that Hertford Town's president, the Rev. Roland Smith, B.A. was 'slightly better, but it will be a long time before he will be out of danger'. How his reverend came to give his time to the club, and what became of his fate, sadly we may never know. For a man of the cloth to be president of a football club was not that surprising: a number of clubs who are today household names had their 19th-century origins in efforts by churches to steer young men away from more sinful attractions. Everton and Wolverhampton Wanderers are examples.

The Club Notes for the fixture with G.E. Romford capture the timeless optimism of fans everywhere at the start of a new season. No matter how dire the previous season, the summer break is a purgative, and as the days begin to get shorter, the club is reincarnated, with everything possible once more. 'Today we enter upon another season in the history of our Club, and in spite of the bad times experienced last season, come up smiling once more, feeling sure that this season we are really going to turn up "trumps",' read the programme, adding that the club were confident of 'making a considerable advance' if only because the previous season had been so abysmal. Always look on the bright side of life, as being a fan teaches you to do.

As these two reprints and 1920s programmes show, there is more to a publication than just the team sheet or a report of the last match. I am reminded of a cringe-inducing record called *Deck of Cards*, recorded in 1948 by Tex Ritter, a Stetson-wearing country and western singer. It recalled the North African campaign in World War II, just a few years earlier, and a 'soldier boy' put on a charge for spreading out his playing cards during a church service. His defence, sombre and devout, is that the cards are a proxy Bible, almanac and prayer book, 'You see, Sir, when I look at the Ace it reminds me that there is but one God,' and so on, with the 52 cards, four suits and 12 picture cards a reminder of how many weeks there are in a year, then in a month, and how 12 months make a year, the kind of things you could easily forget without a pack of playing cards.

I suppose that our collection of football programmes could be my secular deck of cards, though I don't need a front and back page as a sonorous reminder that everything has a beginning and an end. They are ephemera but carry multiple meanings, triggers for memories, signifiers of places and people, markers along a timeline, expressions of cultures. Each is a story of a place and a time and a set of relationships between people – fans, players, managers, directors, advertisers, young hopefuls, old pros, stars and journeymen, local lads and exotic foreigners. They are touched by tales of triumph and of tragedy, of meteorology and technology, of work and play. Sometimes, when I was at the game and can still recall its highlights, the programme provides a tangible and personal connection, but even when a programme was just collected it can still have a resonance, not just for great occasions but also for the rich and banal struggles of everyday lives.

The book takes a broadly chronological approach to this canvas. Chapter 2 begins with programmes which date from World War II. Chapter 3 draws on the programmes from some schoolboy representative games, giving glimpses of 'stars of the future' at the time when I was myself a young schoolboy.

Chapter 4 explores the professional game in the early 1950s when floodlights and foreign opposition were grasped as means to stem the fall in attendances, at a time when Britain struggled to define its place in the post-war world. The next chapter, 'Soccer Diaries', takes its title from the diaries I kept, recording a mid-1950s humdrum life anchored around football, bad spelling and watching ITV. Chapter 6 charts the passage from the 1950s to the 1960s, a period when politicians told British voters that they 'had never had it so good', and football had to compete with other sources of entertainment for the masses. Chapter 7 looks at the careers of England's 1966 World Cup winners, then Chapter 8 reviews the 1960s more generally. Chapter 9 marks my own migration to Scotland and the Scottish programmes in the collection. Chapter 10 covers programmes and experiences from the 1970s, a period marked by industrial unrest, rampant racism on the terraces, but also some great games. Football's status as a 'slum game' is the central theme of Chapter 11 with its focus on the 1980s. It is here that the reason for the preponderance of Torquay United programmes in the collection of a man who has never visited the English Riviera resort not known for its football prowess is revealed. Chapter 12 takes my life and the programme collection to foreign fields, leading to the wider globalisation of the game since the 1990s, the theme of Chapter 13. Finally, Chapter 14, reflects on the gulf between the game in the post-war years, and the state of the industry when Covid-19 induced a lockdown and games were played behind closed doors for a TV audience.

Programmes cited in Chapter 1 that are in the collection:

- 1 September 1906, Aston Villa 4 Blackburn Rovers 2, Football League First Division (reprint)
- 28 April 1923, Bolton Wanderers 2 West Ham United 0, FA Cup Final (reprint)
- 16 September 1926, Hertford Town Reserves v. Wood Green Reserves, (result unknown), Spartan League Second Division
- 27 August 1927, Hertford Town v. G.E. Romford, (result unknown), Spartan League First Division
- 26 December 1952, Manchester United 2 Blackpool 1, Football League First Division
- 7 February 1953, Manchester United 3 Aston Villa 1, Football League First Division
- 20 April 1953, Manchester United 3 Liverpool 1, Football League First Division
- 20 May 1964, Scandinavia 2 Rest of Europe 4, friendly (Danish Football Union 75th anniversary)
- 13 November 1971, Airdrieonians 2 Hibernian 2, Scottish League First Division
- 4 November 1980, Cambridge United 0 Coventry City 1, Football League Cup fourth round replay
- 22 November 1980, Middlesbrough 2 Wolverhampton Wanderers 0, Football League First Division
- 23 January 1982, York City 1 Tranmere Rovers 3, Football League Fourth Division

Chapter 2

Hard Times

BORN IN 1944, I have no first-hand memories of World War II or its immediate aftermath. Like others of my generation, I grew up with narratives about the war, though they rarely came from the men of our parents' generation who were directly involved. From my father, who was not demobbed until I was nearly two, I picked up little more than a sense of camaraderie, and the facts that he had been a Private and that the Army had taught him how to drive. This new skill then defined his role in the armed service: he drove trucks through the Netherlands as the Allies advanced. The ability to drive also helped him get a job after he was demobbed. As a young child I can remember him working nights driving newspaper delivery vans for the *Daily Express*, then switching jobs to do early-morning collections of milk from farms on the Pennine fringe of Manchester – in those days there were still some farms operating within the conurbation itself. He would arrive home late morning with a lorry-load of churns, and then take them on to the dairy in nearby Failsworth.

Meanwhile, my mother would tell the tale of how she turned up for work in a textile factory in town, the morning after the Luftwaffe had bombed Manchester. The works had been hit and she was sent home. Her twin brothers had been prisoners of war, having been captured in North Africa: Arthur, the bus conductor mentioned in Chapter 1, was the elder; Sidney, the younger one, lost fingers in a factory where he was forced to labour, but again neither of these two uncles ever talked about their experiences. I discovered subsequently that 'Uncle Sid' had been awarded the Croix de Guerre for exceptional service at the Battle of Bir Hecheim: I guess that he and his twin brother were among the 845 prisoners taken when the Axis forces finally triumphed after a two-week siege of the old Ottoman fort in the Libyan desert in the summer of 1942. On the home front, my widowed grandmother would recount how she and my mother used to shelter under the stairs in our tiny living room when there was a raid on. Air raid shelters and bombed sites were familiar elements of the townscape of my childhood. Thus World War II was both very near to me during my early years, but also unknown and not frightening. Fragments from our football programmes help to sketch in something of the early years of my life.

Bill Shankly, legendary manager of Liverpool, was one of the generation whose careers were interrupted by military service during World War II. He famously quipped, 'Some people think football is a matter of life and death. I assure you, it's much more serious than that.' It was a good line, but it is sobering to think how football managed to carry on during the war alongside genocide and the everyday dangers that faced civilians in their homes, workplaces and even football grounds. A programme we have from 16 October 1943 encapsulates both the tragedy and the bravery of those distant times. That was the Saturday when the *razzia* began in Rome, the round-up of the city's Jews as a prelude to their extermination. Before that fateful morning there had been no mass deportations of Italian Jews. In May 1943 the Axis powers had been defeated in North Africa, then on 3 September Italy had surrendered at Cassibili. By that October day, the Allied forces were pushing on to the mainland, which was now largely occupied by Nazi forces.

A thousand miles away, in the decorous suburbs of south London, while Rome's Jews were being dragged from their homes, Dulwich Hamlet kicked off at half past three against Belvedere from nearby Erith, in a South Eastern Combination game. The match programme said that Belvedere were a 'very good team' who had beaten the Metropolitan Police 6-0 the previous Saturday. I guess the crowd that autumn afternoon was made up of boys, members of Dad's Army and soldiers on leave. The programme cost them one penny, the same as the Hertford Town programme from almost 20 years previously, which was discussed in Chapter 1: inflation was low for a long time. It is neatly printed on one sheet of A5-sized salmon pink paper; Dulwich played in pink and blue, which seems a daringly extrovert kit for the times. The back side of the programme set out the line-ups, crisply listing each player by his initials and surname. Then, below the names of the referee and the linesmen, and in bold type is written, 'SUPPORTERS WILL PROBABLY KNOW OF THE FOOTBALL ASSOCIATION RULING re STOPPAGE OF GAMES. ONLY IN THE EVENT OF ENEMY AIRCRAFT OVERHEAD WILL PLAY BE STOPPED. SHELTER IS PROVIDED UNDER THE STAND.' These few words capture the stoic spirit of Britain during the Blitz. More than just 'Keep Calm and Carry On', the message also conveys the 'British sense of fair play', and of abiding by the rules. No point in a team two down, ten minutes from time, ear-wagging the officials, 'Ref, I think I can hear an air raid siren.' The official would simply glance to the sky and issue a curt 'Play on!' Only once planes became visible overhead would the game be abandoned, and players and fans sprint to the shelter beneath the stands.

Dulwich's upcoming opponents also spoke of the times. The Royal Netherlands Navy would meet them on 20 November, then there would be an RAF XI on 4 December and 'on Boxing Day we are at home to a strong Army XI'. The London Fire Force had played the RAF a couple of weeks earlier. The previous week's match at Gravesend, which Dulwich had lost 4-1, was described decorously as 'quite a pleasant game', and afterwards the visitors had been 'entertained to tea' and 'both sides spent a happy time together'. The Corinthian spirit throbs through these words.

Despite this chivalry and stoicism in the South Eastern Combination, football during World War II was far from being business as usual. The Football League and the FA Cup had been suspended, and the professional clubs played in regional competitions. In 1943/44, Spurs won the League (South), Lovell's Athletic (the professional team of Lovell's sweet factory in Newport, Monmouthshire – the club continued until 1969) won the League (West), and Blackpool won the League (North) First Championship. In an achievement that defies geography, Bath City were winners of the League (North) Second Championship.

On 4 December 1943, the day that the RAF XI were at Dulwich, on the other side of London Brentford were entertaining Fulham in the Football League (South). Putting out teams was not easy. The raincloud-grey four-page programme pays fulsome tribute to Fulham's manager Jack Peart, 'Who has done more than any London official to keep the game going (with so many difficulties) during the War period.' It records Peart's 'willingness to help any Club in difficulty for players, and at times at the expense of his own Club'. These arrangements were not rewarded with the kind of fees today's agents take from the game. Meanwhile, the Brentford programme's Notes section, told fans that Tommy Kiernan, an Albion Rovers inside-forward, had returned from overseas service and 'has intimated his desire to play for us again'. Doubtless the overseas service had been more demanding and less lucrative than a loan spell in the Belgian Second Division might be today. Kiernan was not the only absentee: 'Peter McKinnon is unable to play today, having gone home on leave,' while 'Doug Hunt was unable to play on Saturday last owing to Military duties'. Reading the rest of the programme conveys a sense of drab times, which presumably were not relieved for the 7,510 crowd as they witnessed a goalless draw that December afternoon. The fixture against Reading a couple of weeks previously on 20 November 1943, had been 'farcical, as little of the game could be seen'; it had been abandoned after 33 minutes, victim of London's Dickensian fog. The next fixture had resulted in a 4-1 victory for Brentford against Clapton Orient, but 'was a very poor one and played under depressing conditions'. It must have been even more depressing for the Clapton Orient fans, as the league table on the back page of the programme showed them to be rock bottom with just two points from 14 games, and a goal difference of -34.

By 5 February 1944, when Arsenal were Brentford's visitors, Clapton Orient had amassed six points from 23 games, having scored 25 goals but conceded 75: clearly, defending was not their strength. Brentford's programme for the Arsenal match (see Programme Spotlights 3) gives further insights into wartime football, and the wider society of which it was a part. It records how George Stewart, who had played at inside-left in the game against Fulham, was unable to play 'owing to his Military Duties'. A.N. Other was listed as the Brentford outside-right. However, Frank Soo, a well-known star at that time who was serving in the RAF and guesting for Brentford, returned to wear the number four shirt against Arsenal. In 1942 Soo had become the first non-white player to represent England. He was captain of Stoke City when war broke out just weeks after the club had cancelled their remarkably inauspiciously planned summer tour to Germany and Poland. Susan Gardiner's book *The Wanderer: The Story of Frank Soo* is the definitive account of Soo's career. It is difficult now to imagine how he might have been treated at a time when there were so few people of East Asian descent in England, but in 1945 he was quoted in the *Evening Sentinel,* the local Stoke newspaper, as saying that he would have made many more appearances for England but for his 'Oriental blood'.

- -

Programme Spotlights 3: Wartime Gunners
Brentford 4 Arsenal 1, Football League (South), 5 February 1944

A crowd of over 20,000 turned out, more than double Brentford's next highest home gate that season. Doubtless Arsenal brought a large following and their glamour attracted others. Ted Drake was probably their biggest star. He scored 42 league goals when Arsenal were champions in 1934/35, and the following season had scored all of the Gunners' goals when they won 7-1 at Villa Park. During the war he was serving in the RAF, as was Bernard Joy, who was the last amateur to play for England (against Belgium in 1936). The Compton playing on Arsenal's left wing was presumably Denis Compton, as that was his regular position – his elder brother Leslie also had a long career with Arsenal, playing in many positions. Denis, a dashing batsman, was arguably England's best cricketer for 20 years from the late 1930s. His Arsenal debut was in 1936.

Brentford's number four, Frank Soo, was the first player of Asian origin to play in the English Football League, and the first non-white player to represent England, which he did nine times between 1942 and 1945. However, as these wartime internationals were deemed to be unofficial, he was never accorded the status or significance he deserved. An injury ended his chances of international selection after the war. His father, Quan Soo, was a

Chinese sailor who became an immigrant and married an English woman, Beatrice, a fellow worker in a laundry. Their son Frank was born in Buxton in 1914, then grew up in Liverpool and played for Prescot Cables before signing for Stoke City in 1933, where he starred alongside Stanley Matthews. Soo scored Brentford's first goal in this game against Arsenal. Centre-forward Townsend got two, and the other Brentford scorer was Dennis Westcott, a Wolverhampton Wanderers forward who was guesting for Brentford and presumably the A.N. Other who filled the right-wing berth.

Though the club admitted 'All members of H.M. Forces in uniform… to all games at reduced prices', Brentford, like others, continued to struggle to find players who could juggle playing professional football with their duties as members of the armed forces.

For their home game against Crystal Palace on Easter Monday, 1944, the programme noted, 'We expect to have difficulty in fielding a representative side owing to the uncertainty of the Service players.' More optimistically, it suggested that Jack Astley, 'an old Bees favourite' and now 'Lieutenant J. Astley serving with the R.A.' would be turning out for the club who had sold him to Coventry City in 1936. In the event, our programme for the game, which Brentford won 2-0, has nine team changes written in pencil to their line-up, with Astley's place at number two being taken by Brown. Meanwhile the back-page league table saw Tottenham Hotspur top, Brentford seventh, and Clapton Orient still bottom – played 25, won two, drawn three, lost 20, goals for 26, goals against 80, points seven.

After the war, football resumed. Unlike most other things, it was not rationed. The first full post-war international to be played in England was staged at Maine Road, Manchester City's ground, on 13 November 1946, when the 'Red Dragons' of Wales were the visitors. Tommy Lawton was the only player who had appeared in England's 7-0 win over Ireland (as Northern Ireland was called) at Old Trafford on 16 November 1938, the last pre-war home international.

The programme for the game at Maine Road included a couple of paragraphs about the referee Willie Webb, highlighting his day job as a Glasgow engine driver who usually worked the Carlisle run. It evokes the steam train, labour-intensive, tenuously connected world of the short film made a decade earlier, *Night Mail,* with W.H. Auden's verse commentary:

> *This is the night mail crossing the Border*
> *Bringing the cheque and the postal order*
> *Letters for the rich, letters for the poor*
>
> *The shop at the corner, the girl next door.*
> *Pulling up Beattock, a steady climb:*
> *The gradient's against her, but she's on time.*
>
> *Past cotton-grass and moorland boulder*
> *Shovelling white steam over her shoulder*
>
> *Snorting noisily as she passes*
>
> *Silent miles of wind-bent grasses.*

The main advert on the front page of the eight-page programme (which cost two pence) was for 'Tizer the Appetizer', a fizzy soft drink brewed locally and imbibed by generations of Mancunians, myself included. Fred Dawes was advertising the new 1946 models of radios with 'free home service and easiest weekly payments': televisions were not mentioned. There was also an advert for the Princess Sports Depot, located in Moss Side, not far from City's stadium, and close to where Aunty Ethel and Uncle Bill used to live. I remember, as a young boy, buying from that shop a sleek clockwork speedboat that cut a dash through paddling pools; and then, when I was about ten, getting a cricket bat there. The bat was subsequently adorned with the autographs of several leading England cricketers of the mid-1950s, which I had garnered during the Scarborough Festival. It stayed in the family for around three decades until my mother inadvertently left it on a Manchester corporation bus after a trip to a park with her grandchildren.

Unlike the Brentford programmes, this one gave the team colours: England 'White Shirts – Dark Knickers', and Wales 'Red Shirts – White Knickers': in today's usage of 'knickers', the terminology suggests an unlikely spectacle. The dark-knickered England team that November afternoon was: Swift (Manchester City); Scott (Arsenal) and Hardwick (Middlesbrough); Wright (Wolverhampton Wanderers), Franklin (Stoke City) and Cockburn (Manchester United); Finney (Preston North End), Carter (Derby County), Lawton (Chelsea), Mannion (Middlesbrough) and Langton (Blackburn Rovers). Their opponents were listed as: Sidlow (Liverpool); Sherwood (Cardiff City) and Hughes (Birmingham City); Whitcombe (West Brom'), Jones (T.) (Everton) and Burgess (Tottenham Hotspur); Jones (E.) (Swansea), Powell (A.) (Leeds United), Ford (Swansea), Powell (I.) (Queens Park Rangers) and Edwards (Birmingham City). In the end Ford did not play, his place being taken by Stan Richards of Cardiff City who won his only cap. What is striking is how the England players in particular were dispersed around a wide variety of clubs, with only Middlesbrough having more than one representative. Only two of the England 11 were with London clubs – Laurie Scott, who had been in the Arsenal side listed in the programme for their 1944 defeat by Brentford discussed above, and Tommy Lawton. The geographical centre of gravity of English football was well north of the capital.

The pen pictures of the teams in the programme shed light on those distant heroes, their tenuous lives and the Britain in which they had grown up. Frank Swift, the legendary goalkeeper, for example, 'A former fisherman, he is now a Manchester innkeeper.' George Hardwick, England's captain,

'During war was badly injured by a flying bomb.' Billy Wright, at 22 'the baby of the team', was still in the Army. Left-half Henry Cockburn 'works as a fitter at Oldham', while Tom Finney, 'a truly great right winger' was famously a plumber by trade who had 'made a big name with Army teams in the Middle East'. On the Wales team, George Edwards stood out as, 'A Bachelor of Arts. George is training to become a schoolmaster, after studying at Swansea and Birmingham Universities. Taught history and geology while in R.A.F.' A further reminder of the times was an advert alongside these pen portraits for the R.E.M.E. Regimental Association (Manchester Branch). The acronym stands for the Corps of Royal Electrical and Mechanical Engineers, which must have recruited strongly locally, given the significance of engineering in the economy of the Manchester conurbation. Significantly, the advert highlighted that the branch had a 'Welfare and Employment Representative always in attendance'. Readjustment to civilian life must have been difficult for many, and while there is no knowing how skilled the representative might have been, there is also a sense of support and sharing among those who had been through war together. It makes me wonder what it must have been like for my own father, returning to a wife and child he would hardly have seen.

Those early post-war years saw massive crowds watching football. The England v. Wales game, which England won 3-0 with one goal from Lawton and a brace from Wilf Mannion, drew a crowd of 59,121 on a Wednesday afternoon. Though Britain still had its Empire, the hardships of war were not followed by prosperity. Football was an escape from shortages and a long working week, often in arduous conditions. Most people lived in rented housing, many of which, like that in which I was brought up, lacked bathrooms or inside toilets; little or nothing had been invested in repair and maintenance since before the war, at least. Willie Webb quite possibly returned to such a home after refereeing the international at Maine Road, before reporting at the station for train driving work the next day.

The programmes from these early post-war years bear the imprint of this world. Chelsea's and Manchester United's home programmes in 1946/47 carried an advert for Afrikander pipe tobacco, 'For the "Piping" days of Peace'. The copywriter's clever pun must have struck a deep chord after the horrors of war. Even so, the weather that winter was particularly severe, and there were fuel shortages and power cuts. As the programme for the mid-table meeting of Chelsea and Sunderland on 22 March 1947 recorded, the ban on midweek league games had seemed 'likely to dislocate the Competition beyond remedy'. There had been talk of declaring the season null and void, or playing postponed games in midweek behind closed doors, a solution resurrected in 2020 when the Covid pandemic lockdown brought the 2019/20 season to a halt and delayed the start of the 2020/21 season. The eventual remedy was to extend the season to 14 June. As an aside, our copy of the match programme for that game against Sunderland was autographed by the entire Chelsea team – with the single exception of star number nine Tommy Lawton.

Reconciliation with wartime enemies was not easy, but in Manchester at least football helped. Although I did not see him play live until 1954, Bert Trautmann had made his debut in goal for Manchester City in November 1949. He had served in the Nazi forces on the eastern front before being brought to the north-west of England as a prisoner of war. City's decision to sign him was not without controversy, but as is so often the case with talented players, his performances on the field soon made him a hero in Manchester. Equally, then as now, opposition fans could be unforgiving: Alan Rowlands's *Trautmann: The Biography* records the taunts of 'Nazi' and 'Kraut' when he played his first game in London later that season at Craven

Cottage. Even in his later years, before leaving City in 1964, Rowlands records that Trautmann was still receiving hate mail directed at his German origins. Over his long career at City, I saw him play many times and remember him as an outstanding goalkeeper, big, brave and athletic. Without doubt he was a legend in Manchester across the blue/red football divide.

Paper itself was rationed from 1940, and newspapers did not regain their pre-war size until 1953. Not surprisingly, the programmes from this period also have few pages, and many are printed on poor-quality paper. This and the passage of time leaves them in a fragile state today. Chelsea's programme was a single sheet of paper, folded three times so as to create eight pages; the origami economised on the need for staples. Like Chelsea, Bury printed in the club colours, blue and white, as did Rochdale, and no doubt others. However, Arsenal's programme for their game against Chelsea on 31 August 1949 was an altogether more lavish affair, perhaps as befitted the club's status and famed marble halls. It was priced at sixpence, when others typically cost two or three pence. It had 14 pages when others usually had four, eight or 12; and was half to one inch wider than the normal formats. In addition, it was extensively illustrated by photos, including from the annual Arsenal v. Middlesex cricket match recently played at Highbury, which featured Denis Compton, the golden boy of English cricket at the time and Arsenal player (see the Brentford v. Arsenal Programme Spotlights, page 43).

Maybe there was more money around in London. To support this hypothesis, occupying the slot filled by an advert for 'Table Soccer' (i.e. Subbuteo, the game where you flicked players that were mounted on plastic bases) in the programme for the Sunderland game, there is an advert in the Chelsea v. Huddersfield Town programme of 19 April 1947 for 'Holidays on the Continent'. Helpfully it added 'Belgium, Holland, France, etc.' (no mention of Germany) for those uncertain of the geography. It was placed by Davies Turner and Co. Ltd. of 4 Lower Belgrave St, SW1. In contrast, and to confirm the stereotypes, Stone-Dri Rainwear was a regular advertiser in Manchester United's programmes. Rochdale's programme for the FA Cup tie against Barrow on 27 November 1948 included an advert for Rochdale Corporation Baths, as well as for the Rochdale Corporation Gas Department, the kind of local institutions that sustained the lives of Rochdale's citizens in those difficult days: many houses in the town would have lacked a bathroom.

In general, adverts for entertainment (other than beer and cigarettes) amounted to little more than local cafes. However, programmes of this era also display a set of social attitudes that leave me feeling uncomfortable today. Cosmopolitan Chelsea carried a regular advert on the bottom-left corner of the team sheet double centre page, for the Kilburn Empire, Maida Vale and the Grand, Clapham. Thus, according to the Chelsea v. Huddersfield programme of 19 April 1947, the Grand was showing *Claudia*, described as a 'Delightfully Daring Comedy'. A month earlier the offering had been *Birds from Paradise*, a 'glamorous review'. It is hard to imagine the scale of titillation on offer, but the official censor, the Lord Chamberlain, would have ensured it erred on the side of modesty. 'To-night', in the Chelsea v. Sunderland programme of 22 March 1947, the Kilburn Empire advertised *Ten Little Niggers*. With similar disregard, the Manchester United programme for their game with Blackpool on 2 September 1950, under a heading 'Smile', includes a 'joke' about a government official going to 'Kingwa' to inspect groundnuts. The fiasco of a UK colonial scheme to grow peanuts in what was then the colony of Tanganyika would have been topical. The punchline of the joke is an 18in tall British colonel, who is invited to 'tell this gentleman how tall you were before you told that Witch Doctor what you thought of him'. No doubt, such casual racism was seen as harmless at the time, but it was racism and fed from and fuelled the kind of discrimination that Frank Soo had suffered. It sat alongside other stereotypes. For example, Chelsea described their own 'Wee Bobby' Russell as 'A typical, canny Scot, dour and reasoning, stolid to a degree,' in their 22 March 1947 programme.

Class also ran through 1940s Britain like the lettering through a stick of Blackpool rock. It was particularly evident in FA Cup Final and international programmes. The front page of the programme for the classic 1948 final, in which manager Matt Busby's first great team beat Blackpool 4-2, had under 'Wembley Empire Stadium' 'Chairman and Managing Director: SIR ARTHUR J. ELIN, MBE.' Turn the page and you are faced by a photo of 'Their Majesties The King and Queen' beneath the heading 'Royal Silver Wedding 1923–1948'. A couple of pages further on was a page bearing the photos of four old men, the officials of the Football Association, headed by the president, The Right Honourable The Earl of Athlone, KG, PC, GCB, GCMC, GCVO, DSO. Football may have been played and watched by working men, but it was organised and overseen by men from a different social class. The programme, as befits the special occasion, was 16 pages and cost a whole shilling.

For all these blemishes, reading the programmes of the 1940s demonstrates that football in those days was indeed the people's game. There was also pride in the way that so many of the players had served in the forces. Chelsea's Ray Goddard, whose pen picture featured in the programme for their game with Huddersfield on 19 April 1947, had undergone 'the rigours of the Burma campaign ... 14 months in the jungle cut off from civilisation'. Wee Bobby Russell had served in the Middle East and been taught 'all there is to know about tanks'. Even for the new generation, the professional game was not that far removed from everyday life. Chelsea's programme for their game with Stoke City on 15 November 1947 included an invitation, 'We have vacancies for boys of between 15 and

17 years of age who really possess outstanding ability, for the positions of backs, halves, and inside and outside forwards.' The 1948 FA Cup Final programme records how George Dick, a Scot and Blackpool's number ten that day, had worked as a waiter in the town where he decided to ask the club for a trial.

- -

Programme Spotlights 4: An epic cup final
Blackpool 2 Manchester United 4, FA Cup Final, 24 April 1948

The programme for this epic FA Cup Final had a suitably dramatic front cover. The sketch of the goalkeeper leaping to save conveys the drama of a match, an image enhanced by the diagonal naming of the clubs, and then the expanding, red backgrounded 'Empire Stadium'. Similarly, the font, the size and the colour of 'Final Tie' and 'Wembley', and the white flashes on the green background build the excitement – you feel the energy, something is going to happen. The depiction of the stadium at an angle (paralleling the keeper's upper body just as the Blackpool v. Manchester United line follows his legs) draws on Expressionism in its rejection of realism and its use of boldly contrasting colours. The cover is in stark contrast to the rest of the programme, which is very conventional in its content and design.

The match was indeed dramatic. Blackpool took an early lead when Stan Mortensen broke through and was tripped by centre-half Chilton as he reached the area: Shimwell's spot-kick went underneath Crompton's dive to his right. Jack Rowley equalised after lobbing the ball over Joe Robinson in Blackpool's goal, then following it for a tap-in. However, Mortensen gave the Seasiders a 2-1 half-time lead. United dominated the second half. Jack Rowley equalised with a classic centre-forward's header from a free kick before inside-left Stan Pearson scored with a powerful shot. Finally, right-half John Anderson, a less celebrated name from the era and a local from Manchester, scored from distance.

- -

Charlie Mitten and Jack Rowley had played in that 1948 final, with Rowley scoring twice (see Programme Spotlights 4). They were stars of Manchester United and at the peak of their careers. Our collection of football ephemera includes a copy of the illustrated magazine *Sport* for the week 8–14 July 1949. It shows Rowley and Mitten at Butlin's Filey Holiday Camp, surrounded by a dozen women in bathing costumes (though the flags in the background suggest a stiff breeze was blowing, and Mitten is sensibly wearing a sweater!). Boosting wages over the summer by working at Butlin's and enjoying the delights of the British seaside was as good as it got. The following summer, Mitten and his family flew to Bogotá. Luis Robledo, the Cambridge-educated son of a millionaire Colombian cattle baron, and married to the daughter of an English earl, was the exotic figure behind the improbable migration.

It is easy to understand the lure of Bogotá for Mitten. Richard Adamson's book *Bogota Bandit: The Outlaw Life of Charlie Mitten: Manchester United's Penalty King* tells how, a year after his stint at Butlin's, Mitten was in a New York hotel room on a summer tour with his club, when he received a telephone call from Neil Franklin, England's centre-half in that first post-war international against Wales at Maine Road. Franklin had already moved to Independiente Santa Fe, along with his Stoke team-mate George Mountford, who had vied with Stanley Matthews for the Stoke number seven shirt. Colombia had withdrawn from FIFA, so were not obliged to pay transfer fees when signing players internationally. The terms on offer to Mitten were a £5,000 signing-on fee, a £5,000-a-year contract plus £35 win bonuses. These compared with the £12 a week he was earning at Old Trafford. Though his Manchester United contract had expired, there was no doubt it would be renewed for the forthcoming 1950/51 season. So, there in New York, Mitten packed his trunk, got a team-mate to take it back to England, and flew to Bogotá with only hand luggage. His wife, back in their house rented from United, heard the news from reading the newspapers. Mitten returned home, collected his family and together they headed off, not to the bracing Yorkshire seaside but across the Andes to the capital of Colombia at over 8,000ft above sea level.

Around this same time, I remember the Manchester United goalkeeper, Jack Crompton, running a sweets and tobacco corner shop in the 19th-century terraced street next to the one we were living in at the time in the Moston area of the city. Then, as now, Moston was not a fashionable part of town. In the Manchester United v. Portsmouth programme for the FA Cup fifth round tie on 11 February 1950, Crompton was lauded for his 78th-minute penalty save in the last game of the previous season against the same opponents. The goalkeeper's heroics had secured United a second-place finish, and so a bonus for the players of £440, £110 more than if they had slipped to third. The 1948 FA Cup Final programme said Crompton was studying accountancy: I guess his ambition was efficient book keeping to support his planned future as a small shopkeeper, but not a career dealing in financial derivatives in the City of London.

However, we need to beware of slipping into rose-tinted nostalgia for a simpler, more equal though poorer era. In a game against Newcastle United in which Mitten scored in front of a crowd of 70,787, Matt Busby, in his manager's column in the *United Review* of 4 December 1948, mentioned Charlie playing for England against Scotland at Maine Road in a game staged for the Bolton Disaster Fund. On 9 March 1946, a crowd estimated at 85,000 had crammed in to Burnden Park for an FA Cup sixth round second leg match between Bolton Wanderers and Stoke City. The terracing at the Railway End was more like a bank of ash with some flagstones; my personal recollection is that it was not much better more than a decade later. There was desperate overcrowding, barriers collapsed, people were crushed underneath. Many were injured, and 33 fans died. It happened at Bolton, but the conditions there were not exceptional. It was the people's game, but the people were not treated like human beings. It would take more than four decades and more tragedies before fans in the UK were treated better.

Nor were the people angels. 'The Football Association is concerned at the growing practice of throwing missiles at Officials and players,' reported Chelsea's programme on 15 November 1947, while adding somewhat sanctimoniously, 'While we are singularly free from such incidents at the Bridge, a fact of which we are justly proud... Such conduct is a blot on the game.'

Nostalgia is an integral part of being a football fan, and was just as prominent in the post-war period, as our oldest Scottish programme, Heart of Midlothian versus Partick Thistle from August 1950, shows. The text in the programme, under the heading 'Random Reflections and Notes from my Diary', was written by George Robertson, who is listed on the cover as one of the Edinburgh club's directors. It is mainly given over to stories about one Isaac Begbie, of whom Robertson wrote, 'To many he is only a name, but to me and thousands of Hearts old-timers he was one of the greatest half-backs that ever kicked a ball at Tynecastle.' The story goes on to explain how Begbie's family were 'in the dairy business', and so Isaac 'was a 4 a.m. man, and many a time I have seen him sitting on the top of a cart of turnips collected from a field out Gorgie way'. It is a reminder of the 19th-century municipal geography of Edinburgh, that Tynecastle was then outside the city boundary: it is less than two and a half miles from the very centre of town. In 1890/91, Begbie had been in the first Hearts team to win the Scottish Cup. It is also interesting to read that, in Robertson's view, 'The introduction of the inside-forward coming back to assist his half-back was the result of Begbie slowing up.'

Programme Spotlights 5: Hearts' Edinburgh roots

Heart of Midlothian 2 Partick Thistle 0, Scottish League Cup, 26 August 1950.

The single-sheet, eight-page programme, printed in Hearts' maroon colours, depicts sketches of iconic Edinburgh landmarks on the front cover – the Scott Monument, St. Giles Cathedral and Edinburgh Castle. These images indicate the club's close identity with the city. Unusually, the teams are listed on the front, and are not set out in the conventional 2-3-5 formations of the day, but instead, in the modern way, are simply names by number.

The Hearts side included the legendary trio of Alfie Conn (Senior), Willie Bauld and Jimmy Wardhaugh; over their careers, they scored more than 900 goals for the club.

As somebody diligently typed in on the programme, Wardhaugh scored one of Hearts' goals that beat Partick Thistle, right-back Parker getting the other. However, the damage to the Jam Tarts' chances of qualification had already been done by drawing 1-1 with Thistle at Firhill in the opening fixture two weeks previously. Motherwell won the group and went on to land the cup, beating Hibernian 3-0 in the final.

Robertson continued his reminiscences by recalling that Scotland's first international against Ireland had been played 66 years previously, in 1884. It was a game Scotland won 5-0 at the Ulster Cricket Ground in Belfast. In an off-hand comment that intrigues, he observed that Scotland's formation that day was 'two half-backs and two centre-forwards'. Robertson also pointed out that the Scotland team had been drawn mainly from village sides. These were not the picturesque villages of southern England. Scotland's players came from Vale of Leven

(West Dumbartonshire, which became one of Scotland's 'Little Moscows' as unemployment rocketed in the 1920s), Abercorn (a West Lothian coastal village), Annbank (in South Ayrshire, then a mining village), Arthurlie (Barrhead, south of Glasgow) and Lugar Boswell (East Ayrshire, a settlement that grew around an ironworks). It is a reminder of just how important these industrial villages were to Scotland's economy and culture in the second half of the 19th century, and to its subsequent politics. No doubt religion would also have held a fierce grip on village life. Indeed, the Hearts programmes in the 1950/51 season carried an advert from the Church of Scotland – 'A Good Supporter is Loyal – Do you support YOUR Church?' Hearts were traditionally the Protestant team in Edinburgh.

Like the Manchester United programme from that same season mentioned above, Robertson's column in the Hearts programme also included a joke. A bugler and a piper had to sound reveille at Edinburgh Castle one dark, frosty morning. The piper had a hangover and was afraid of slipping on the ice, so said to the bugler, 'Ginger, you go in front and I will go before you.' End of joke. Much has changed since those post-war years, and perhaps that includes our sense of humour.

Programmes cited in Chapter 2 that are in the collection:
- 16 October 1943, Dulwich Hamlet v. Belvedere, South Eastern Combination (result unknown)
- 4 December 1943, Brentford 0 Fulham 0, Football League (South)
- 5 February 1944, Brentford 4 Arsenal 1, Football League (South)
- 10 April 1944, Brentford 2 Crystal Palace 0, Football League (South)
- 13 November 1946, England 3 Wales 0, Home International Championship

- 22 March 1947, Chelsea 2 Sunderland 1, Football League First Division
- 19 April 1947, Chelsea 1 Huddersfield Town 0, Football League First Division
- 15 November 1947, Chelsea 4 Stoke City 1, Football League First Division
- 24 April 1948, Blackpool 2 Manchester United 4, FA Cup Final
- 27 November 1948, Rochdale 1 Barrow 1, FA Cup first round
- 4 December 1948, Manchester United 1 Newcastle United 1, Football League First Division
- 31 August 1949, Arsenal 2 Chelsea 3, Football League First Division
- 11 February 1950, Manchester United 3 Portsmouth 3, FA Cup fifth round
- 26 August 1950, Heart of Midlothian 2 Partick Thistle 0, Scottish League Cup first round Group Three
- 2 September 1950, Manchester United 1 Blackpool 0, Football League First Division

Chapter 3

Schoolboy Dreams

MY FIRST career ambition was to become a fisherman. The inspiration came from my first holiday by the seaside, which was probably about 1950. We went on a motor coach from the bus station in the centre of Manchester to Scarborough, for a week of sand, donkey rides and fresh air. Throughout her life, whenever we were at the coast, my mum would always tell me to 'breathe in the sea air'. While she never seemed to realise that holding my breath for a week was not an option, air quality in industrial Manchester made it easy to understand why she would have seen sea air as good for you. Back home, the air carried two contrasting fragrances, sweet from the biscuit works or acrid from the dye factory. Scarborough was bliss: sand pies, paddling and ice creams. I began to dream of ways to stay there permanently. Eureka, be a fisherman!

My intention lasted about a year, until our next holiday and a trip 'round the bay' seated at the front of a small open-top boat, the seat any six- or seven-year-old would grab. Once outside the harbour, there was a swell on the North Sea. Each time the boat crested a wave I gazed down to the chasm of dark green water into which this fragile vessel was about to plunge. Then we lurched violently up again as the craft struck the next wave. On disembarkation after my 30-minute ordeal, any colour the week's fresh air had put into my cheeks had quite drained away. I decided against the life of a mariner.

So from the age of about six or seven, football filled the void in my career aspirations. I would become a footballer. Those childhood years were spent among the terraced houses, back alleys and corner shops that had developed as Manchester spread into surrounding villages and countryside during the last quarter of the 19th century. Like most working-class lads in similar places across Britain, I played multi-age group football in the streets and on scraps of open space near home. Cars were rare in the late 1940s and early 1950s; few people in such neighbourhoods owned one, and carts drawn by horses remained a feature of the streetscape.

At the age of about nine or ten, for the first time I took part in an 11-a-side game that was refereed. This was entirely due to Malcolm Darlington. He was a maybe two or three years older than me, the best footballer within a few streets' radius of where I lived, and would eventually go on to represent Manchester Boys, play a few games on the left wing for Manchester City, then spend most of his career as a part-time player with non-league Hyde United. Malc formed a team, Abbotsford United, named after the street where he lived (and one of the places where we played football). We played several games in the David Lewis Recreation Ground against a local Boys' Brigade outfit, who had the advantage of responsible adults overseeing their side, one of whom would referee our encounters. They also provided wooden stands that served as goalposts with a rope for each crossbar.

No replica shirts in those days. Indeed, as a spontaneous start-up from a gang of lads, we had no football shirts between us. The solution was that we would wear white shirts, because every boy was likely to have one, if only for special occasions. My ambition was to play at centre-forward, the glamour position of the day. I must have been remarkably persuasive, as Malc, our manager/coach/captain/star player agreed that I could play there. As probably the youngest member of this mixed-age team, and of no more than average stature for my age, I was exceptionally unsuited to the position. In those days, centre-forwards were big, strong and expected to score goals, if necessary by clattering the goalkeeper, ball and all, into the net. My mum cut a black number nine out of some material and stitched it on the back of my white shirt. Maybe it was this camouflage which hid my deficiencies and helped me to retain my position.

I can still clearly recall scoring my first goal for Abbotsford. I collected a pass just inside the opposition half and found myself running unopposed (was I offside?) towards their goalkeeper, who was a big, stout lad who seemed to get more enormous with every pace I took. Panic setting in, I swung my right foot (the only one I could kick with) at the heavy case ball, and it soared high to the keeper's left and into the top corner just below the rope. Our goal celebration was as undemonstrative as those of our heroes – my team-mates politely shook my hand, and said, 'Well done', but, all those decades later, I can still picture the ball going in, and hear Malcolm Darlington congratulating me for placing the shot so precisely (I didn't feel obliged to confess that it could have gone anywhere). The fact that this moment literally became a memory of a lifetime says something about what football can mean to young boys and old men.

Like the rest of the Abbotsford XI that day, my football boots had probably come from the local Co-op, the Blackley Cooperative Society on Moston Lane, the nearest thing to a department store, located on the nearest thing to a local High Street. At the Co-op you had a number, which was recorded with every purchase to build up your dividend, embedding thrift into shopping. The boots may even have been Timpson

'Knock-Out' boots, 'Built for Speed, Comfort and Accurate Kicking', as the advert in the *Manchester Schools FA Handbook* put it. Whatever boots I was wearing that blissful afternoon would not have ensured 'accurate kicking'. They were made with stiff leather that remained inflexible no matter how much greasy Dubbin was smeared into them. They reached ankle height, and had heavy toecaps – hence the need for ankle protection from the toecaps of others. The design had not changed from the pre-war era, and exemplified the manly virtues of the British game.

Each weekday I made the short walk from home, past Abbotsford Street and up Church Lane to Alfred Street Elementary School. Opened in 1905, it did not have a playing field on site like newer, more suburban schools had. However, it did have a schoolyard and a core of male teachers who were dedicated to football and to developing the talents of the older boys. My copy of the *Manchester Schools FA Handbook* for 1954/55 hints at the commitment of teachers at Alfred Street to schools football. They, and others like them teaching in schools across the city, freely gave their time to the benefit of generations of boys and the game as a whole. A. Hudson, Alfred Street Boys School, Manchester 9, was vice-chairman of the Manchester Schools' FA that year. 'Archie' taught me in 1952/53. He was a forceful man with a shock of white hair, and prone to intoning repetitive advice that I can still recite by heart. 'It'll do won't do, only your best will do,' was one, and another, was, 'If you want the liquorice, you can have the liquorice.' This was not a prelude to distribution of sweets. The liquorice was his strap of black leather, which he used to punish miscreant eight-year-olds by beating them behind the knees.

The system of secondary education created by the 1944 Education Act had been phased in gradually, while new schools were being built. Performance in the '11-plus' examinations sifted children into different education paths. Nationally around 25 to 30 per cent who 'passed' would move on to grammar school, while the remainder would go to a technical school or a secondary modern school, or, until those schools were built, would stay on at the elementary school until they reached 15, the school-leaving age. Thus while I was still under ten, there were boys also at Alfred Street who were approaching 15 years of age. There were girls too, though, while boys and girls attended the same school, they were taught separately from the age of seven and had different playgrounds, so I never remember seeing the older girls. It was these 14- and 15-year-old boys who represented the school in competitive football against other local schools. My age group never received any coaching from teachers, we just played informal games in the schoolyard with coats for goalposts, and anything spherical for a ball; most usually it was a tennis ball.

Despite, or perhaps because of, his position in the Manchester Schools FA, Archie Hudson did not coach the school team. That task was shared by Mr Callaghan, the art teacher, and Mr Weekes. Callaghan was a chirpy, mercurial figure, who went on to become the Labour MP for Middleton and Heywood, a couple of miles up the Rochdale Road from Alfred Street. Weekes, more chubby, had been my class teacher in 1951/52. The headmaster at Alfred Street, Mr J. Anderson, was a vice-president of the Manchester Schools FA and its representative on the Council of the Lancashire Schools FA. The handbook lists his home telephone number. At that time no more than ten per cent of British households had a phone. For most of us, a phone was something in a big red box about half a mile away from your home, not something that you carried in your pocket to take photos and mail them to friends. I have no recollection of where the nearest public phone box to our house was; I guess we knew nobody who had a phone, so had no need to use the phone box.

A school had to pay two shillings per annum to be a member of the Manchester Schools FA, according to the rules listed in the handbook. Rule 18 was unequivocal, 'All teams must be under the direct and sole control of the teachers of the schools, and the training and tuition of teams or refereeing of matches by anyone other than a teacher shall be a disqualification.' So, no parental involvement in those days, and seemingly no school unable to provide a teacher to take on these extra-curricular roles.

The handbook contains photos of nine school teams who had won trophies in 1953/54, and the four area select teams (North, South, East and West) and the Manchester Boys team from that season. There are no black or Asian faces among these portraits from all parts of this large industrial city. A Royal Commission on Population had reported in 1949 that immigrants of 'good stock' would be welcomed into the UK, in an effort to plug labour shortages. A year earlier, the former German cruise ship, the SS *Empire Windrush*, had docked at Tilbury with its cargo of 400 or 500 people from the Caribbean. Although migrants from the New Commonwealth began to arrive in increasing numbers in the 1950s, the pictorial evidence in the handbook suggests that they had made no impact on schools football in Manchester in the first half of that decade. And were there any girls featuring in games under the aegis of the Manchester Schools FA? Of course not. Schools football in Manchester, and probably everywhere else in the UK, at that time was a male, white activity. Like children, ladies were admitted for half price when Manchester played Barnsley in the English Schools Trophy semi-final at Maine Road in April 1950. My flimsy four-page programme for that match (kick-off 11am) records that another Alfred Street lad, Hallett, played centre-half for Manchester.

With my class-mates, I would go to support Alfred Street's teams in their football matches against other schools. The games were staged on local park pitches, or in the case of knock-out finals at the Newton Heath Loco ground, a venue famous all across the north of Manchester. The name did not imply insanity; 'Loco' was an abbreviation for Locomotive, just like Lokomotiv Leipzig or similar exotic-sounding clubs from central and eastern Europe. Newton Heath Loco had been formed by railway workers in the Motive Power Division of the Lancashire and Yorkshire Railway, whose steam trains were lined up in the goods yard behind the Loco ground at Ceylon Street, just off the Oldham Road. Their fellow workers in the Carriage and Wagon Department played as Newton Heath LYR (Lancashire and Yorkshire Railway) at North Road, on the other side of the tracks, and became Manchester United. The Motive Power Division never reached such heights, and the Loco ground was redeveloped for housing after 2008, but for schoolboys like me in the early 1950s it was our Wembley.

Those years were something of a golden age for schools football in our part of Manchester. This would have made my own dream of being a footballer credible, had it not been for my lack of ability. In 1953, Wilf McGuinness captained Mount Carmel, which was the local Catholic school, Manchester Schoolboys, Lancashire Schoolboys and England Schoolboys, before signing for Manchester United when he left school. He made his first-team debut as a 17-year-old. A serious injury in December 1959 ended his playing career when he was still only 22. In all, he made 81 appearances for United and won two full England caps, and then had an unhappy 18 months as United manager in 1969/70.

While playing at the highest level, McGuinness continued to live locally in our part of north Manchester, and so when he made his debut for England, as a 20-year-old wearing the number six shirt against Northern Ireland at Windsor Park, Belfast, in a 3-3 draw on 4 October 1958, he kindly brought me and a school pal of mine, who lived just round the corner from him, a copy of the match programme. It remains in our collection, and includes a lovely story by Malcolm Brodie of the *Belfast Telegraph* about that summer's World Cup finals in Stockholm. Northern Ireland had been based at Tylösand, now publicised globally as the name of an IKEA sofa, but in 1958 just an obscure coastal settlement convenient for Halmstad where the Irish team would play. Brodie described how, as the team arrived, a local boy 'rather timorously' approached goalkeeper Harry Gregg with a piece of paper asking in English for his autograph. Gregg obliged, and so 13-year-old Bengt Jonasson 'became unofficial translator and general factotum to the Ireland party. He went with them on training stints… travelled in the bus to the matches… attended civic receptions… advised them on prices when they went on shopping sprees… and assisted Gerry Morgan in unpacking the hampers.' At the players', officials' and press reporters' expense young Bengt was a guest at Windsor Park that October afternoon, among the crowd of 58,000.

Programme Spotlights 6: A programme gifted by Wilf McGuinness from his England debut

Northern Ireland 3 England 3, Home International Championship, 4 October 1958

The Ireland team included three outstanding performers. Harry Gregg was the world's most expensive goalkeeper following his £23,000 move from Doncaster Rovers to Manchester United in 1957. Right-half and captain Danny Blanchflower would lead the all-conquering Spurs team of the early 1960s, while Jimmy McIlroy was the archetypal creative number ten, and the maestro of Burnley's league championship-winning team in 1959/60.

The game was played in heavy rain on a muddy pitch. The home team took the lead after 16 minutes when Wilbur Cush (Leeds United) ran on to a defence-splitting pass from McIlroy. A fierce right-foot drive from the edge of the penalty area by Bobby Charlton made it 1-1 on 31 minutes. In the second half, Celtic wing-half Bertie Peacock restored the home team's advantage with a drive, before Tom Finney latched on to a back pass (always a risky option on a sticky pitch) and scored his 30th international goal, breaking the England record at the time. Ireland came back again when England's goalkeeper McDonald (Burnley), under the kind of aerial challenge that was allowed in the UK in those days, dropped a cross, allowing centre-forward Tommy Casey (Portsmouth) to bundle the ball home through the mud. It was left to man of the match Charlton to hit another unstoppable shot, this time with his left foot, past his club-mate Gregg, following a pass from Fulham's Johnny Haynes.

In another echo of the times, the BBC's Northern Ireland sports editor explained in the programme how Northern Ireland's crucial group stage play-off with Czechoslovakia in the World Cup finals that summer had been broadcast in the province. He estimated that more than 250,000 were glued to their radios with the game tied at 1-1 when the commentary was cut for the nine-o'-clock evening news. Telephone lines to Broadcasting House, Belfast were jammed as fans protested. No doubt the gentlemen who ran the BBC were surprised, but unmoved, by the complaints.

Another local tyro was Joe Dean, goalkeeper for Alfred Street, Manchester Boys, Lancashire County and England Boys. His twin brother David played with him as the strong, bustling centre-forward in our school team. In 1954, Joe kept goal for England Schoolboys against Scotland at Wembley, a game that was televised, and in which he made a name for himself after throwing the ball as far as the halfway line. He also kept goal against Eire Boys in a 3-3 draw in Cork, where another member of the England team was Terry Beckett, from St. Patrick's in Collyhurst, just down the Rochdale Road from Alfred Street, and the school that also educated World Cup winner Nobby Stiles, and later Brian Kidd, a scorer in the 1968 European Cup Final. On leaving school Beckett had offers from Wolves and Spurs but opted for Manchester United, where he was a member of their 1955 FA Youth Cup-winning team alongside McGuinness, Bobby Charlton, Duncan Edwards, Eddie Colman and Shay Brennan, some of the most famous names in the club's history. He scored one of the goals in their 4-1 victory over West Brom in the first leg of that final. In Tony Whelan's *The Birth of the Babes*, Beckett explained how Mr Mulligan, a teacher at 'St. Pat's' and a United fan, had close links with Joe Armstrong, United's chief scout at that time.

Naturally, all of us at Alfred Street were proud of what Joe Dean had achieved, and so it was that I went to stand low down on the open terrace behind the goal at the scoreboard end at Maine Road on 15 May 1954 to watch him keep goal for England Schoolboys against Wales Schoolboys. Of course, I bought and kept the programme and still have it. The programme tells me that Joe, then just a month over 15, stood at 6ft 1in, and weighed 12st 5lb (roughly 78.5kg). I was nine years old: no wonder he seemed like a colossus in the schoolyard.

The match was part of the celebrations for the Golden Jubilee of the English Schools Football Association (ESFA). The eight-page programme cost threepence, and is printed black on white. The first inside page contains photos of three elderly-looking men. W.H. Morgan was the chairman of the ESFA, and had been awarded an MBE in recognition of his work with schools football. The programme comments on his integrity of purpose, and his portrait bears the mark of a man you would not want to upset. His hair is short and sparse, and although his rectangular face is full on to the camera, his eyes are directed to his left, as if he were a teacher giving out dictation while keeping a reproachful watch on miscreant boys in the back row. The treasurer, Alderman R. Charlton from Andover, looks more avuncular, has lost less of his hair and, slightly side-on to camera, even manages a smile: a geography teacher, maybe? Secretary W.R. Ward, Esq, (Birmingham) is pictured in heavy glasses beneath a receding hairline and puffing on a pipe. You can imagine him commanding the stage in a chemistry lab behind a haze of smoke, the stink mingling with the acrid aromas left from the experiment, and using all his grizzled experience to push no-hopers to pass their examinations.

Of those playing in front of Joe Dean that May afternoon, only three names are familiar. The 'golden boy' was Alick Jeffrey from Rotherham, playing at inside-left. He was two-footed and strong in the air. The programme that day noted that he had 'headed a grand goal for England against Wales at Watford'. He went on to make his senior debut for Doncaster Rovers later that year while still only 15. When Doncaster travelled to Eastville to meet Bristol Rovers in an FA Cup fourth round tie in 1956, Jeffrey was described in the programme as follows, 'Regarded as the best young footballing prospects [sic] in the country at the present time and indeed is a brilliant player. Has already gained schoolboy, junior, intermediate and amateur honours in two seasons and likely to gain more. This fine, well-built lad celebrates his 17th birthday tomorrow (Sunday) but is likely to remain an amateur. Is a danger with head and feet, and can he shoot!'

A transfer to Manchester United was mooted, and Peter Whittell's book *Alick Jeffrey – The Original Boy Wonder* (2003) claimed that they made a payment of £200 to him ahead of signing. However, Jeffrey then suffered a badly broken leg while playing for England Under-23s against France in October 1956, ending the prospect of the move and a glittering career. He offered to return the money – equivalent to 20 weeks' wages – but United's manager, Matt Busby, told him to keep it and buy something nice for his mother: he got her a washing machine. After spells with Skegness Town (where he again broke his leg) and in Australia, Jeffrey returned to Doncaster Rovers in 1963. The Gillingham v. Doncaster programme on 22 February 1964, which is in our collection, described him as 'much travelled, unlucky youngster'. Jeffrey went on to play for Lincoln City before retiring in 1970 to run a pub, after a short spell with Worksop Town. He died in Doncaster, aged 61. Despite his misfortunes and set-backs, he managed 132 goals in 284 Football League appearances.

Derek Temple, whose 'clever ball control and powerful shot' was highlighted in the schools match programme, lined up as England's number nine, alongside Jeffrey. He had better luck in his professional career, spending a decade with First Division Everton and winning an England cap against West Germany in 1965. Scoring the late winner that enabled Everton to beat Sheffield Wednesday 3-2 in the 1966 FA Cup Final was his moment of glory, before he moved on to Preston North End and then Wigan Athletic. One of the boys that Temple kept out of the team against Wales Schools was Alex Dawson from Hull, who also went on to score a goal in an FA Cup Final, albeit for the losing team, Preston North End, who went down to West Ham United in 1964. Though representing England Schools, Dawson had actually been born in Aberdeen.

Playing on the left wing for Wales Schools was Kenneth Morgan – it should have been Morgans – who was only 5ft 6in tall and weighed 9st 7lb (just over 60kg), and as the programme said, and as his later career with Manchester United and Swansea would prove, could play on either wing. Writing Morgans' obituary in the *Daily Telegraph* in 2012, Jim White described him as 'a spring-heeled winger, capable of prodigious accuracy with his crossing'. That captures my own memories of him.

Joe Dean's own professional career had barely started before he suffered a setback. He left Alfred Street school that summer of 1954 and joined Bolton Wanderers. When he made his First Division debut as a 16-year-old on Saturday, 11 February 1956 at a snow-covered Molineux, against Wolverhampton Wanderers, he was the youngest goalkeeper ever to appear in the Football League. Wolves went on to finish the season in third place, and were the division's top scorers with 89. It was never going to be an easy baptism. Dean was hit on the head in the first few minutes and was reported as saying, 'I hardly remember a thing until half-time'; presumably there was some concussion. While the circumstances of the collision are not recorded in the newspaper cutting I had pasted in my scrapbook, at a time when the charging of goalkeepers was legal and routine, it is not too cynical to imagine toughened pros setting out to put in an early physical challenge on the young, inexperienced stopper.

Worse was to follow, as Dean palmed a Wolves corner into his own net to open the scoring. In the second half he was off the field for ten minutes with a cut over his left eye that required stitches. He also injured a knee, and was treated on the field by the trainer with the eponymous magic sponge. Dean's manager, Bill Ridding, was consoling, 'He gave a creditable show and did just as well as we expected him to do against such strong opposition.' Back at Alfred Street, a 13-year-old pupil, under Mr Callaghan's tutoring, had spent two weeks painting a 15ft-long watercolour depicting a yellow-jerseyed Dean pushing a cross over the bar as attackers closed in. He gave it to Dean as a present.

Although he made 17 first-team appearances between 1956 and 1960, Joe Dean never really established himself in the Bolton team. He was behind Eddie Hopkinson, who was a few years older, and who made his debut on the first day of the 1956/57 season, during which he played in every game.

Hopkinson went on to keep goal for the Trotters in 518 league games before retiring in 1969. He was ever-present in five of his first eight seasons in the Burnden Park team, won the FA Cup in 1958 and was capped 14 times by England. Dean was his understudy, though Dean was in the Bolton team sheet for their 2-0 home defeat to Manchester City on 5 April 1958, another of our programmes.

More generally, Dean was Bolton's Central League goalkeeper. As such he is mentioned in the 21 September 1957 Manchester United v. Arsenal programme, in the report of the previous weekend's reserve game at Old Trafford which ended in a 2-2 draw. With the game goalless, 'Bolton's goal had a remarkable escape, Dean saving three times in quick succession.' With Bolton leading 1-0, he was beaten by a penalty, then a minute into the second half by 'a low shot'. Dean also figured in the write-up of the return game the following January, in the programme for United's FA Cup tie against Ipswich Town. The reserve teams had again drawn 2-2. Dean was credited with turning away a centre from under the bar, and also saving a 'full-blooded drive', before being beaten twice in a minute by Liam Whelan, one from close range, the second through a crowd of players from 25 yards.

Dean moved to Carlisle United in 1962. He played for them until 1970, making 137 appearances. At the age of 31, he signed for Barrow and turned out for them 41 times in a two-season stay. What happened to him after that, I do not know. While his football abilities earned him a living for the best part of 20 years, like so many others who represented their country as schoolboys, he did not progress to become a full international. The programme for that day when the boys of England and Wales faced each other at Maine Road contained the telling statistic that of 640 schoolboy internationals up to 1953, only 23 had achieved senior caps.

Among these ancient programmes of schoolboy matches is one of my personal favourites. It's probably worth nowt, and I have no idea how I acquired it, as I was too young to have gone to the actual match. Alongside sports photos that I had cut out of newspapers, it is sellotaped into the scrapbook that I would assemble in the winter evenings. Those cuttings also have their own stories, 'Bill Whelan sticks out a foot to score Manchester United's second goal' (the opposition's left-back obscures all of Whelan but his left leg). Then there is Spurs' goalkeeper collecting a high ball in a game at Maine Road, in the distinctive green – the paper not the keeper – of the *Manchester Evening News 'Green 'Un'*, which was published as the matches ended, and carried the results and reports before anyone else. On another page, I pasted in a photo of West Ham's number five, Brown, launching the kind of two-footed tackle on Sheffield United's outside-right that today would warrant not just a red card, but prosecution for assault. Nestled among this ephemera, folded, tatty and too fragile to detach, printed black on white paper, tenuously attached by sellotape holding down the top and bottom corners of its spine, is the programme from a game played at Boundary Park, 'By kind permission of the Directors of Oldham Athletic', as it says on the front, on Saturday, 6 May 1950. It was probably a drab and windy afternoon: even May afternoons at Boundary Park are often like that. The match was a schoolboy international between England and 'Ireland', who were actually Northern Ireland (see also the programme from Windsor Park in 1958, Programme Spotlights 6). The school leaving age in Northern Ireland at the time was still 14, an indication of the society's disregard for skills beyond those required for labouring work.

One tattered page in that programme instructed readers, 'These boys are the stars of today – keep an eye on them – they will be the stars of tomorrow.' England's centre-forward was

----

Programme Spotlights 7: The mental, moral and physical development of schoolboys

England Schools v. Wales Schools, Schools Jubilee International, 15 May 1954

This game, which I attended as a nine-year-old boy, was part of the celebrations for the golden jubilee of the English Schools Football Association. The Corinthian spirit was echoed in the text of the programme. 'The main objects of the Association are the mental, moral and physical development of schoolboys and the observance of the highest sporting traditions,' it noted. Up to two substitutes were allowed for players 'who shall have left the field owing to injury before the 38th minute', and in addition an injured goalkeeper could be replaced at any time. Substitutes were not allowed in English league games until 1965/66. The star youngster on show was Alick Jeffrey from Rotherham.

----

still only 13. 'Strong and two-footed. Splendid distributor, especially with long cross passes to wings,' was how he was described. There are not many of us left now who saw him play, but that pithy pen portrait of the number nine from Worcester County, reignites my mental picture of the great Duncan Edwards. This was his first international appearance, though two years later he was still in the England schools team, captaining them from left-half against Scotland at Wembley on 5 April 1952. England beat Ireland 5-2 that afternoon at Oldham, and at outside-left, benefiting from those diagonal passes from his centre-forward, was David Pegg, 'A fine winger. Well up to the tradition of Yorkshire stars of the past,' as the programme described him. Like Edwards, Pegg went on to become one of the 'Busby Babes' at Manchester United, where he was playing in the first team at the age of 17, and later was capped by England.

Programme Spotlights 8: A reluctant 13-year-old puts football before Morris dancing

England Schools 5 Ireland Schools 2, Schools International, 6 May 1950

Because the school leaving age was still only 14 in Northern Ireland, the cut-off for selection for this schools international at Boundary Park was boys under 14 on 1 September 1949. The plain black on white printing was the norm for England's home schools internationals for some time, though by the 1954 game against Wales mentioned previously, the quality of the paper had improved and pages were larger.

The programme is notable because the game marked the first international appearance of 13-year-old Duncan Edwards who played at centre-forward for England, and would soon become a star with Manchester United and England.

James Leighton's book *Duncan Edwards – The Greatest* (2012) tells how that afternoon at Oldham, 'Edwards delivered a display that belied his tender years... Launching himself at the Irish defenders, Edwards had them quaking in their boots every time he set off on a run.' However, Leighton also describes how Edwards only 'reluctantly' chose to play, as it meant he could not take part in the national Morris and Sword Dancing Championships in Derby that same day! His local newspaper welcomed his England selection, of course, while adding, 'At school Duncan is also a star member of the Morris, sword and folk dancing teams and last year competed at the Leamington and Birmingham festivals.'

How thrilled and proud these lads from working-class families, growing up in the industrial heartlands of Britain, must have been to be wearing their country's shirt, and playing at the ground of a league club. World war had stamped their childhood: air raids, rationing, kick-abouts in the streets and parks. Stepping out as internationals, these adolescents must have spied their chance of a lifetime, and for the moment lived their dream of becoming a footballer. Some would achieve greatness, some face tragedy, others just disappointment and a more ordinary life. But, just as I still treasure my first goal for Abbotsford United from a shot that gets more powerful every time I think about it, they will have had memories of glorious times when they were still boys.

Programmes cited in Chapter 3 that are in the collection:

- 6 May 1950, England Schools 5 Ireland Schools 2, schools international
- 7 April 1950, Manchester Schoolboys v. Barnsley Schoolboys, English Schools Trophy semi-final (result unknown)
- 5 April 1952, England Schools v. Scotland Schools, Schools International (result unknown)
- 15 May 1954, England Schoolboys v. Wales Schoolboys, Schools Jubilee International (result unknown)
- 28 January 1956, Bristol Rovers 1 Doncaster Rovers 1, FA Cup fourth round
- 21 September 1957, Manchester United 4 Arsenal 2, Football League First Division
- 25 January 1958, Manchester United 4 Ipswich Town 0, FA Cup fourth round
- 5 April 1958, Bolton Wanderers 0 Manchester City 2, Football League First Division
- 4 October 1958, Northern Ireland 3 England 3, Home International Championship
- 22 February 1964, Gillingham 1 Doncaster Rovers 1, Football League Fourth Division

Chapter 4

Light at the End of the Tunnel

AFTER ENDURING a world war, it is perhaps understandable that Britain turned inwards. Fighting men had to be demobilised and reintegrated into employment and civilian life; a welfare state was being built, but, as previous chapters have shown, there was still rationing and hardship; national debt soared. The post-war boom that made the USA so prosperous and began to revive the economies of western Europe was slow to take hold in the UK.

As a child I had no real inkling of such things, even when our household received a food parcel, I think from Australia. What I did know accorded rather well with the perspective of UK policy-makers at the time: we had won the war and had an Empire. These blinkers proved inappropriate at a time of rapid change in international relations. However necessary and inspirational Churchill's 'finest hour' speech was when he delivered it on 18 June 1940, it fashioned a mindset that depicted Britain as a global power, a pretence which continues to resonate in England, but was flawed even before the end of the 1940s.

The emotional crescendo of Churchill's great speech was, 'If we can stand up to [Hitler], all Europe may be freed and the life of the world may move forward into broad, sunlit uplands. But if we fail, then the whole world, including the United States, including all that we have known and cared for, will sink into the abyss of a new dark age made more sinister, and perhaps more protracted, by the lights of perverted science. Let us therefore brace ourselves to our duties, and so bear ourselves, that if the British Empire and its Commonwealth last for a thousand years, men will still say, "This was their finest hour.'"

However, soon after 1945 the Empire was unravelling, the USA and the USSR had emerged as antagonistic superpowers that the impoverished UK could not keep pace with, and by 1951 six continental countries were cooperating economically in the European Coal and Steel Community that would soon morph into the European Common Market.

The two generations before mine, the adults in my childhood world, had been defined by direct experience of world wars, which imprinted assumptions about hostility and triumph in relation to foreign countries and their peoples. While these attitudes hung over my own generation as we grew up, for us they were received wisdoms not lived experiences, and therefore more shallow and less resilient in the face of changing facts and new possibilities. The cocktail of hubris and insularity that pervaded the Britain of my childhood years was strongly embedded in football, which was, as we were regularly reminded, a game invented by the British. As a youngster, it was more from football than from any treatise on political economy, that I constructed my understanding of Britain's place in the world in which I was growing up. New technologies, specifically television and floodlighting which fed off each other, exposed British football and its followers, such as me, to the game and a world beyond these shores.

The home countries did not take part in the first three World Cup competitions (1930, 1934 and 1938) and during those years they were not members of the international governing body, FIFA. They had withdrawn in 1920 because other members would not agree to their demands to cut off relations with Germany and its World War I partners. In 1946 membership was resumed, and for the 1950 World Cup FIFA offered places in the finals to the winners (England) and runners-up (Scotland) in Britain's Home International Championship. The Scottish Football Association (SFA) had already declared that they would only accept FIFA's offer if they won the championship, so England's 2-0 win at Hampden Park meant Scotland stayed at home while England went to the Finals in Brazil. A 1-0 defeat in Belo Horizonte by the part-timers representing the USA meant England failed to progress from the group stage: fans back home assumed the score had been misreported. By the time I became aware of it a few years later, that result had been almost forgotten, an aberration rarely mentioned and treated like some eccentric relative who turns up unexpectedly at a family funeral.

A year after that ignominious defeat in Belo Horizonte, during a couple of weeks in May 1951, British football clubs made direct contact with the foreign game on an unprecedented scale. It happened through an unlikely route. I had just about learned to read, and remember reading about the Festival of Britain in the *Daily Mirror*. The event ran for five months until September 1951. It was designed to showcase British business and boost national morale by looking to a future full of possibilities; in today's language it was an attempt by the government to create a 'feelgood factor'. A travelling exhibition, as part of the festival, brought a sample of displays for a three-week showing in Manchester. I was not aware of this, and nor did I read the *Manchester Guardian*'s review, in which the display of 'a basket-work skeleton wearing the last word in beach clothes and a great raffia sunhat' drew the pithy dismissal, 'Far from Blackpool!' We northerners were not easily impressed by such frivolities. The travelling exhibition also went to Leeds, Nottingham and Birmingham, but the South Bank in London, bombed during the war, was the real focus of the festival, with the Royal Festival Hall, the futuristic Skylon, the Telekinema, and a short distance upriver at Battersea Park there was a funfair.

Football was accorded a part in these festivities, with the English Football Association inviting continental, Irish and Scottish teams to play friendlies between 7 May and 19 May 1951, at very different levels. We have the programme from a game on the opening day. Taking advantage of the longer evenings with a 6.30pm kick-off, league champions Tottenham Hotspur played host to FC Austria at White Hart Lane. An extensive table of results compiled online by Javier García and Andrea Veronese reveals that on that same Monday evening South Liverpool were thrashing Cork Athletic 5-1, while a couple of days later Derby County were held to a 1-1 draw by Borussia Dortmund. With the domestic season finished, the single sheet four-page Spurs programme gushed, 'Continental Soccer will invade and pervade Britain.' VE Day was only six years in the past, so the word 'invade' was perhaps unfortunate. Austria itself remained under occupation with US, British, French and Soviet zones. Vienna was still the febrile city in ruins, as immortalised in the film *The Third Man,* and the place where intelligence agents from the Cold War powers brushed shoulders. In April 1951, the month before the game at White Hart Lane, Bela Bajomi, a Hungarian working for British intelligence, had been executed by the Russians, having been captured by them in Vienna; probably he had been betrayed by double agents inside the UK's own spy agency.

This brief but immersive engagement of English clubs with continental counterparts was a novelty. The Spurs programme noted that this was the first time the club had faced a team from Austria, and that the match would provide 'the opportunity to judge the "Continental Style" of play compared with our own type'. The programme reveals a palpable sense of the unknown, observing, 'We are told that FC Austria play "old style" soccer with an aggressive centre-half; they put everything into attack, without by any means neglecting defence, but without the close man-to-man marking that we see in our own style of football.'

Britain was an island: in British football the full-backs wore numbers two and three and marked the opposing wingers, who wore numbers seven and 11. Centre-halves were number five and marked the centre-forward, wearing number nine, while the wing-halves (four and six) jostled with the inside-forwards (eight and ten) in midfield. 'The Continent' might have been visited by players as soldiers a few years before, or become a holiday destination for Chelsea supporters as mentioned in Chapter 2, but as far as football was concerned it was *terra incognita*. It seems clear that Spurs knew little about their opponents that May evening, and certainly had never seen them play, even on film. The aggressive centre-half was Ernst Ocwirk (Ocvirk in the programme) who played as a central midfielder, and would score for Austria in their victorious 1954 World Cup third-place play-off game against Uruguay, before making a big-money move to Sampdoria in 1956, where he became an icon. The Festival of Britain match at White Hart Lane was not the first time Ocwirk had appeared in London, as he had represented Austria in the 1948 Olympics.

Austria's pre-war 'Wunderteam' had reached the semi-finals of the 1934 World Cup. They were runners-up in the 1936 Olympics. So the tone struck in the Spurs programme welcome sounds slightly patronising when it spoke of Vienna's '"old style" soccer' and said 'football in that country has reached a very high standard' and went on to describe football as 'one of our national games that has been taken up so enthusiastically and successfully by them'. Football was still 'our game', even if enthusiastic foreigners were now reaching a high standard.

Programme Spotlights 9: England's best meet strangers

Tottenham Hotspur 0 FC Austria 1, 7 May 1951, Festival of Britain friendly

Spurs were the newly crowned champions of England, having secured the title for the first time in their history, with a 1-0 home win against relegated Sheffield Wednesday on 28 April. The 'push and run' team, so called because of their passing, had only won promotion from the Second Division the previous season. The front cover of the four-page programme shows a cartoon with manager Arthur Rowe shaking hands with skipper Ron Burgess, who had played for Wales in the 1946 international at Maine Road discussed in Chapter 2. On either side of them are the caricature portraits of 11 players and the trainer. Inside, the programme advertised Spurs' next game, against Borussia Dortmund, the following Saturday afternoon, which they won 2-1.

Bill Nicholson, who would go on to manage Spurs' 1961 Double-winning team, was listed to play at right-half. The programme also set out the visitors in the 2-3-5 formation that all British teams used at that time, despite the fact that the 'centre-half' had ceased to be a 'half-back' and instead become a 'stopper', or what we would now call a centre-back. Thus the great Ernst Ocwirk was listed as a centre-half because he wore the number five shirt, despite the fact that he would play in Vienna's midfield, with a totally different role than Clarke, Spurs' number 5.

When they hosted Belgium on a Wednesday afternoon in November 1952, apart from Home Internationals, England had played only three matches at Wembley since the end of the war. Our programme for this match, Belgium's first full international against England, related that there had been a 'spirited and interesting' 2-2 draw with France in May 1945. Then in May 1951 Argentina had visited and were beaten 2-1, a game remembered for 'the acrobatic display by the visiting goalkeeper, Miguel Rugilo, whose gestures amused the 100,000 crowd'. Unfortunately the programme for the Belgium game provides only this tantalising reference to the antics of Señor Rugilo, but there is a newsreel of highlights of the win over Argentina online. The Argentina game was a part of the Festival of Britain celebrations. The newsreel film gives prominence to the moustachioed Rugilo, describing him as 'the goalie with the deadpan face', while adding 'This Rugilo is good!' We see him saving at his near post from Jackie Milburn, swinging on his crossbar as a Mortensen header goes over it, flapping wildly at an out-swinging corner, getting treatment and then being beaten by late goals from Mortensen and Milburn after the visitors had led at half-time.

The third post-war foreign guests to the Empire Stadium had been Austria, who drew 2-2 in November 1951, a game in which 'England gave a glorious fighting display', and the 'England attack had given the Austrians a terrific battering'. The newsreel from this match shows Ocwirk setting up Austria's first goal with a diagonal pass from an inside-left position. The Pathé commentary talks of England playing long passes to match Austria's 'clever stuff'; wily fellows, these foreigners.

An article by John Graydon in the programme for the Belgium match spoke of the progress of the visitors as 'among the most heartening features of post-war football': the previous season they had beaten Italy 2-0 in Brussels. However, Graydon was quick to point out that 'an Englishman, Mr. William Gormlie, has played a major role in the advancement of Belgian football', adding, 'In so small a country as Belgium

Mr. Gormlie has not a great reserve of top-grade players.' This was rather confirmed with England 5-0 winners.

So England were still, it seemed, pre-eminent. Yet, a more careful scrutiny might have challenged that complacency. A note in the programme for the Belgium match explained, 'According to International rules, under which this game is being played, it is possible to change the goalkeeper at any time during the match and to replace any other player up to the 44th minute.' In contrast the programme for England v. Wales at the same venue two weeks earlier made no reference to such a rule, because the British football associations chose to override it for Home Internationals. The manly British game would resist the introduction of substitutes right through until 1965. Internationally, things had moved on, but the British had not.

The England v. Belgium programme also included a page advertising other attractions at Wembley. These included the United States Air Forces in Europe Grid Iron 'Football' Championship Final, which would include 'American Bands – Cheer leaders – Drum Majorettes' and a display by 'Crack American Drill Squad'. The opposite page was a full page advertisement for Pepsi Cola, which was about to be launched on the UK market. On a white background, the centre of the page was the cap of a Pepsi bottle, in its trademark red, white and blue: below to its left, the index finger of a red hand points to the cap, alongside the injunction 'Look for the Signs'.

On the back of the same page, the back cover of the programme, was an advert for Bovril. While claiming it was 'an international favourite among athletes' and lauding its 'concentrated goodness of beef', the advert began in a very British fashion, 'If you're feeling a bit November-foggyish inside, nip into the bar and have a hot Bovril.' The match was taking place just weeks after Britain had exploded its first atom bomb on islands off Western Australia, a comfort blanket for retaining 'great power' status. Yet in this programme you could discern the post-war reality: it was the men supping Pepsi and playing grid iron that dominated the defence of Europe, and Yankee commercial glitz was reshaping consumption and popular culture in a Britain struggling to escape from a year-round state of November-foggyishness.

A still more telling insight into Britain's failure to keep pace was provided in John Graydon's article. On a recent drive to Brussels airport in the company of England manager Walter Winterbottom, he had noted the 'large number of practice pitches, several of them fitted with floodlighting'. Englishmen may have taken football to foreign parts, but even a small country like Belgium was now outstripping the mother country in investment in infrastructure and new technologies. Belgium had floodlit practice pitches, while, as the Pathé newsreel showed, their game at England's national stadium in 1952 finished in fading light on a grey afternoon in late November.

The pivotal moment that destroyed forever the fog of complacency that still enshrouded the British game came in the fading light of another November afternoon in 1953. I remember arriving home from school just in time to catch, on our new TV with its 12in screen, Alf Ramsey slotting home a penalty in the closing minutes. It was England's third goal: Hungary had already scored six. Forty years later, I would pay my own homage to that epic game, by going to a small bar in Budapest that goes by the simple name of 6:3. The inside is adorned with photos of the 'Aranycsapat', the golden team, the Mighty Magyars. Oh my Bozsik and my Puskás long ago, long ago.

We have a BBC videotape of excerpts of big games from the 1950s and 1960s for which Ken Wolstenholme was the commentator, and it includes the 6-3 game. As they lined up to kick off, Koscis and Puskás indulged nonchalantly in 'keepy-uppy'. Wolstenholme's jaw appeared to drop as he said prophetically, 'If we see a lot of that, I think we're going to have a lot of trouble.' Just 42 seconds later, Nandor Hideguti had picked up a pass from Bozsik in midfield, strode forward, feinted then shot from the edge of the penalty area to put the visitors ahead. Wolstenholme repeated ruefully the conventional wisdom, 'Everyone's always said these continentals can't shoot,' a conviction that Hungary's 24-game unbeaten run had failed to overturn. 'Well, they can now,' Wolstenholme might have added, if he had anticipated his famous 'it is now' line at the end of the 1966 World Cup Final.

When the teams took the field, England skipper Billy Wright had spotted something strange. In the book *Puskas on Puskas: The Life and Times of a Footballing Legend*, Wright was quoted as saying that he noticed that the Hungarians 'had on these strange, lightweight boots, cut away like slippers under the ankle-bone'. This prompted him to remark to Stan Mortensen, 'We should be all right here, Stan, they haven't got the proper kit.'

Ferenc Puskás in particular destroyed the Blimpish fallacies. For Hungary's third goal, he did an eloquent drag-back (leaving Wright sliding past into nothingness), followed by an explosive left-foot finish. 'I've never seen such tremendous ball control,' said the dazzled Wolstenholme. Wright probably thought the same. A closer look reveals that the artistry of the finish simply complemented the pace and the fluidity of the build-up. The number eight, Kocsis (who was really the centre-forward), picked the ball up from deep and passed to left-winger Czibor, who was overlapping Budai (the right-winger) on the left of England's bemused defence. Czibor's low cross then set up Puskás. After 27 minutes, with the score 4-1, our commentator told his audience, 'Before the game everyone was telling me it was a lot of ballyhoo about these Hungarians – England would win.' Puskás's exquisite lob setting up Hideguti for his hat-trick was still to come. On top of all that, goalkeeper Grosics would regularly roll the ball out rather than hoofing it downfield.

With today's ubiquitous TV coverage, video and exhaustive statistical analysis of every aspect of the modern game, it is hard now to imagine how the Olympic champions, who since 1950 had been beating all comers, could arrive at Wembley as virtual unknowns for their opponents. Like FC Austria two years previously, the numbers on the shirts of the Hungarians baffled, belying the positions England expected them to occupy on the field. The number nine, Nandor Hideguti, playing deep, presented the English, and particularly his official marker, centre-half Harry Johnson, with a conundrum that seemed not to have been anticipated. Should I stay or should I go? The English FA had sent a team of seven to the Hungary v. Sweden game at the Nepstadion, just ten days before the Wembley encounter. The Hungarians used it to practice with an English ball and with different tactics than they would employ at Wembley. England's confusion endured as six months later the Hungarians won the return game in the Nepstadion 7-1.

Writing in the programme for the match at the Empire Stadium, John Graydon had again sounded warnings. He had witnessed that game against Sweden in the Nepstadion. He noted that despite a high wind and use of the larger English ball, 'Everything the Hungarians attempted had "Class" written all over it.' He praised their passing, speed of thought and movement and stamina. He rightly predicted 'a match worthy of a memorable occasion'. Elsewhere in the programme, journalist Geoffrey Green had stated, 'England faces perhaps the greatest challenge yet to her island supremacy.' Graydon wrote the pen portraits of the visitors. He referred to goalkeeper Grosics's 'accurate throws to his colleagues'. Despite Graydon's explanations of who played where, the pen portraits and the centre pages 'Plan of the Field of Play' assigned the Hungarians to the standard 2-3-5 formation that England would play. Thus Lorant, described by Graydon as 'a powerful "stopper" centre-half', was 'left-back'. Bozsik was 'centre-half' because he wore the number five. Graydon noted that the midfielder was about to become the 'first Member of Parliament ever to play in an International match on the famous pitch'. Crucially, in terms of the confusion caused for England's defenders, Graydon explained that Hideguti, listed as centre-forward, 'usually lays well behind his inside-forwards, feeding Puskás and Kocsis with the kind of through passes they turn into goals'. Of Puskás he said 'able to combine superb artistry and an astute positional sense with terrific shooting power'. On a later page in the programme, Harold Palmer was less overawed. English professionals 'have shown superior stamina' compared to 'foreign players', adding, 'Apart from the slightest variations to meet particular opposition we do not have to worry unduly about tactics. The English game is all right. Our crowds would not want to see the Continental style all the time.'

The combination of complacency and humiliation made a huge impression on my young mind and sense of national identity. Things like poverty, rationing and bomb sites were how things were, the natural order of things, so familiar as to pass as unexceptional. 'We' had won the war, extensive areas on the world maps on classroom walls were coloured pink, denoting the British Empire, which my school celebrated each year with a parade on Empire Day. 'We' had invented football and led the world in it. That narrative was exploded by 6-3, followed by 7-1; if the football bit was a hollow boast, might the rest be no more than the same? The emperor had no clothes. England did not rule the world. The conventional views of the generation before ours were at best suspect, at worst bluster. We were a nation in decline, placing faith in outdated methods and muscle, while other European countries used imagination. The Aranycsapat had prepared me for the debacle of Suez that came in 1956, when the British attempt to use force to regain 'our' Suez Canal that had been nationalised by Egypt's President Nasser had to be aborted once the USA put on pressure.

From 1953 onwards, though still a boy, I ceased to buy into notions that 'Britannia rules the waves' My generation that came of age in the 1960s was the first to grow up with a sense that Britain was a country in decline, and that those in authority were not to be trusted or even respected, rather their pretensions to grandeur made them appear ridiculous.

If the Festival of Britain and then England's double humiliation by Hungary had unlocked the door to football in other countries, it was the technology of floodlights that took Britain across that threshold, while also creating a new way for fans to experience the game. Journalist Tom Jackson's regular article in the Manchester United programme for their fixture with Blackpool on 2 September 1950 had mused on the possibilities of playing under floodlights. The club had recently returned from a close-season tour of the USA, where they had 'played several matches under the giant arc lights, and in some instances it was later than ten o'clock at night when they took the field'. To many, the prospect of 'illuminated football' being staged at a time of night when British football fans would have been going to bed, ready for an early start in the factory or coal mine the next morning, might have seemed outlandish. However, Jackson reported that the United players and management were convinced that playing under lights 'would revolutionise the sporting scene over here'. He quoted a 'serious prediction' from United manager Matt Busby, that 'once illuminated football was tried in a big way here, it would come to stay'.

Despite this early enthusiasm, Manchester United would not install floodlights until 1957. Others moved more quickly.

Arsenal played under their lights in 1951/52, against Glasgow Rangers and against the Israeli side Hapoel, attracting large crowds on each occasion. We have the programme from their third such enterprise on Wednesday, 22 October 1952 when the Gunners played the Scottish champions, Hibernian, at a floodlit Highbury, and won convincingly, 7-1, with outside-left Dan Roper helping himself to five of the goals. Just as significant as the floodlights was the fact that the second half of the game was televised live, and was the first floodlit game at Highbury to be shown on TV. The novelty may have swelled the crowd that night, with over 55,000 packing the stadium.

The Football League and the English FA were never enthusiasts for innovation; they did not like floodlights and not until 1956 were they willing to sanction league matches being played under lights. This meant that, though Arsenal had installed floodlights in 1951 they were forbidden to use them for league matches. This was the reason why the Gunners, and other clubs, began to play midweek friendlies under the lights. The screening of a live floodlit match suggested a sea change in the way football could be presented, and it is astonishing to think that live televising of games remained the exception for another 30 years.

The Arsenal v. Hibs programme (see Programme Spotlights 10) explained that the meeting was the idea of the Duke of Edinburgh to raise funds for the Central Council of Physical Recreation and the National Playing Fields Association. The programme advertised a Royal Performance of Bertram Mills Circus that the Queen and her husband would attend (tickets 7/6d upwards) to support the same good causes. On the same charitable theme, Messrs. Stuart Surridge and Co. Ltd. had presented 'two white footballs' for use in the match; this rare commodity was another innovative element to this game.

The worthiness of the good causes was explained by Vice Admiral Sir William Agnew, KCVO, CB, DSO, writing in the programme in his capacity as general secretary to the National Playing Fields Association. He pointed to 'the great and increasing shortage of public playing fields for boys and girls after they have left school'. While he did not put it this way, this was a problem created by the welfare state. The more egalitarian post-war education system was introducing more schoolchildren to more sports, but the cities were still unreconstructed from the pre-war era. Older working-class neighbourhoods were densely packed with houses, factories, shops, churches and pubs, and the inter-war suburbs, while more spacious, were similarly bereft of playing field provision. Geographical access to a sports field depended a lot on historical accidents of philanthropic provision, or the Victorian enthusiasm for public parks and recreation grounds as decorous and health-giving spaces.

The second problem identified by Sir William was the shortage of public playgrounds for pre-school and school age children, 'Every year thousands of children are killed and maimed on the roads.' Children had previously had the run of the streets, but with car ownership rising and motorised delivery vehicles replacing the horse and cart, there was now dangerously unequal competition for space outside the home.

Wolverhampton Wanderers were another club to install floodlights early, doing so in September 1953, and play televised midweek friendlies against international opponents. They went on to win the league that season, playing a muscular direct style of football, the epitome of the British game. Thus there was great interest in their meeting with the Hungarian side Honved under the Molineux lights in December 1955. It was a chance for a national redemption after the routs that the Hungarian national team had inflicted on England. To the delight of 55,000 fans packed into the ground, Wolves won 3-2, after being two down at half-time on a muddy, bumpy Molineux pitch. This was one of several triumphs they racked up over foreign teams in these home floodlit friendlies. We have the programme from their meeting with Moscow Dynamo on 9 November 1955, a game Wolves won 2-1. Notes by 'Wanderer' on page three begin, 'History is made tonight,' without quite going on to substantiate the claim. Wolves had lost 3-2 in Moscow in August, and there are a description and photos of that trip, including one with the tag, 'Somewhere among this big crowd in the grounds of the Kremlin are members of the Wolves touring party.' Players didn't get paid for their image rights in those days.

Reading the programme (see Programme Spotlights 11) again imparts a sense of just how exotic these foreign teams were, not just to the fans but to the correspondents and players professionally involved. 'Wanderer' commented on how different the Moscow contingent would find 'the surroundings at Molineux' from 'those of their own splendid stadium' which had a capacity of 80,000 and a running track around the pitch. Indeed, 'Track events were provided to fill the time at the interval and after the match.' The dressing rooms in Moscow were described as an 'eye opener to the party from England. They were like spacious lounges with rugs and carpets, settees and easy chairs. By comparison the English dressing room will probably appear austere with their bare, but practical benches, and plain floors.' In the same programme, journalist Ivan Sharpe also gave a first-hand account of the experience of watching Dynamo play at home, 'Like most Continental grounds there is little or no covered accommodation for spectators… If, as tonight, it is a floodlit match, the lights gleam on two huge pictures of Lenin and Stalin.'

More importantly, there were differences on the pitch, reaffirming the arguments made previously in this chapter. The

Wolves manager, Stan Cullis, was quoted as saying of Moscow Spartak, 'Every man was a soccer technician,' implying that such comprehensive skills were not a normal part of equivalent teams in England. Similarly, Sharpe observed, 'The emphasis is on slick movement, positional play and distribution of the ball. Like the Hungarians, they have the knack of mixing the short-and-long-passing game. The through ball between centre-half and full-back is ever in mind.' He also noted that the goalkeeper did not expect to be charged by an opponent, a phenomenon that would be 'an interesting new phase' for Soviet fans: in reality, it was another backward-looking feature of the British style of play through the 1950s, eventually tamed by playing European matches.

The programme notes elaborated that it was as though Soviet teams 'train themselves to play in any position' before settling to that which best suited them. They were 'crisp, nippy, mobile players, all pulling together all the time', and 'fit as fiddles', despite being 'not full-time players'. This latter observation was probably naiveté rather than politeness. Dynamo was the club of the Ministry of Internal Affairs and the internal security service.

This gave them a rather special pulling power in the USSR transfer market. Lavrenti Beria, Stalin's notorious head of the secret police, had been Dynamo's patron until he was toppled and executed in 1953, following Stalin's death. Disappointing him could have consequences. In theory, Wolves were facing a team of amateurs, but playing for Dynamo brought pressures quite different from turning out for Corinthians. At the very least there would have been a security presence among the group visiting from Moscow, and it is easy to speculate that the trip to the Midlands would have been an unmissable opportunity to gather some first-hand information about transport, industry and aspects of UK life, if not more.

Programme Spotlights 11: The charge of the light brigade
Wolverhampton Wanderers 2 Moscow Dynamo 1, 19 November 1955, friendly

The back page of the programme is illustrated in the picture section. Similar cartoons were often used in 1950s programmes, though it is unusual to find them on the back page. This one plays on the idea of lights, which were still a novelty and only used for friendly matches. It is not clear whether the cartoonist recognised that the Charge of the Light Brigade at the Battle of Balaclava in 1854 had been mounted against the Russian forces, but it seems an unnecessary reminder of past hostilities between the countries. Wolves' half-back line of Slater, Wright and Clamp would be England's in the 1958 World Cup. Bill Slater gave Wolves the lead after 15 minutes, with left-winger Jimmy Mullen scoring the second in the second half, before Vladimir Ilyin pulled one back. The Moscow team included legendary goalkeeper Lev Yashin (see Chapter 1). In contrast to other British programmes of this era, the line-ups displayed across the centre pages showed Dynamo playing a back three, numbered two, three and four, with Boykov (number five) and Sokolov (six) as midfielders, then five forwards. Presumably Wolves had learnt about this formation from their previous meetings with Soviet teams.

Ivan Sharpe's article in the programme for the game at Molineux provided a timeline of 'The Foreign Challenge to our position in these Islands as pioneers and premier Soccer players'. It amounted to 'a disturbing story – shattering to some... a complacent British public refused for years and years to believe' that the defeats were anything more than blips, 'false form by tired teams'; the 'chess-like football' of the foreigners was thought to be something that 'wouldn't suit our crowds'. Even as late as 1957, a journalist writing in our programme of the Charity Shield final between Manchester United and Aston Villa propounded the view, 'The Continentals may go in for the extra frills… the British way of soccer [is] a model for the rest of the world.' Similarly, the *Manchester Evening Chronicle* journalist Alf Clarke, in his Casual Comments page of our Manchester United programme for the 18 September 1957 game against Blackpool, referred to criticism being heaped on to the reigning league champions and then current league leaders for starting to 'play around' when in the lead. Clarke pointed out that the tactics were the same as those deployed by the famous Hungarian side that had trounced England in 1953. He pointed to a simple logic that was to underpin the dominance of Barcelona and Pep Guardiola's Manchester City decades later, 'If we have the ball our opponents cannot score.' The fact that points like these needed to be made says a lot about football in Britain in the 1950s.

Some insight into the issues that midweek floodlit fixtures posed can be discerned from the programme for the final floodlight trial match for the Olympic XI, between Luton Town and the England Amateur XI, on 17 October 1955. Luton were a First Division team, and their 'foremost thought' when asked to play extra matches like this one was, 'How will this match affect us from the injuries point of view?' Squad depth and rotation had yet to be invented. However, the programme writer reassured readers that there was 'no need to worry in this respect tonight, for this Amateur side will be only too keen to play their football on the style of the famous Corinthians'. Alick Jeffrey (see Chapter 3), described in the programme as 'an inside-forward of great promise', was in the Olympic XI. In the Olympics they appeared as Great Britain, though all the players were from England, the other British associations having withdrawn support, a stand-off indicative of institutional tensions that existed even at a time when Unionism was virtually unchallenged within the UK.

The vogue for floodlit friendlies against foreign teams soon spread. Chelsea hosted the Red Army team, CDSA (Central Sporting Club of the USSR Ministry of Defence) Moscow, on 7 November 1957. According to our match programme, it was an (unnamed) Englishman who had brought football to Russia at the turn of the century, while working there as the managing director of an Anglo-Russian textile mill near Moscow. 'Why should we worry if our one-time pupils have become as good as their teachers?' asked the writer. The one-time pupils won 4-1, despite the appearance of a youngster called Jimmy Greaves as a second-half Chelsea substitute; Greaves would go on to have a stellar goalscoring career, and appear in the Rest of Europe team in Copenhagen (see Chapter 1). It was the visitors' first win on their tour, having gone down 6-5 before a crowd of 52,000 against West Bromwich Albion, then 3-1 against Bolton Wanderers earlier in the week. Meanwhile, Chelsea's next floodlit match was advertised as being the following Tuesday against Beogradski, who at that time were a prominent Yugoslavian club. Access to hard currency would have been a strong incentive for eastern European teams to play these friendlies.

Our programme collection contains several of these floodlit friendlies. Cardiff City, another First Division team at the time, inaugurated their floodlights on 5 October 1960 with a 2-2 draw against the weirdly named Grasshopper Club Zürich (the origin of the name is obscure). This was just a couple of weeks after Leyton Orient had staged their own first floodlit friendly against foreign opposition, Israel's reigning champions Hapoel Petach Tikva. Coventry City hosted Akademisk Boldklub from Copenhagen, beating them 1-0 on 6 March 1957. The single folded sheet, black and white *Bantam* programme promised 'a football treat' based on the performances that the Danes had already delivered at Luton and Grimsby. The pen portraits of the visitors on the back page were sparse, suggesting that many were unknown quantities, for example, 'Jan Hansen (Goalkeeper). Aged 26', though readers were told that 36-year-old Knud Lundberg (inside-left) had 'played in 39 internationals'.

A similar air of mystery hung over the visitors to Home Park on 30 October 1961. Club Always Ready La Paz were on 'an extended tour', taking in this fixture which had been 'arranged at short notice'. The programme announced them as twice champions of Bolivia, and runners-up the previous season. They were the first Bolivian club to tour in Europe, with games against some familiar European clubs (AEK Athens, Olympiakos, Anderlecht), and some rather vaguely specified sides, which included Sofia and Warna (sic) from Bulgaria, and Aalborg of Denmark. There were also matches against a Selection Sofia and a couple against Selection Bucharest. Gantoise Gent, Olympique Lille and Alemannia Aachen had all beaten them, as had FC Altona of Hamburg. In the UK they had drawn 3-3 at Aberdeen and had then lost 3-1 to Exeter City. It seems likely that the proximity of Plymouth to Exeter was a factor in arranging the otherwise improbable meeting that October night.

The tour had begun well in terms of results for Club Always Ready, with a win at Aalborg and two wins and a draw in Bulgaria, with an aggregate goal difference of 14 for and six against. Things were still going well in Athens with a win and a draw, a pattern repeated when they played in Belgium. From there it was downhill: the next three contests resulted in one win, one draw and one defeat, but the remaining five games yielded an aggregate of two draws and three defeats, in which they conceded 14 goals. The travel must have taken its toll; to get from Bucharest to Aberdeen in 1961 must have been a draining experience. The decision to follow that with a 600-mile trip to Exeter suggests a measure of masochism, with the 3-1 defeat by the then-Fourth Division side scarcely a surprise.

Only 11 La Paz players were profiled in the Plymouth programme, and the same 11 were listed on the team sheet. So it seems possible that a squad of just 11 señores from La Paz headed halfway across the world for a tour in which they criss-crossed the Iron Curtain to reach Home Park for a friendly against mid-table Second Division opponents. Their home games would be played at over 11,000ft above sea level; their tour games were mainly played at venues just above sea level.

Sometimes glamour foreign friendlies did not work out. Our Leeds United programme for 16 November 1957 against Manchester City told of how negotiations for a floodlit game on 3 December against Lanerossi Vicenza, then standing second in the Italian Serie A, had been scuppered. Italy had called up the club's entire half-back line for a World Cup qualifier against 'Ireland' in Belfast on 4 December. As Vicenza would not be able to field a full-strength team the proposed fixture was shelved. Incidentally, the same programme spelled City's home Maine Road as Main Road: such slips were not uncommon in programmes of the day.

Stoke City's programme for their Second Division fixture against Lincoln City on 23 February 1957 informed fans that Stoke had declined three recent offers to host floodlit friendlies against German sides, 'Munich F.C., the Werder Bremen F.C. and the Schweinfurt F.C., Southern Germany' (the Bundesliga was not formed until 1963). Instead Stoke wanted to concentrate on getting promotion, an ambition boosted by beating Lincoln 8-0. However, the club were also putting a proposal to the annual conference of the Football League that would allow clubs with adequate floodlighting to determine the time of their Saturday kick-off up to 3pm, and that if there was mutual agreement with opponents until even later. Even at that point, use of floodlights for a league game depended on the agreement of both clubs, and, as the programme editorial noted, four clubs had already refused to play under Stoke's lights, with a consequent £1,000-a-game loss to the Potteries side.

Floodlights and fans' appetite for games against foreign opposition paved the way to the European Cup, the Cup Winners' Cup and the Inter-Cities Fairs Cup. As England's 1955 champions, Chelsea were invited to take part in the first European Cup competition. However, the Football Association successfully warned them off any such dalliance with continentals. Hibernian, who had won the Scottish League, therefore became the first British club to play competitively in Europe. Hugh Shaw's team reached the semi-final before going out 3-0 on aggregate to Reims.

On 26 September 1956, Manchester United played Anderlecht at Maine Road because Old Trafford still had no floodlights. I was only just 12, and was not allowed by my parents to go across town for a night game, so missed seeing the first European Cup game played on English soil, and an epic match.

However, I did get the programme, now highly sought-after, through others at school. It is unremarkable, following the standard format that the club used for many years. The photo on the front page showed the Anderlecht team. Their pen portraits, written by Tom Jackson of the *Manchester Evening News*, revealed that these really were part-time players: goalkeeper Felix Week was an electrician; there was a motor mechanic, an upholsterer, a tailor, three bank employees, an office worker, and five who were employed by local or municipal governments, including the captain Joseph Mermans, 'Belgium's soccer idol', who had 57 caps and had represented the Rest of Europe.

Programme Spotlights 12: What is the European Cup?

26 September 1956, Manchester United 10 Anderlecht 0,
European Cup preliminary round. second leg (aggregate 12-0)

Journalist Tom Jackson's regular programme article began 'What is the European Cup?' It went on to explain the previous (inaugural) season's competition, without mentioning that the Football League had deterred English champions Chelsea from entering, and still less dwelling on United's defiance in accepting the invitation to take part in the 1956/57 competition.

Twenty teams from 18 countries were entered, meaning that ten got byes from this preliminary round. Glasgow Rangers were the other team from the UK, and Spain had champions Athletic Bilbao, plus Real Madrid who qualified as winners of the 1954/55 competition. They were organised into three broadly geographical groups – Group A from eastern and central Europe ('far-away places like Turkey, Poland, Rumania, Czechoslovakia, Yugoslavia and Bulgaria' as Jackson put it); Group B, which had the UK teams, the Scandinavians, the French and Belgian representatives and Real Madrid; and an odd assortment in Group C which might have been southern Europe but included Borussia Dortmund and CA Spora from Luxembourg. Of the major footballing nations, there was no representative from the USSR or from East Germany.

In the game itself, Dennis Viollet scored four, Tommy Taylor three, Liam Whelan two and John Berry one. In the closing minutes, United were still chasing more as the team sought to set up a goal for David Pegg (mentioned as a schoolboy international in Chapter 3), the only forward not on the scoresheet. In *There's Only One United* (1978), Geoffrey Green wrote that from the left-wing Pegg 'ran absolutely wild that night, turning the opposition inside out and contributing directly to seven or eight of those goals… what a performance!'

Lest this should diminish the 10-0 victory of the Busby Babes, it is worth recalling that the West German team that had won the World Cup just a couple of years previously was also made up largely of part-timers. Meanwhile, Anderlecht had beaten several foreign teams, including Reims (the previous season's finalists), and Arsenal at Highbury. Furthermore, Anderlecht's captain was reported in the match programme as having been confounded by the way United had played in their 2-0 away leg win in Brussels, 'With the precision of the Russians or the Hungarians, and at twice the speed!' Instead of playing long passes, United had moved the ball around the field, 'trying to find gaps in the home defence'.

A further indicator of how novel the European Cup was, and the problems of organising the competition even in the next season, 1957/58, can be gleaned from our Manchester United v. Portsmouth programme of 19 October 1957. It records how manager Matt Busby had travelled to Madrid the previous week for the draw for the next round of the competition. After eliminating Shamrock Rovers 9-2 on aggregate, United drew Dukla Prague, but no representative of the Czech army club was there. 'It was virtually a wasted journey... because negotiations had to be opened by post later. Subsequently, Mr. B. Miklos, who runs a travel agency in London... took up the reins, and by this time something more definite may have been arranged between the clubs.' An update appeared in our United programme of 2 November, saying the date for the Old Trafford leg had been agreed, but finding a date for the return game had been a problem. Dukla said their floodlighting system was 'not too good', while a midweek afternoon was out of the question because 'the majority of the club supporters could not get off from work'. Dukla therefore suggested a Saturday or a Sunday, leading United to point out that 'the European Cup could only be played on midweek dates by the majority of competing clubs'. Eventually, Dukla accepted United's original suggestion of Wednesday, 20 November and set about upgrading their lights, though at the time of going to press the programme was unable to confirm whether it would be a night game or an afternoon game. The 16 November United v. Sheffield Wednesday programme informed us that the work on Dukla's floodlights had not been completed, and so the return leg would kick-off at 2.30pm.

The advent of European football competitions in the 1950s can be seen as a step towards seeking to end the horrific wars that had ravaged the continent in the first half of that century. The Treaty of Rome, which set up the European Economic Community, dates from 1957. Of course, the geographical span of that political treaty was less than that of the football competition, but both shared a vision of Europe in which people lived together in peace. Since that time, there have been flashpoints and tensions in politics and in the football, but those floodlit matches in the 1950s did indeed open eyes to the possibilities not only of how and when to watch football, but also of new and better ways of being Europeans.

Programmes cited in Chapter 4 that are in the collection:
- 2 September 1950, Manchester United 1 Blackpool 0, Football League First Division
- 7 May 1951, Tottenham Hotspur 0 F.C. Austria 1, Festival of Britain friendly
- 22 October 1952, Arsenal 7 Hibernian 1, charity match
- 12 November 1952, England 5 Wales 2 Home International
- 26 November 1952, England 5 Belgium 0, friendly
- 25 November 1953, England 3 Hungary 6, friendly
- 17 October 1955, Luton Town v. England Amateur XI, final trial for 1956 Olympics

- 19 November 1955, Wolverhampton Wanderers 2 Moscow Dynamo 1, friendly
- 26 September 1956, Manchester United 10 R.S.C. Anderlecht 0, European Cup preliminary round second leg
- 23 February 1957, Stoke City 8 Lincoln City 0, Football League Second Division.
- 6 March 1957, Coventry City 1 Akademisk Boldklub 0, friendly
- 18 September 1957, Manchester United 1 Blackpool 2, Football League First Division
- 19 October 1957, Manchester United 0 Portsmouth 3, Football League First Division
- 22 October 1957, Manchester United 4 Aston Villa 0, FA Charity Shield
- 2 November 1957, Manchester United 1 Burley 0, Football League First Division
- 7 November 1957, Chelsea 1 CDSA Moscow 4, friendly
- 16 November 1967, Leeds United 2 Manchester City 4, Football League First Division
- 16 November 1957, Manchester United 2 Sheffield Wednesday 1, Football League First Division
- 19 September 1960, Leyton Orient v. Hapoel Petach Tikva, friendly (result unknown)
- 5 October 1960, Cardiff City 2 Grasshoppers Zurich 2, friendly
- 30 October 1961, Plymouth Argyle v. Club Always Ready La Paz, friendly (result unknown)

Chapter 5

Soccer Diaries

IN 1955, I scraped in to the local boys' grammar school, after a borderline resit exam and then an interview for one of the final few places. We also moved house, back to Moston, about a mile up the road. This double dislocation projected me as a young 11-year-old into new and unfamiliar worlds, where teachers wore gowns and I had to wear a school uniform. The school had its own playing fields and aped Britain's private schools, so I was assigned to a house, which would shape my formal sporting activity for the years ahead. I remember still the headmaster addressing us as the new intake to the school, and telling us that we needed to discard our old friends as, unlike us, they would not have homework to do. The move back to Moston had already severed those old links for me: my career with Abbotsford United (see Chapter 3) was over. Our new next-door neighbours were City fans with two boys around my own age and a car, so as well as watching United, I began to be taken to City home games as well.

Perhaps my entry to North Manchester Grammar School for Boys explains why I was given not one but two diaries that Christmas. One was a *The Legible Soccer Diary*; the other, inscribed as a gift by Aunty Ethel and Uncle Bill, was the *Letts*

School-Boys Diary. This latter struck an earnest educational tone. It included a frightening range of mathematical tables – not just logarithms but also antilogarithms, square and cube roots and reciprocals, along with trigonometrical ratios. The countries of the world were listed, along with their capitals, population numbers, areas in square miles, and principal exports. Sovereigns from the Normans to Elizabeth II were set out in sequence. British Prime Ministers since 1757 were there too: for example, the Marquess [sic] of Rockingham occupied the post for less than a year in 1782. There were also tables of Latin and German verbs and of French irregular verbs, and a list of careers for boys and sources of information about them. These included colonial service, the army, holy orders and accountancy and similar professional occupations, though there was no mention of the kind of manual jobs that the adult males in and around my family were doing. Thankfully, the suggestions of books to read included works by Enid Blyton, which just about defined my literary range at the time: I had been awarded *Five go to Smugglers' Top* for coming top of the class in 1954!

I guess the *School-Boys Diary* was all just too much for me. My entries in it were sparse, though opposite a picture of the Queen, I had filled in the fact that I was 4ft 9in tall on 21 December 1955 and weighed 5st 6lb. I had also made use of one of the pages provided for recording examination marks. It makes grim reading: in Physics I had got 50 per cent and was 15th in the class, Maths 48 per cent and 29th, English 50 per cent and 28th, Religious Instruction 54 per cent and 17th, and so on with all the marks hovering around the 50 per cent mark, demonstrating, at best, consistency.

In contrast, I filled in the *Soccer Diary* assiduously, though some days detentions by teachers were the only event deemed worthy of writing about. During the summer term, the ability to spell 'athletics' correctly eluded me regularly. My contact with literature was mainly focused on comics, supplemented by visits to the library (variously spelled as 'librey', 'libery', 'liberery' or 'liberly'). My reading took in 'Assosaion Football' (at least I spelled half the title correctly), Frank Swift's *Football from the Goalmouth*, *Chips the Alsation* (sic), Rex Milligan's *Busy Term*, and later Biggles. It was quite a limited literary canon. At the same time, I was sending off letters to football clubs asking if they could please let me have a copy of their programme: thankfully, no record of my spelling in those missives survives.

My first diary entry was on 1 January 1956, in capital letters, 'NO FOOTBALL BUT YESTERDAY UNITED BEAT CITY 2-1 AT OLD TRAFFORD. TAYLOR AND VIOLLET SCORED.' My programme from that game provides a further insight into the developing relationship between football and television. An article by television commentator Kenneth Wolstenholme, who is also mentioned in Chapter 4, began, 'There were many people in the television world who said we were mad for attempting to put on two sports news programmes on BBC television on Saturday evenings. They said it was impossible to put on 15 minutes of news and film in *Today's Sport* at 7.10pm and another 30 minutes of **different** news and film in "Sports Special" at ten o'clock' (original emphasis included). No such endeavour had ever been attempted before anywhere in the world, he added.

- -

Programme Spotlights 13: Pushing TV technology to the limits

20 August 1955, Manchester City 2 Aston Villa 2, Football League First Division

This programme was from one of my earliest visits to Maine Road. The cover illustration (see picture section) records for posterity what the old ground was like in the 1950s, with its extensive open terraces. We used to stand on the uncovered terrace behind the goal at the scoreboard end. Floodlights are not shown, though they had been installed in 1953. Over the years that followed, the terraces were covered and seats were added, with the long stretch opposite the main stand becoming the Kippax, legendary as the epicentre of home support. The stadium was set among the terraced streets of the Moss Side district of the city. It was built on the site of a former brick works in 1923, and was City's home for 80 years before they moved to the stadium that had been created for the 2002 Commonwealth Games.

I have absolutely no recollection of the Aston Villa game, though I had used a red biro to write in Villa's four team changes and the half-time scores, and a blue pen to record the result of the match. Like so many in my early days as a collector, this programme had been sellotaped into a scrapbook, as the residual bits of sellotape show.

What makes the 12-page programme of historic significance is that this was the first game where the BBC experimented with recording a live commentary on to the film, instead of dubbing the commentary on afterwards, making it possible to transmit that same evening the five minutes of highlights permitted by the Football League. The other reason why this is a landmark programme is that it introduced for the first time a ticket coupon which needed to be saved to gain priority for tickets to sell-out matches. As City went on to win the FA Cup that season, the fans got to make use of these vouchers, though the voucher remains intact in my programme.

City's team included Bert Trautmann in goal (see Chapter 2) and Don Revie at number nine. However, following the example of the great Hungarian team (see Chapter 4), this 'centre-forward' was actually playing in midfield. Dubbed 'The Revie Plan', it was a system that City had introduced in 1954/55, and which had taken them to the FA Cup Final in that season. In 1955/56; they went one better and won the cup.

Wolstenholme explained the technical barriers that had to be overcome. It took two hours to process film, and that could only be done in London, though he did not explain why. Then another two hours were required for editing. Finally commentaries had to be dubbed on to the film. The breakthrough had come in the first game of that season at Maine Road, when commentaries were put on the sound track of the footage as it was being shot (see Programme Spotlights 13). The problem was that the commentator could not see what the camera was shooting, so had to say more than in a live TV commentary. Wolstenholme also described how only 30 minutes of film were shot, in 30 separate 'takes'. Also, as ever, there were obstacles enforced by the Football League, which prescribed that only five minutes could be shown.

There was still the problem of getting the film to London for editing. The answer that the BBC had come up with was two aircraft and a helicopter, though this still left the producers at the mercy of the British weather. Wolstenholme recounted how after Wales v. England, 'thick cloud and rain' meant that the plane had 'circled London for 15 minutes at 350ft'. Back in those days planes queuing to land at Heathrow were the exception not the norm. All of this meant that only London games, where film of the first half was rushed to the processing centre by motorbike, could be shown in the 7.10pm slot. The weather 'more than once stopped our covering a northern or Scottish game', while 'often the film is not ready until the last second – literally'.

The rest of my entries to my *Soccer Diary* for that first week in January 1956 focused on the lead-up to the weekend's FA Cup ties. The only personal event recorded was the acquisition on the Thursday of the Wolves v. Moscow Dynamo programme discussed in Chapter 4. On the Tuesday and the Wednesday, I blocked out in capitals the City and United line-ups for the forthcoming third round matches, misspelling some of the names. Then on the Saturday it was BRISTOL ROVERS 4 UNITED 0. On a gluepot of a pitch it was the upset of the round; while Rovers would finish the season sixth in the Second Division, United would go on to win the league by 11 points, a record margin in the 20th century at that stage. As consolation I wrote in my diary that goalkeeper Wood and wing-half Colman had played well.

In the 1950s, it was not uncommon for football to be disrupted by the weather, and particularly by fog. The cartoon in my Manchester United v. Burnley programme on 2 November 1957 includes 'Real Old Trafford fog' being sold for 'Ten Bob a Jar' to the 'Sunny South' of Europe. Smog, acrid, impenetrable and laced with the pollutants of industrial Britain, was a frequent uninvited guest at football grounds in those days. It forced postponements and abandonments. It could arrive suddenly – the players would come out to warm up and you could see from end to end, then by the time of the kick-off ten minutes later a yellow-grey blanket would have descended. This is exactly what happened at the Manchester United v. Arsenal FA Cup fourth round tie in 1962. The four-page 'emergency' programme for the rescheduled game the following Wednesday explained on its front page that there were 50,000 of us inside the ground, when 'minutes later, literally nothing at all was in view'. The fog also disrupted the bus services, so after that match was called off, with my pals and thousands of others I had to walk back into the city centre to get transport home. If the fog descended during a game and you were standing behind the goal (as I usually was in those days), you tugged your scarf more tightly around your nose and mouth, and relied on the noise of the crowd at the opposite end to provide the commentary on what was happening. The new floodlights were of little help: the fog seemed to reflect back the light rather than be penetrated by the lamps.

A couple of weeks after I had stood behind the goal at Maine Road before choking fog had brought Manchester City's cup tie with Blackpool to a premature end, I went to my first United away game. My *Soccer Diary* records the build-up. On Sunday, 15 January I had 'Lernt [sic] to play WHIST'. On Monday I 'Got the TIGER': this was not an exotic pet but a weekly comic that featured Roy of the Rovers, whose goalscoring would continue to inspire awe in readers over a career that extended more than four decades, only to end tragically when he lost his renowned left foot in a helicopter crash. My Cardiff City v. Manchester City programme from the previous weekend arrived on Tuesday, where I also recorded the retirement of England cricketer Len Hutton. The only Wednesday entry was the 5-1 victory of our school football team against a school from Bolton. Thursday, 'Got a CHARLTON A. v. SPURS programme', then Friday brought the cancellation of the games period at school, presumably due to bad weather, but also 'Got the tickets for PRESTON'. These were the tickets from the local newsagent for the bus to the game at Deepdale the following day, one for me and the other for my mum, who yet again was taking me to pastures new.

Saturday, 21 January 1956, 'PRESTON 3 UNITED 1. I saw UNITED's match. CITY 1 HUDDERSFIELD 0'. This brief entry does less than justice to an event I can still remember. First, we went down to the newsagent's to be picked up, at one of several collection points across Moston and Harpurhey. Then the journey took in the western edge of the Pennines at Belmont, a wild landscape that was strange to me and usually spoken of in terms of near dread. The coach parked in the car park adjacent to the stadium, we bought a programme (see Programme Spotlights 14), and stood right at the front and near the halfway line. When the teams came out to warm up, this enabled me, like scores of other youngsters, to duck under the barrier I was leaning on and run on to the pitch. Autograph book in hand, I made a beeline for Duncan Edwards (see Chapter 3). Our conversation went, 'Can I have your autograph, please?' to which the left-half replied, 'After the game.' Waiting after the game was not an option, as I had to return to the bus and the subdued journey home after United's defeat. However, a few months later I did get Edwards's autograph along with several of his team-mates at Old Trafford.

Programme Spotlights 14: A disappointing afternoon at Deepdale

21 January 1956, Preston North End 3 Manchester United 1, Football League First Division

The programme from my first United away match is unusual in having a cartoon-style advertisement on the front cover. More generally covers carried depictions of the stadium or photos of recent games, rather than this verbal/visual pun on 'Inside the "POST"'. The gaunt features of the goalkeeper convey a sense of desperation, contrasting with the faces of the fans.

The A5-sized programme, printed in black-and-white, observed that United had won every one of the last eight matches, with North End's previous win over them at Deepdale being in September 1947. It added that 'they were last here in March 1955 in mud and rain'. Conditions were pretty much the same that January afternoon, where I was part of the crowd of 28,047.

There were two United team changes that I wrote neatly into the programme. Colin Webster replaced Tommy Taylor at number nine, while Jackie Scott came in for what would be his last appearance for United, on the right wing in place of Johnny Berry. Tom Finney wore the number seven shirt for the home team. An advert for his plumbing and electrical requirements business was on page 13, above ones advertising the British Rail trains to Sheffield for the following week's game at Bramall Lane, and for the next two home reserve matches.

I cannot remember much about the game except that Liam Whelan scored United's goal, and that standing at the front, right next to the pitch, gave me a close-up, wince-inducing view of Preston's tough-tackling Scottish right-back Willie Cunningham and his equally uncompromising fellow Scottish international (and future United and Chelsea manager) Tommy Docherty at right-half. In front of them was the immaculate Tom Finney.

Willie Cunningham was a former miner from Hill o' Beath in Fife, who had captained Scotland in the 1954 World Cup, and was renowned as a hard-as-nails defender. This small Fife industrial village was also the birthplace of two other famous Scottish internationals, Jim Baxter and Hibs and Celtic midfielder Scott Brown.

On Saturday, 27 October 1956, I wrote in my *Soccer Diary*, 'Got ITV', little realising what a momentous change in British media and life this meant. Access to this new world of entertainment was made possible by a kind of decoder box that sat on top of our 12in black-and-white TV. This technological and cultural innovation clearly made a deep impact on my daily life, as it triggered a stream of *Soccer Diary* entries: 28 October 'Watched ITV Played conkers'; 29 October 'Was on cross-country. Came 10th. Watched ITV.' 'Cross-country' was not a slow, over-crowded train service with outmoded rolling stock; rather it was running undertaken as part of the games period at school, though the 'country' element in inner Manchester was a leap of the imagination. Next day I 'watched *Do You Trust Your Wife* and other shows,' then on Wednesday *The Shooting Star* which is more likely to have been a Western than a discourse on astronomy. Then 1 November brought a trip to the cinema to see *Reach for the Sky* ('It was good. Played football'): again it was not astronomy, but rather about the World War II fighter pilot Douglas Bader. On the Friday, I 'watched ITV' and 'played football'.

Such changes in entertainment were taking place in households across Britain. The foreword in the 1956 *Soccer Diary* ruminated on how television was impacting on British football. It began, 'The menace – or benefit (whichever way you like to look at it) – of television grew during 1955.' While millions more had watched the televised matches, 'thousands less turned up at the gates of league and cup matches'. Bad weather in December, January and February accounted for part of the fall in attendances. However, televised games against continental teams 'whetted the public's appetite for really big matches'. There was talk of a European league and of an 'all-British floodlight league'. In contrast, the diary related how the Scottish Cup semi-finals (Airdrie v. Celtic and Aberdeen v. Clyde) had attracted poor crowds, and 'bad weather hits hard at those clubs which have little covered accommodation'.

Football fans were charged an Entertainment Tax, which was finally removed by Chancellor of the Exchequer Peter Thorneycroft in the Budget in the spring of 1957. My Manchester City programme for their game with Preston North End on 13 April gave Thorneycroft 'three rousing cheers', adding that the tax 'has been slowly crippling the professional game in Britain'. However, the relief was not to be passed on to the fans. 'Clubs are in agreement with the theory that a cut in prices at the turnstiles would not induce some of the "missing millions" to return to the terraces.' A cartel was operating, though the programme did not describe it that way. Rather it noted that admission prices had indeed risen. The minimum had been hiked in 1951 by three pence, to one shilling and sixpence, then the following year fans had to find a further threepenny bit to purchase admission; and in 1955, to meet the inflation of maintenance costs and rising salary bills, this charge went up to two shillings. With such claims of penury from the clubs, it is a surprise that our Chelsea programmes in 1956/57 First Division carried no adverts.

Despite the 'rising salary bills', clubs' expenditure on player wages was not particularly generous. In 1955, the average male manual worker's wage in UK was about £10 per week, roughly twice that of their female equivalents. In 1956/57, a Manchester United and England player such as Roger Byrne would have earned £744 in wages, £72 in league match bonuses, £45 in league talent money, £60 in European Cup bonuses, £150 in accrued benefit, £80 from Provident Fund credit, £56 in FA Cup bonuses, £50 in FA Cup talent money, £400 from international match fees, and £20 from inter-League match fees. While this totals £1,677, or roughly three times the average annual wage of a male manual worker, the earnings of the vast majority of players whose careers fell short of such elite status would have been much more dependent on the basic wage. Notifications of fundraising events for player benevolence were common in programmes.

The Manchester United programme for their game with Aston Villa in February 1953, the second big game that I went to, included an advertisement for a dance at the inner-city Gorton and Openshaw local men's club to raise money for the players' testimonial fund. Tickets cost three shillings and six pence and could be obtained from Stan Pearson (the England international who lined up as United's number ten that afternoon) 'or any of the players… Buses from Piccadilly, 218 and 219'.

While clubs struggled to sell tickets for run-of-the-mill matches, there was still high demand for big fixtures, notably in the FA Cup. Typically fans would camp out overnight outside the ground to be sure of being near the head of the queue on the morning that sales commenced. To better and more fairly manage the sale of tickets, and to boost attendance and programme sales throughout the season, clubs began to introduce tokens and token sheets in their home programmes, including reserve team games.

My first programme to contain a token was Manchester City's 2-2 draw with Aston Villa on 20 August 1955, mentioned above. The editorial on page three got straight to the point and explained the new scheme. 'After long and careful deliberation, the club' had decided that each programme would carry a voucher with a number and appropriate date. 'You are asked to collect and save these vouchers until such time as you are called upon to send them to Maine Road with your application for a ticket.' However, having the vouchers would not guarantee a precious ticket. The editor went on to explain that those travelling to a first team away game could send the programme from that game in lieu of the reserve team token that day. Stern advice was proffered, 'Don't try and be clever and send a voucher and programme from the same day! And it is no use trying to beg vouchers from other people – only one will be accepted for each date.'

However, the system was by no means foolproof, though City had had the nous to include the date on their tokens, so for example, that first one at the Villa game was 'No.1 – 20.8.55'. United were less savvy, and so it was that as a 12-year-old the following season I was able to crack the Manchester United voucher scheme quite easily to get tickets for the glamour European Cup semi-final with Real Madrid. My *Soccer Diary* did not tell the full story, saying simply 'Got a voucher' (Friday, 29 March 1957), then 'Got a REAL MADRID ticket' (Monday, 1 April).

So how did we do it? Firstly, you could indeed beg vouchers from other people if they had ones you didn't have – or you could swap them if you had spares. If all else failed, you could offer to buy their programme. Thus multiple tokens and spare token sheets could be accumulated. Collaboration with school pals ensured that all this was in place, with the voucher obtained on 27 March probably the last piece of the jigsaw. The design of each token was a grey football set in a small white square, and on the ball was written 'Manchester United Football Club, League 1ˢᵗ Division, 1956/57 Token'. No doubt this was seen as enough to prevent fraud in an age before photocopiers. In the middle of the ball, in a white panel was the number of the token, e.g. 'No. 21'. You could stick your tokens into the numbered squares on the token sheet with sellotape. When you presented it to the ticket office to buy a ticket, they punched a hole through two adjacent numbers, so that you couldn't reuse that set of tokens again for a ticket for the same match.

My recollection is that for the Madrid game they were stamping through tokens five and six. So the first visit with my pals to the ticket office on 1 April 1957 was with a sheet with a sufficient number of vouchers, including five and six. One hole, one ticket. However, we also had spares of tokens 15 and 16, and a razor blade which was used carefully to scratch off the first digit in each case, transforming 15 and 16 into five and six. The holed vouchers five and six were then replaced on the token sheet by the counterfeit versions, with added sellotape for disguise. The next trip, to a different window in the ticket offices, was tense, but successful. The reward for this juvenile entrepreneurialism came on Thursday, 18 April, when I recorded in my *Soccer Diary*, 'Sold Madrid ticket for 10/-. Played football. Scored. Draw 2-2.' Ten shillings for a two-shilling ticket represented a considerable windfall to my budget. The match was televised live. Madrid had won the first leg 3-1, and scored two first-half goals at the Stretford End to put the outcome beyond doubt.

The following season, United's tokens spelled out the number, rather than using numerals. Somebody must have spotted our manipulations!

In general, my diary entries for 1956 and 1957 record a humdrum life, as the excerpts already cited suggest. In winter I played football, in summer cricket, with the entry for 26 April 1956 striking a note all cricketers will recognise, 'No cricket practice. It rained and snowed.' Undeterred, the following day I 'Played cricket. Scored 1'. The loss of practice clearly impaired my performance. On school days there were regular entries in the diary recording detentions, examinations or absences with a range of minor illnesses. There were other days when I went fishing for tiddlers in a mill lodge. Transporting my haul home in a full bucket of water on the top deck of a bus was a hazard, which on one occasion resulted in the conductor coming upstairs to locate the source of the water that was dripping on the heads of lower deck passengers. These expeditions would be followed by days in which high rates of fish mortality were recorded in the diary: keeping the sticklebacks in old paint cans meant that lead poisoning probably hastened their demise.

This pattern followed into the start of 1958: homework; snow; football scores; watching ITV, etc. There was extra work to do in Latin as some sort of punishment. I never recorded the reasons for detentions and similar sanctions; they seemed to be random though frequent. 'Bladder burst' on Wednesday, 22 January 1958 was not the medical crisis it might appear, just the inside of an old football meeting its demise.

On Monday, 27 January I got a cold and so was off school for the rest of the week, then on Saturday, 1 February, 'ARSENAL 4 UNITED 5', an exceptional score, of course, but a game whose significance nobody could have realised that weekend. We have the programme (see Programme Spotlights 15), and, although there was a crowd of 63,578 that day so there are likely to be many copies, I have seen the programme of that game advertised for as much as £150. It was to be the last league game the Busby Babes played before the Munich disaster.

Programme Spotlights 15: I had never seen an English side do the things they did
Arsenal 4 Manchester United 5, First Division, 1 February 1958

Any game ending 5-4 is likely to stick in the memory, but this one has added poignancy as it was the last time Manchester United played in England, five days before their plane crashed on the runway at Munich airport, with eight players among the 23 dead.

United were trailing Wolves in the race for the title, but had struck a rich vein of form since Christmas. They went 3-0 ahead in the first half. Duncan Edwards opened the scoring with a low drive from distance after ten minutes. The second came from a classic counter-attack: Gregg, recently signed for a record £23,000, made a diving save from a Groves header, and quickly threw to Albert Scanlon who raced 70 yards up the left wing and provided the cross that Bobby Charlton smashed home. Then Tommy Taylor made it three after another break by Scanlon, followed by a chip from right-winger Ken Morgans.

Game over? The drama was still to come. Arsenal scored three times in two and a half minutes around the hour mark. Centre-forward David Herd volleyed home, then Jimmy Bloomfield got two close-range goals, the second from a diving header. At 3-3 the home crowd roared on their favourites, only for Dennis Viollet to head United back in front from another Scanlon cross a few minutes later. On 71 minutes, Taylor, perhaps the most mobile centre-forward of his day, dribbled in from the right and beat Jack Kelsey at his near post from a narrow angle. Still, Arsenal fought back and scored a fourth from Derek Tapscott, described by journalists as being a worthy match-winner on any other day.

No doubt defending fell short by modern standards: wingers did not drop back to aid their full-backs, so Scanlon's dominance of his marker, Stan Charlton, gave the visitors a constant advantage. The quality of their play was expressed by David Herd, who later transferred to United in 1961. Herd is quoted in *The Lost Babes: Manchester United and the Forgotten Victims of Munich*, a book by Jeff Connor, 'I had never seen an English side do the things they did. We were all attacking teams in those days, raiding wingers, two potential strikers and a midfield that tended to pour forward. But United did it all at a different pace.'

- -

I went back to school on Monday, 3 February, then on Wednesday it was 'RED STAR 3 UNITED 3 so UNITED in SEMI FINALS'. Thursday, 6 February 1958, in my scrawly handwriting my diary says, 'UNITED plane crashed on take-off. BYRNE, TAYLOR, BENT, JONES, WHELAN, COLMAN, PEGG killed. Went to BARBER'S. More badly injured.' The plane carrying Manchester United players, staff and travelling journalists on a flight from their European Cup game in Yugoslavia, had crashed on take-off at Munich Airport in snowy weather, after stopping there to refuel. Twenty-three people died in the accident, and the 21 survivors were forever haunted by the trauma of the events.

I was getting my haircut when I first heard of the tragedy, at about 4.30pm. Somebody opened the shop door and shouted in the news. Of course everyone was stunned, maybe disbelieving. I raced home, and bit by bit that evening some details filtered through: the radio and television understandably named those known to have survived, leaving you to infer the worst for those not mentioned. My diary entry was probably written the next day, as the full list of casualties was not known when I went to bed, amid the newspaper photos of the United team that were pinned on my bedroom walls. Those of us lucky to have been too young to experience the horrors of the wars of our parents and grandparents had no preparation for the shock and grief that came that afternoon. Even now, it is something that has never left me, and the same is true for friends who are my contemporaries. Since that day, wherever

I have been, no 6 February has passed without profoundly sad thoughts about the tragedy.

I had stood so many times at the small fence surrounding the Old Trafford pitch, with my red and white scarf and knitted bobble hat, cheering them on, whirling my rattle, painted red and white, when they scored or got a corner. I had seen them on bad days, as when the young side succumbed 5-1 to Bolton Wanderers on a cold January Saturday afternoon in 1954, the only consolation being the rasping sound as Tommy Taylor's powerful header hit the net just yards in front of me. But I had also seen them develop into not just the best team in England, but something special. Their speed, so notable when you are standing close by the touchline; the fluid passing; the prodigious power of Edwards in particular. Watching them play was the nearest I had to an education in aesthetics and drama, participating in the sounds made by the crowds of 40,000 or more people that rose with the spectacle of which we were each and all a part. Too young to have seen Busby's first great team at their peak, this was the side that I had grown with and identified with like no other, before or since. It gave me pride in being from Manchester; it helped me to understand who I was. Four minutes past three on 6 February: so many were dead, others would never play again. It marked my own life.

David Pegg had been England Schools' 'fine winger' that afternoon at Boundary Park against Ireland in 1950 (see Chapter 3). I remember his dashing dribbles down the left. He had torn apart the Anderlecht defence in that 10-0 rout in 1956, the game in which Tommy Taylor had bagged a hat-trick and Liam Whelan had netted twice (Chapter 4). Some fans sometimes got frustrated with Whelan, because he liked to hold the ball, but he was a quality player. Roger Byrne, left-back and captain, was mentioned earlier in this chapter. I still have an image of him timing his tackles to perfection. Geoff

Bent was his capable deputy. Salford-born Eddie Colman, small, quick and elusive, was a favourite. Mark Jones was a big but mobile centre-half.

There are poignant stories among survivors. Ken Morgans, whom I had seen in that Welsh Schools team that met England Schools at Maine Road in 1954 (Chapter 3), had played in the game in Belgrade on 5 February. The following day, he lay unconscious, his head badly injured, in the battered fuselage that had come to a halt beyond the runway at Munich Airport. He was there for five hours in the freezing cold. As the news came through with the names of the dead and the survivors, Morgans was not on either list. He was only discovered after the official search had been concluded, when some journalists were allowed to visit the tangled wreckage to look for canisters of film from the game in Belgrade. Today it sounds unbelievable that his rescue depended on such a tenuous arrangement.

Morgans had sat in a window seat as the Elizabethan made its third and fatal attempt to take off. In his old age, he told the *Daily Mail*, 'I can remember us going through the fences. I was by the window and I'll never forget the screeching noise as it ripped through the fencing. I couldn't remember anything after that.' He was unconscious for three days and in hospital for six weeks. There was no counselling to address the trauma he must have suffered. The only therapy that the stand-in boss, his fellow Welshman Jimmy Murphy, knew was to get back playing football. The doctors had told Morgans that he should not play again until the following season, but he appeared in nine games during the few remaining weeks of 1957/58, and played in the European Cup semi-final against AC Milan. But Munich crushed the innocence and spontaneity. Thereafter, he played mainly in the reserves, with just four more first-team games for United. His grief for team-mates who had perished was deep and long. Years later he said, 'Because of what happened to them, I just didn't seem to care. I tried, but the players were just not the same.' In 1961, he joined Swansea Town for a small fee, and then dropped out of league football at the age of 28. He spent a decade as a pub landlord, then worked as a ship's chandler, retailing supplies and equipment to ships.

The morning of 7 February 1958 at school was like no other. The normally boisterous, rowdy playground, where impromptu games of football merged together amid scuffles and banter, was hushed. We huddled in small groups and spoke softly, hardly daring to take in what had happened to our heroes. My diary records 'MATT BUSBY still VERY ILL. It snowed.' It also notes that school assembly was cancelled that day: maybe the staff also were too stunned and grief-stricken to face it. On the following Tuesday, the diary says, 'UNITED dead brought home'. The FA Cup fifth round tie with Sheffield Wednesday had been rescheduled by ten days to Wednesday 19 February, the first day back at school after the mid-term break. My parents rightly anticipated that it would be a packed and emotional crowd at a match under floodlights on the other side of the city, and there was homework to be done and school next morning. My entreaties to be allowed to go were turned down, though I did get the programme (see Programme Spotlights 16).

After the elation of the game in which the second half was televised, two days later my diary recorded perhaps the saddest news of all, the death of Duncan Edwards (see Chapter 3) who, after two weeks, finally succumbed to his injuries. I had been taken into the city centre by my mother on the Tuesday ('Got KEN DODD's autograph'), and absorbed from the headlines of the newspaper sellers on the street corners that Edwards' condition was deteriorating, but the news that Friday was just too awful to take.

In the sixth round United managed a draw at The Hawthorns. So it was that on Monday, 3 March, as well as watching ITV, an event still sufficiently exotic to warrant entry into my diary, 'Got DAD to let me go to see UNITED v. WEST BROM'. So on the Wednesday, as soon as school finished, my school friend Roy Dean and I called in at our house to get some essential nourishment prepared by my mother, then caught the bus to Old Trafford. Around two hours before kick-off we had our place on the barrier at the Stretford End; about halfway up the terracing there was a horizontal passageway with the barriers two to three feet above it. If you were small, like we were, this height advantage let you see over the crowd in front of you. It was another emotional rollercoaster, with the young makeshift United side hanging on against one of the leading teams of the time as the goalless game entered the last minute. Then Bobby Charlton, another crash survivor, set off on a long run down the right wing towards the Scoreboard End. He cut it back for Colin Webster to tap in from close range. Delirium! The Pathé newsreel commentator finished with '60,000 people will never forget it as long as they live'. Correct, I can still see Charlton's sprint, with time suspended for the split second before Webster scored. The crowd surged and swayed, people half-hugged, half-hung on to one another, hats were thrown into the air; noise, bedlam, delirium, ecstasy mingled with the pain of remembrance. Emotion on a scale I have never experienced in a football ground before or since. Towards the end of that month, sandwiched between 'Had a POLIO vaccination' and 'Got a BILLY BUNTER book from libery [sic]' United beat Fulham 5-3 in the semi-final replay, with young Alex Dawson (see Chapter 3) scoring a hat-trick. The dream was ended at Wembley when Bolton won the final 2-0. Because of postponements and replays, the patched up team played 13 games in 36 days between 22 March and 26 April, before the Cup Final on 3 May. The Final programme commented on the cup run, 'Such was the sympathy for United's plight it was not easy to play against them.'

Programme Spotlights 16: Ghosts
Manchester United 3 Sheffield Wednesday 0, 19 February 1958, FA Cup fifth round

The United team sheet was blank as the club did not know who they could put out. In the end they lined up with Gregg; Foulkes, Greaves: Goodwin, Cope, Crowther; Webster, E. Taylor, Dawson, M. Pearson and Brennan. Incredibly, Gregg and Foulkes were survivors from the crash, which had happened less than two weeks previously. In his autobiography *Harry's Game,* Gregg said that playing again saved his sanity. Ernie Taylor (see Chapter 1) was an emergency signing from Blackpool nearing the end of his career who had been an FA Cup winner in 1953, while Stan Crowther had been signed that afternoon from Aston Villa. The rest were reserves or young third team players. Alex Dawson had been one of the England Schools reserves at the 1954 meeting with Wales (see Chapter 3), while Shay Brennan was part of the 1955 FA Youth Cup-winning team (Chapter 3). The front of the programme carried a message from the chairman, Harold Hardman, under the headline 'United will go on'. Apart from the page giving pen portraits of the Sheffield players, the rest of the programme carried tributes to the players, club staff and journalists who had been killed, with the back page listing the memorial services – inter-denominational, Protestant, Jewish and Catholic. There was also a one-page message to those who had survived the crash.

The surreal quality of the game was captured perfectly when reserve right-back Brennan, playing on the left wing, opened the scoring direct from a corner on the left. In an age when more were believers, many ascribed it to divine intervention, as if Sheffield Wednesday did not already face an impossible task. The reality was that Ryalls, the goalkeeper, helped it in with a mistimed punch. Twenty-year-old Brennan added a second before Mark Pearson, after a dribble into the area from the right, set up Dawson for the third.

It was around this time that I became aware that there was a conspiracy against Manchester United, led by the Football League and the FA. Surprisingly few people realised that such unfairness existed, but my finely tuned antennae enabled me to trace and explain otherwise unremarkable incidents for decades thereafter. Three facts first alerted me to what was going on. My suspicions had first been raised by the attempt to block United's entry to the European Cup in 1956, and the animus with which the Football League treated the club thereafter. Not least in this was the insistence that there could be no rearrangement of United's league fixtures to allow for travel back from European games. Would the fatal third attempt at take-off in the snow at Munich have been made if the following Saturday's scheduled league match could have been postponed? Then, the second fact is that in those desperate weeks after the crash United sought to borrow Puskás, Czibor and Kocsis, members of the great Hungarian team (see Chapter 4) who had defected after the 1956 Hungarian uprising had been brutally put down by the USSR. They were serving a two-year ban by FIFA for leaving their Hungarian club without permission. Puskás, in his edited autobiography, says that after about six weeks of arguing the FA refused to sanction their moves. Finally, lest there be any shred of doubt left, in a gesture of sympathy and respect United had been granted a place in the 1958/59 European Cup and drew Young Boys of Berne in the first round. The English authorities protested on the grounds that United were not the champions. United were forced to withdraw, and though they fulfilled the fixtures with the Swiss opponents, they were played as friendlies.

Years later, when I became old enough to appreciate the irrationality of caring passionately about the performance of a football team, I would return to the tragedy of Munich for an explanation. I was 13 at the time of the crash, and still innocent about so many things. The crash bound me emotionally to United in a way that I have never been able to break from, though the takeover by the Glazer family has stretched loyalty to the limits. My adulation of the Busby Babes was unreserved; in a sense I was growing up with them. I had seen them so often it seemed like I knew them personally. Of those who died at Munich, all but Tommy Taylor had come through the youth team. Their story was a great one, that fans everywhere still cherish, of young players in their teens emerging from the youth team to take the football world by storm. It was not just about success, but also about style. They played the new type of football that we had glimpsed from Hungary and then from Real Madrid: a fast, fluent passing game based on attack.

One positive outcome of the disaster was that, like Bert Trautmann becoming a City hero (see Chapter 2), it helped the people in Manchester to put World War II behind them. There was huge respect and gratitude for the skill and care of the doctors and nurses at the Rechts der Isar Hospital in treating the injured. This echoed through the United programmes, beginning in that for the Sheffield Wednesday cup tie. Three days after the epic sixth round replay, West Bromwich Albion won 4-0 at Old Trafford in a match where Professor Georg Maurer, the chief surgeon, his wife Erika, and his team of surgeons and nurses were guests of honour, an event celebrated by the front page photo when United entertained Sunderland on 4 April, showing Bill Foulkes, the new club captain, presenting a bunch of red and white carnations to Mrs Maurer. Then the programme for the game against Wolverhampton Wanderers on 21 April welcomed the award of the CBE to Professor Maurer. I am convinced that within Manchester, Trautmann and Munich created a spirit of reconciliation at a time when other channels of mass communication, notably the cinema, were still replaying wartime enmities.

Programmes cited in Chapter 5 that are in the collection:

- 7 February 1953, Manchester United 3 Aston Villa 1, Football League First Division
- 23 January 1954, Manchester United 1 Bolton Wanderers 5, Football League First Division
- 20 August 1955, Manchester City 2 Aston Villa 2, Football League First Division
- 31 December 1955, Manchester United 2 Manchester City 1, Football League First Division
- 31 December 1955, Charlton Athletic 1 Tottenham Hotspur 2, Football League First Division
- 7 January 1956, Manchester City 1 Blackpool 1, FA Cup third round, match abandoned
- 14 January 1956, Cardiff City 4 Manchester City 1, Football League First Division
- 21 January 1956, Preston North End 3 Manchester United 1, Football League First Division
- 13 April 1957, Manchester City 0 Preston North End 2, Football League First Division
- 2 November 1957, Manchester United 1 Burnley 0, Football League First Division
- 1 February 1958, Arsenal 4 Manchester United 5, Football League First Division
- 19 February 1958, Manchester United 3 Sheffield Wednesday 0, FA Cup fifth round
- 5 March 1958, Manchester United 1 West Bromwich Albion 0, FA Cup sixth round replay
- 8 March 1958, Manchester United 0 West Bromwich Albion 4, Football League First Division
- 4 April 1958, Manchester United 2 Sunderland 2, Football League First Division
- 21 April 1958, Manchester United 0 Wolverhampton Wanderers 4, Football League First Division

- 3 May 1958, Bolton Wanderers 2 Manchester United 0, FA Cup Final
- 31 January 1962, Manchester United 1 Arsenal 0, FA Cup fourth round

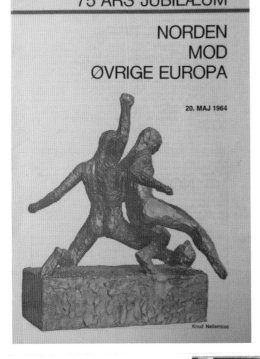

*Programme Spotlights
1: A star-studded line-up
showcased by Danish design*

*Programme Spotlights
2: Time for a rhyme:
Sportopia, 1980*

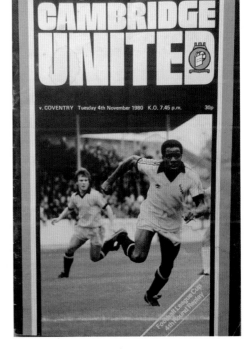

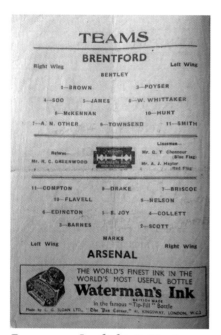

Programme Spotlights 3: Wartime Gunners

Programme Spotlights 4: An epic cup final

Programme Spotlights 5: Hearts' Edinburgh roots

Programme Spotlights 6: A programme gifted by Wilf McGuinness on his England debut

Programme Spotlights 7: The mental, moral and physical development of schoolboys

Programme Spotlights 8: A reluctant 13-year-old puts football before Morris dancing

Programme Spotlights 9: England's best meet strangers

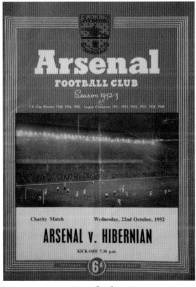

Programme Spotlights 10: Illuminated football

Programme Spotlights 11: The charge of the light brigade

Programme Spotlights 12: What is the European Cup?

Programme Spotlights 13: Pushing TV technology to the limits

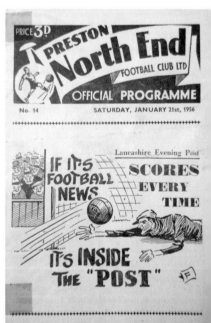

Programme Spotlights 14: A disappointing afternoon at Deepdale

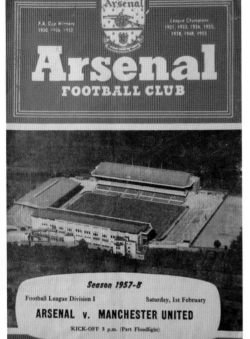

Programme Spotlights 15: I had never seen an English side do they things they did

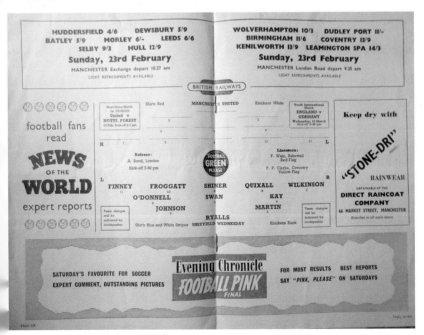

Programme Spotlights 16: Ghosts

Programme Spotlights 17:
Independence day

Programme Spotlights 18: Bridging
the north-south divide

Programme Spotlights 19: A
directory of a local economy

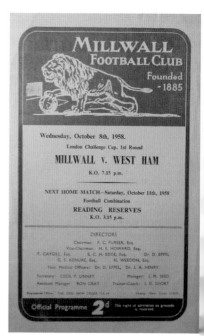

Programme Spotlights 20: Life in
the fast lane

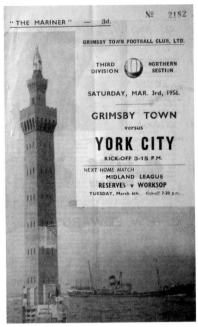

Programme Spotlights 21: A tiger on the terrace

Programme Spotlights 22: A night on the (Grimsby) Town

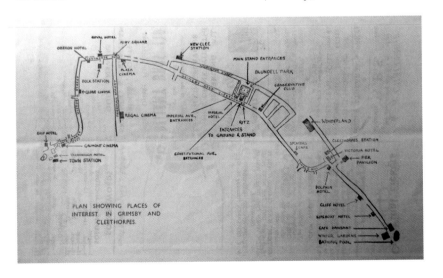

Programme Spotlights 23: A star is born

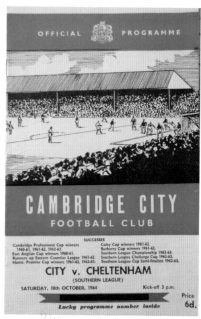

Programme Spotlights 24: Home killed meat

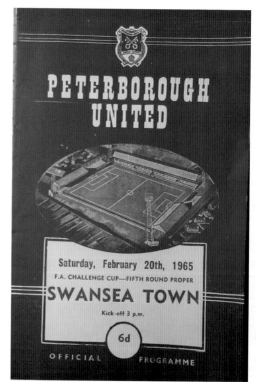

Programme Spotlights 25: A Posh crowd

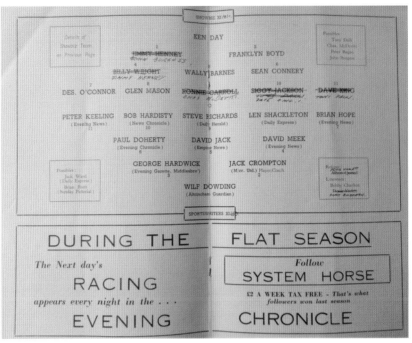

Programme Spotlights 26: 007 plays by the rules

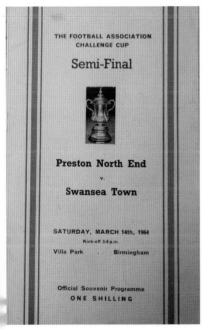

Programme Spotlights 27: Repercussions of the five-day working week

Programme Spotlights 28: A fraught homecoming

Programme Spotlights 29: North Terrace, Row 18, Seat 301

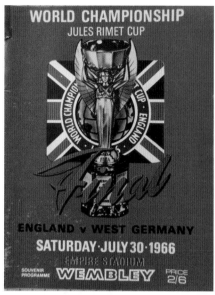

Programme Spotlights 30: Suck a Mintoe and think of England

Programme Spotlights 31: From 0-5 in the reserves to World Cup winner

Programme Spotlights 32:
Opportunity knocks

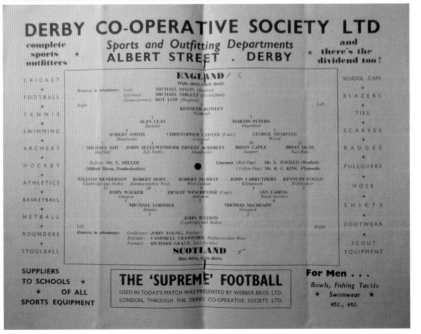

Programme Spotlights 33: From base one to a home run

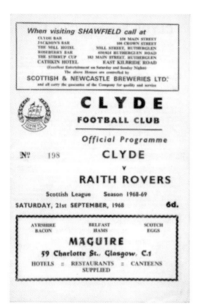

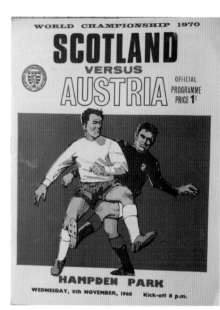

Programme Spotlights 34: A win for the Bully Wee, but not for public health

Programme Spotlights 35: Law changes

Programme Spotlights 36: Should have been a red card

Programme Spotlights 37: The big picture

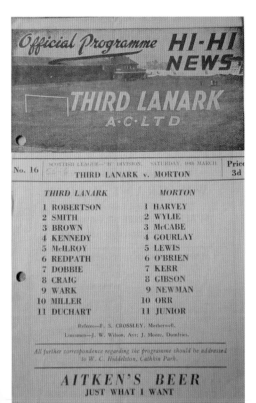

Programme
Spotlights 38: Hi Hi

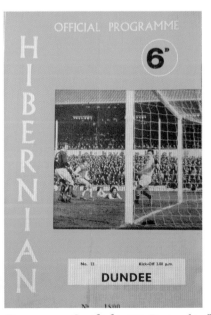

Programme Spotlights 39: Decimal inflation

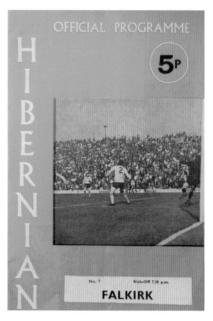

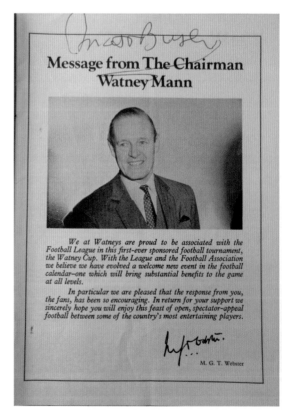

Programme Spotlights 40: Don't trust a keeper to take a penalty

Programme Spotlights 41: Big oil comes to town

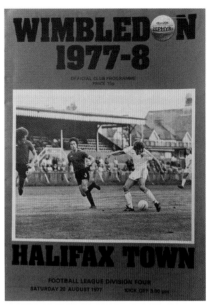

Programme Spotlights 42: The stripper skipper

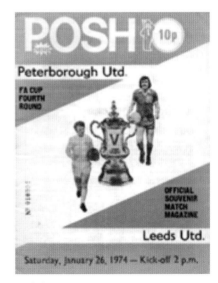

Programme Spotlights 43: More elastic needed

Programme Spotlights 44: Young, gifted and black

Programme Spotlights 45: The Falklands War Cup Final

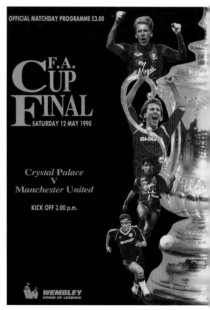

Programme Spotlights 46: Place branding

Chapter 6

You've Never Had It So Good

THE LATTER years of the 1950s were a period in which Britain at last began to experience some post-war prosperity. The Conservatives, led by Harold Macmillan, famously won the 1959 General Election with the slogan 'You've never had it so good'. The football programmes of this period reflect both the continuities, but also the transition, that characterised the country. These were my early teenage years, a period when I began to travel to Manchester United's away games in the north and Midlands with a group of friends from school. In other respects my life continued pretty much the same as that sketched in the previous chapter. My diaries continued to be dominated by the football and cricket scores, and while there were marginal improvements in the spelling and examination results, my recorded existence remained an uninspiring sequel of detentions, getting a haircut, colds and similar minor ailments, cancellations of games periods due to bad weather, and watching TV shows. These schooldays fell well short of being the clichéd 'best days' of my life.

I still played informal games of football in my spare time, mainly with coats as goalposts, which were liable to extend horizontally, and so be the focus of multiple disputes about whether or not a shot was inside, or on, the post. Sometimes we would venture on to a public playing field with goalposts but no nets or referees, and on these occasions our star man was Fred Eyre, who lived locally and was at the same technical school, Ducie Avenue, as Mark, my pal who lived next door to us. After representing Manchester Boys, Fred went to Manchester City where he became their first apprentice. He was with City for a couple of years without playing in the first team, but then achieved some fame in the 1980s through a series of amusing books, most notably *Kicked into Touch*, which sold over a million copies. It celebrated his unsuccessful career, and helped make him something of a cult figure, especially for City fans. Before he was 21, Eyre had been given free transfers by City, Lincoln City and Huddersfield Town. He then went from one non-league club to another, serving under a mammoth 112 managers and coaches across 20 clubs.

Dave Wagstaffe's career was much more successful than Eyre's. Wagstaffe was in the year ahead of me at North Manchester Grammar School, so I knew of him by reputation rather than his being part of the crowd that I hung out with. That reputation though was considerable within the school, where the rugby union team of which he was a part were beating all comers. Then suddenly several members of that team, including Wagstaffe, were expelled. All we were told was that there had been an 'incident' on the waste ground behind the local cinema involving these boys and some girls from the nearby secondary modern school. Wagstaffe transferred to Ducie Avenue, and in a matter of months was playing on the left wing for Manchester Boys, and then he joined Manchester City. I saw him play for City in, and have the four-page programme for, the FA Youth Cup third round tie in December 1958. They lost 4-0 to a United youth team that included future stars Nobby Stiles and John Giles. The City team also included Alan Oakes, another who would make it to become a first-team regular. As a winger, Wagstaffe made 144 first team appearances for City, before being sold to Wolverhampton Wanderers in 1964, where he played more than 300 games over the next 12 years. Landmarks in his career included scoring in the second leg of the UEFA Cup Final of 1972 against Tottenham Hotspur. While with Blackburn Rovers in 1976, he achieved the dubious distinction of being the first player in the Football League to be shown a red card.

Michael Batty was a third contemporary from my early teenage years who made it into professional football. He was in the same year as me at the grammar school, and frequently played football with a crowd of us in the school yard for about an hour after lessons ended and before we made our ways home to eat our tea and do our homework. Batty was big and played 13 games as a centre-half for Manchester City between 1962 and 1966, before moving to non-league Rhyl. At the start of the 1961/62 season I went to watch City beat Leicester City 3-1. The programme has a list of their playing staff, which includes Eyre, Wagstaffe and Batty, the latter then being 17 and listed as standing at 6ft and weighing 13st and 3lb (84kg). I was still a 16-year-old wimp, wearing glasses and with missing teeth.

These associations would be the nearest I would get to the professional game. I continued to plod through my homework and dutifully record the football and cricket scores in my diaries, which reveal the occasional flash of a new consumerism in the world around me. For example, on 9 May 1959, during a visit to the speedway at Belle Vue (in those days the north of England's premier zoo and entertainment complex), I 'got a 1/2 pint of milk from a machine': a vending machine was a technological novelty. Nor was that all, for less than two weeks later, Aunty Pat (who lived across the road from us) 'got a fridge', and then on Tuesday, 2 June I 'Got a

BIC biro'. Even as a harbinger of the demise of the fountain pen, recording the getting of a biro testifies to a remarkably boring life for a 14-year-old.

Excitement came on Saturdays, the best day of the week, especially when I would travel to United away games in the north and Midlands with a crowd from school (see Programme Spotlights 17). We went by coach at first, but then more often we would travel on a British Rail Football Special. Mindful that a significant proportion of the clientele for such trains were scruffy, careless kids, the nationalised rail industry used their oldest and most threadbare third-class carriages to transport us.

To economise and ensure our wellbeing, mothers would have prepared packs of sandwiches and flasks of tea or coffee. It didn't take much of a knock for the flask to break, spilling its liquid down your coat or trousers; I recall one particularly uncomfortable return journey from Blackburn. We would play cards, mainly poker, and have a sweepstake on who would score the first goal. Though only small change was involved, for one surviving on 'spends' the results could make a difference.

Disembarking, we would just follow the crowd exuberantly to the stadium, chanting 'two, four, six, eight, who do we appreciate? U-N-I-T-E-D. United! Terrace songs only began, I think, when 'The Spurs (went) marching in' on their way to the Double in the early 1960s. As you got near the ground, the streets became narrower and more crowded, and it was there that you would find a programme seller. Remember, you might need the programme cover to substitute for a reserve team token to purchase tickets for big games, though in those early years after Munich there were few such occasions. You joined the queues at the 'Juniors' gates to get in for half price, even after you were over the age limit, memorising your revised date of birth in case of interrogation at the turnstile. Safely through, you ascended the stairs to the terrace, there to command a spot right behind the goal.

There was no segregation of fans, so our 'gang' were often standing alongside home supporters. There would be banter with the opposition's stalwarts, but I saw no violence; rather fans would often reminisce about past matches between the teams. I can remember particularly standing on the Holte End terrace at Villa Park in what the programme tells me was September 1960, and listening to an old Aston Villa fan rhapsodise about the FA Cup third round tie in 1948. The home team had scored within seconds of the kick-off, but United led 5-1 by half-time. Villa again got a quick goal and kept scoring, so that the score was 5-4 as the clock ticked down, only for a last-minute United sixth to settle the tie. It's easy to see why the game stayed long in memories: dramatic swings of fortune, high tension, skill, personalities, all stirred by being there that day and witnessing, even being a part of, something special. Memories are cherished and passed down through the generations.

- -

Programme Spotlights 17: Independence day
Leeds United 1 Manchester United 2, 1 November 1958, Football League First Division

This programme is memorable for me because it was the first away match that I went to independently, by which I mean not in the care of a parent, but rather as part of a teenage group of friends from school. Apart from the programme, that has kept the memory alive, I remember three things about that autumn day long ago. First that the coach in which we travelled to the match stopped at a pub somewhere in the Pennines, where some of our group drank something called 'mild'. I was still way too young to do that. Then I remember standing on the open terrace behind the goal into which Freddie Goodwin volleyed the winner from just inside the penalty area. Like many players in those days, Goodwin was also a professional cricketer, playing at first-class level with Lancashire as a seam bowler. Finally, I remember that our 'gang' then threw improvised streamers in celebration. The streamers were rolls of white paper on which Manchester Corporation bus tickets were printed by bus conductors. I don't know how those rolls had been acquired: theft cannot be ruled out.

The cover of the 16-page programme, despite being in blue on a yellow background, is decidedly dull and static, and remained the same for every game. A coat of arms rarely excites. Yellow and blue were Leeds's colours until Don Revie became manager and went for an all-white, Real Madrid lookalike strip.

The inside of the programme is black printing on very ordinary quality white paper. It contains quite a lot of text relative to advertising. There are a couple of paragraphs recalling the meetings of the teams in the 1956/57 season, and in particular 'a devastating shot by John Charles' for Leeds's goal in a 2-1 home defeat. Welsh international Charles had since moved to Juventus, where he achieved legendary status playing at either centre-forward or centre-half. One slightly odd touch in the programme is on a typical page of adverts from small local businesses that included a Ford dealer/horticultural engineer (an unusual combination), wine lodge, outfitters, and painting and cleaning contractor. These are all aligned in the conventional horizontal way, but then in the bottom right quarter of the page with the image and text aligned vertically, is an advert for latex foam rubber. The discordant alignment gives a clumsy, slightly amateur look to the page.

My generation was a lucky one in so many ways. Our fathers and grandfathers had fought in wars, and boys just a few years older than me had to spend two years doing National Service.

Conscription of males aged 17 to 21 had continued after 1945. Indeed, in 1950, during the Korean War, the period of compulsory service in the armed forces was extended from 18 months to two years. The call-up ended in 1960, so I was not required to spend months on end being drilled into obeying orders. This dividing line was surely a factor in shaping the cultural changes that defined the 1960s, and the angry (and even envious?) reaction that they provoked.

National Service impacted upon the careers of footballers. The Crystal Palace programme for their Third Division (South) encounter with Leyton Orient on 24 March 1956 gave an insight into how careers could be affected. It included a feature on Harry Gunning. Like me, Harry was 'a Lancashire lad' whose 'early soccer tuition' had been 'gained on waste patches'. There the similarities ended. He had progressed to sign amateur forms with Blackpool, but 'being called up for National Service broke his spell with Blackpool and he signed amateur forms with Bolton Wanderers, but here again his national service interrupted his career, for he was moved South, and not being re-signed by Bolton at the end of the season, he then signed for Gravesend and Northfleet'. From there he went to West Ham as a professional, then on to Crystal Palace in 1954. He was listed to wear the number 11 shirt for Palace in that day's game against Leyton Orient.

Gunning had similarly lined up on the left wing for Palace's floodlit friendly on 13 February 1956 against Second Division Rotherham United. This programme gives a further insight into the relation between National Service and professional football, for it reports on Palace's game the previous Wednesday evening against 'a very good Army side'. The 19-year-old goalkeeper for the Army had been Alan Hodgkinson, who had already appeared for Sheffield United in the First Division, and who a year later was keeping goal behind Tom Finney and Stan Matthews in the England team that faced Scotland. The Palace programme described Hodgkinson's performance for the Army team as 'really brilliant'. Bill Foulkes, Manchester United's regular right-back and a full England international, who as mentioned in Chapter 5, became club captain, 'had a very harassing time against Gunning but showed strength and class in recovery and distribution'. Bobby Charlton and

Duncan Edwards played alongside Hodgkinson in the Army team, though the Palace programme makes no mention of whether they had featured in the Selhurst Park match.

The programmes of the late 1950s show that, for those completing National Service, there were plenty of secure male jobs on offer. Doncaster Rovers' programmes in 1956/57 carried a prominent recruitment advertisement just below the team sheet. 'WANTED', it read, 'Colliers and Men who like good well paid jobs. See any colliery manager or ask at your local employment exchange.' Also in the South Yorkshire coalfield, the Sheffield Wednesday home programmes in 1961/62 were announcing, 'There are careers for you in coal – ones with a real future.' The advertisements spoke of the 'thriving Yorkshire coal industry' and the prospects it offered of 'an interesting, well paid and SECURE life' for young men and boys leaving school. The emphasis on security suggests that memories of the dole queues of the 1930s remained. Yet 30 years later those young men and school-leavers would be characterised in the films *Brassed Off* (1996) and *The Full Monty* (1997), struggling to make a living after the bitter strike in 1984/85 failed to save their jobs in coalfields in South Yorkshire and other traditional hotbeds of football.

Similarly, Manchester United's home programmes in 1961/62 season included a half-page advert from the Metropolitan-Vickers Electrical Company in nearby Trafford Park, which was headlined 'SECURE EMPLOYMENT FOR SKILLED MEN'. The same advert appeared as a full page in the Manchester City home programmes. The company were offering 'excellent conditions with good rate of pay including piece-work and incentive bonuses' for a bewildering array of technical jobs that included the intriguingly named 'Horizontal Borers'.

On the same page of the United programmes was a quarter-page box in which Handley Page Ltd. from Cricklewood in

YOU'VE NEVER HAD IT SO GOOD

London sought to recruit fitters. At that time the company was still one of Britain's leading manufacturers of aircraft. To tempt the United fans south, the company offered 'Good Pay – Bonus and Security; Non-contributory Life Assurance and Retirement Benefits Scheme; Payment during illness Benefit Scheme; Canteen; Medical and Welfare Services; Wide range of Sports and Social Interests', and the prospects of 'Long Term Engagements [being] offered to approved applicants'. In the programme for United's first floodlit game at Old Trafford on 25 March 1957 (a 2-0 defeat by Bolton Wanderers where the gates shut after I had bought my programme, but before I could get to the turnstiles, and I was left outside to return home, like thousands of others), Handley Page were advertising degree and Higher National Certificate level vacancies in their Flight Test Department at St Albans. By 1970, Handley Page had gone out of business. Barclay's Bank had called in the receiver as Britain's oldest aircraft company hit cash flow problems, having sought to buck the trend of mergers which created bigger competitors.

While the demise of Handley Page was a story replicated across much of British manufacturing industry in the years that followed, their advertising in far-away Manchester was the exception. In general, local businesses were much the most common advertisers in programmes, especially among the smaller clubs, who presumably canvassed hard for their support. The advertisements shine a light on local economic specialisations, even to the point of cliché. Fishermen's outfitters Dobsons Limited took a half-page slot in Grimsby Town's programmes. The back page of Sheffield United's programmes extolled the qualities of Wardonia Blades, 'Sheffield's Sharpest Shavers', which were manufactured only at the Wardonia Works, Sheffield 1. Stanley Tools from the Stanley Works, Sheffield 3, also were a regular in the Blades' home programmes.

Programme Spotlights 18: Bridging the north-south divide

Chester 5 Accrington Stanley 1, 30 April 1958, Football League Third Division (North)

At the end of the 1957/58 season there was a significant restructuring of the Football League. The teams finishing in the top half of the Third Division (North) and Third Division (South) would form the new Third Division, with clubs finishing in the respective bottom halves going into the new Fourth Division. This Chester programme for their last Third Division (North) game struck a cautious note, 'Time will tell whether the changing of the 3rd Division League structure has been a wise move, or otherwise. Extra travelling will have to be done, and naturally expenses will be much higher. We shall entertain 12 New Clubs at the Stadium next season, and this will create a new interest. We shall find out if the so-called superiority of the Southern Clubs is in fact the case, or merely wishful thinking.' It proved not to be wishful thinking. In the first season of the new Third Division, southern clubs took ten of the first 15 places. Plymouth Argyle were champions, while the bottom seven were all from the north. Likewise in the Fourth Division, Watford and Aldershot were the only teams from the south to finish in the bottom half that first season.

Chester's programme is typical of those of smaller clubs at this period, consisting mainly of small adverts placed by local firms. It makes for a very cluttered look. Fixtures, results, and league tables for the first and reserve teams were also included, along with a record of that season's league appearances and goalscorers. The pen portraits of the visitors occupied a little over half a page, but provided sufficient background on each player to demonstrate Accrington's strong links to Scotland – the former clubs of the 11 players listed included Stirling Albion, Dunfermline, Third Lanark, Stenhousemuir and Hibernian, with two others identified simply as Scots.

It wasn't just in the big cities and coalfields that jobs were on offer. Chester's 5-1 home win over Accrington Stanley on 30 April 1958 (see Programme Spotlights 18) was the last Third Division (North) game the sides played, and so the programme is a collector's item. Despite the result that day, Accrington would start the following season in the new Third Division, while Chester were part of the new Fourth Division. The structure of football competition was changing as the post-war boom extended travel patterns. The match programme included a prominent advertisement next to the team sheet in the centre pages. 'DO YOU KNOW?' it asked, 'There are some good jobs going at DE HAVILAND AIRCRAFT Co. Ltd. BROUGHTON.' Wanted immediately were miller setter operators, bench detail fitters, trainee miller operators, and fitters (airframe). Prospective employees were invited to call at the works for interview Monday to Saturday.

Although I only sensed it dimly at the time, this was the world of work that I was heading towards. Even from the grammar school only quite a small minority of pupils were going on to university. Most would be prepared for, and steered into, skilled and semi-skilled jobs in manufacturing, of which there were plenty in Manchester in those days. There were some clerical-type white-collar jobs too, but throughout those schoolboy years I drifted along, giving little thought to any future career. Looking back now, I realise how spectacularly unsuited I would have been to the employment opportunities advertised in the football programmes that I was collecting. As a dedicated wimp, I would have been utterly miserable and a danger to my colleagues if I had gone to work in a coal mine or in the heat of a steel mill, while my school performance in woodwork amply demonstrated that I lacked the precision and dexterity required to make the grade as a horizontal borer. If De Haviland Aircraft had taken me on as a fitter (airframe), there would probably have been a small but lethal gap between the wing and the plane, or take-off and landing would have been complicated by a significant misalignment of one of the wheels.

While I was part of the joyous crowd revelling in the champions, the Busby Babes, beating Sheffield Wednesday 4-1 at Old Trafford on 15 September 1956, about 30 miles to the north Accrington Stanley were facing Chesterfield. The programme for that Third Division (North) encounter gives an insight into small town life in the north of England in the 1950s. As well as those advertisements on the cover (see Programme Spotlights 19), on the next page the eye is immediately drawn to Magnet Pet Foods of Blackburn and Liverpool. Beneath that is W.W. Bleasdale and Co, Qualified Radio and TV Engineer, 7 Blackburn Road, Accrington; then, at the bottom of the page is Rennards, Wine and Spirits Merchants, 7 Birch Street, Accrington. Page three is mostly devoted to 'Our Visitors', but atop the page is 'Floodlighting - - - Peel Park Ground carried out by Dent's The Electricians, 3/13 Burnley Road, Accrington'.

Page four has four adverts, one for the supporters' club, another for a local hotel, a third for a catering service, and another for luxury coaches. The remaining pages included promotions for another couple of hotels; the British Railways train to the match at Chester the following week; the *Northern Daily Telegraph* (in the familiar font of what is now just the *Daily Telegraph*); the 'Largest Local Importer of Scottish Fish'; a Ford dealership; an Accrington petrol station; a joiner and funeral director; farm bottled milk; Shaun's Popular Clothing Club; a carpet and lino specialist; a firm dealing in Slasher Sizing Machines and offering 'alterations to most machines' (I have no idea what a sizing machine was, but my mechanical skills were such that I couldn't have handled one without courting disaster).

Page 15 has another ten adverts: timber merchants, floral tributes, baby carriages, a laundry, a baker and confectioner, heating engineers, private dancing lessons, property repairs, haulage contractors and the Café Royal – the one on Blackburn Road, Accrington. Finally, the back page, which like the rest of the cover pages is printed in Stanley's red and white colours, has a tailor, the Majestic Ballroom, Clarkson's Tyres (who were vulcanising specialists!) and more exotic still, given the time, the place and the climate, an offer from M. Wood and Co. to 'Make Your Home the Present of a Cacti Garden'.

It is a whole, locally owned and locally networked economy of small-to-medium-sized businesses that reads like a Joycean stream of consciousness, defining life styles and the day-to-day business of this small, industrial town in the mid-1950s. It speaks of a buoyancy and cohesion with the football club, which had been formed in 1891, at the heart of a community. However, there were no advertisements from the town's cotton mills, an industry that had peaked before World War I, but which was enjoying what proved to be a temporary revival in the 1950s before its demise in the face of foreign competition by the 1980s. Similarly, the local outlets of national chain businesses, for example the Odeon cinema, Burton's menswear or Woolworth, did not advertise in the programme. Less than a decade later, in 1962, Accrington Stanley was bankrupt, owing transfer fees and the Inland Revenue, and resigned from the Fourth Division of the Football League. The club was reformed in 1968 and regained Football League status in 2016.

- -

Programme Spotlights 19: A directory of a local economy

Accrington Stanley 1 Chesterfield 1, 15 September 1956, Third Division (North)

This 16-page programme, printed red on white, carries an extensive range of small advertisements from local businesses, as is already evident on the cover page. Squeezed in among the adverts comes a page of Club Notes – the defence was giving cause for concern due to the absence of centre-half Jimmy Harrower. The teams spread over pages eight and nine, beneath an advert for the *News of the World*, are surrounded by no fewer than 17 other advertisements for enterprises located in or adjacent to Accrington. They include cafes and bars, a funeral director and the Cemetery Hotel (separate businesses), a hardware shop, a coal merchant, Len's 'For good bacon and ham', and my personal favourite, 'We shall have Rain. Get your rainwear from Arthur Dawson, Arcade Rubber Stores.'

Stanley had made a good start to the season, with 11 points out of a possible 14, and had scored 22 times in the seven opening matches. However, the Club Notes reveals that some fans were still grumbling about missed chances – 'no good wi' 'is feet' as the writer put it in the local accent. The programme also reveals some of the problems for 'border' places with the north/south split of the Third Division, noting that in 1951/52 Chesterfield had taken the place of Shrewsbury Town who had been transferred to the southern section.

The new affluence and job security of the mid-1950s was widely marked by advertisements for consumer goods, most notably cars and televisions, in football programmes across the land. Some of these promotions were quite basic. For example, Portsmouth's programme from December 1955 (v. Manchester United) has a simple instruction, printed in white on Pompey's navy blue background, 'Buy your television from Weston Hart Ltd. It's cheaper in the long run.' Rental was the stepping stone to mass TV ownership, purchase was the option for the thrifty able to save for such luxuries, or get them on credit through hire purchase. There was no such thing as a credit card. Luton Town's programme for their Boxing Day game with Manchester United in 1957 depicted on the front page a 17in screen Murphy TV, with the enticement, 'For years now the Christmas Broadcasts have been as much a part of this happy festival as roast turkey and plum pudding. Now television joins the party in an ever increasing number of homes.' Meanwhile the bulky new models of the leading manufacturers of mass market cars were also being advertised widely in the pages of programmes.

In January 1957, Sheffield Wednesday carried an advertisement for a fully automatic car wash. For as little as six shillings and six pence (just over £8 in 2020 values), the new, modern, automated car washing system would thoroughly clean 'inside, outside and underneath' in only 20 minutes. It was, claimed the advertiser, 'unique in this country'. A similar sense of transition can be discerned in the advert, in the Coventry City programme of 1 November 1958, for concrete garages and coal bunkers.

Julians for Motor Cycles advertised in the Reading programme in 1955/56, with a sketch of an un-helmeted young man astride a motor bike that now looks distinctly old-fashioned, but no doubt was cutting-edge design in its day. 'A motor cycle, scooter or sidecar of your choice' was advertised in Newcastle United's 1957/58 programme against Manchester United, again with a sketch, but this time with a woman riding on the pillion behind her man, and again neither wears a helmet.

By 1961/62, an advertisement in the Fulham programme promoted not just motor cycles and scooters but also mopeds and bubble cars; the car depicted, like most of these micro-cars, had only one rear wheel. The bubble car was a further indicator of the transition from post-war austerity to mass consumerism. It offered a more affordable form of car ownership, and was cheaper to tax than a conventional four-wheeler. It was the precursor of, and overtaken by, the Austin Mini a decade later. Some footballers were able to indulge in more luxurious vehicles (see Programme Spotlights 20).

Programme Spotlights 20: Life in the fast lane
Millwall v. West Ham United, 8 October 1958, London Challenge Cup first round

This four-page Millwall programme, printed blue on white, captures the zeitgeist of the times. In it Jimmy Seed, the Millwall manager, wrote, 'I saw a report that Stan Anslow would be asking for a transfer. The Anslow boy received a benefit last season of £600. He is now the proud owner of a Ford Zephyr car.' The Anslow boy's Zephyr would have been built at Ford's huge Dagenham plant, not so far from Millwall's home at The Den. As the manager implied, it was no standard economy car; rather it was the largest passenger car in Ford's UK range, with a six-cylinder, 2,262cc engine, that could attain speeds of 80mph! Who wouldn't be impressed?

Anslow, born in Hackney, had signed for the Lions in 1951, and had been converted from a full-back to centre-forward. He made his name in 1957 by scoring twice against Newcastle United (FA Cup winners three times in the previous six seasons), in a fourth-round tie in which the London team pulled off a shock 2-1 win before a record crowd of 45,646. His career was cut short by a broken leg sustained early in 1957/58, and he retired at the end of that season. Meanwhile, West Ham progressed to the final of the London Challenge Cup in 1957/58, where they lost to Tottenham Hotspur. The competition was discontinued in 1974.

Products likely to appeal particularly to women rarely appear in the programmes of the 1950s, but there are some exceptions. Leicester City in 1956/57 had a full-page advertisement for The Three Sisters, which retailed waistslips, petticoats, pantees (sic), briefs and nightdresses, as well as knitwear and nylon stockings. In the same season, Babydom were in the Hull City programme against Rochdale, offering prams, folding carriages, and toys for (wince) 'all the young "players'" needs'.

The tobacco companies assiduously chased the disposable income of fans. The health risks associated with smoking were still not widely acknowledged. It is no coincidence that cigarettes were widely advertised in the match programmes of the day; fans were a substantial market for big tobacco. The Stoke City v. Lincoln City game on 23 February 1957 was one of our son Euan's teenage 'strategic purchases', standing out because Stoke won 8-0, with Tim Coleman getting seven of them, which still stands as a Stoke record. On his day Coleman could be a mesmeric dribbler, but like so many wingers he was notoriously inconsistent; he followed his outstanding feat against Lincoln by failing to score again that season as Stoke went goalless in six of their next seven fixtures. The programme for Coleman's most memorable outing carried a banner advert for Players cigarettes across the bottom of the middle pages beneath the team sheet, 'In league with pleasure – Players Please.'

The whole back page was an advert for Park Drive cigarettes, 'It's quality, quality all the time with Park Drive. They're so well made.' There was also an inside-page advert for Mennex Snuff. The same product was advertised on the back page of the West Bromwich Albion programmes in 1957/58. Senior Service cigarettes were promoted on the full inside front page of the Sunderland programme for the Christmas Day game with Aston Villa in 1956. The front page of the 1956 Sunderland programme carried the proud strapline 'Only Club which has never played in any other than the First Division', but that record lasted only until the end of 1957/58 when Sunderland were relegated. Second Division Bristol Rovers' programmes in 1955/56 advertised Anstie's Gold Flake cigarettes (five for eight pence) above the team line-ups. Selling in packets of five was a means to reach people short of money, including new young smokers such as some of my teenage class-mates.

- -

Programme Spotlights 21: A tiger on the terrace
Hull City 2 Rochdale 0, 25 August 1956, Football League Third Division (North)

I have always loved this programme which, like many others, I got as a boy by writing to the club requesting a copy. There are a number of things that make it stand out. The orange and black of the club colours are unusual, and are used throughout the programme on a white background, giving a clean, fresh and easily navigable quality to the whole thing. The use of good quality shiny paper was not that common in 1956, and it adds to the feel and visual presentation.

The cover page demonstrates all these qualities; contrast it with the covers of the Chester and Accrington Stanley programmes shown earlier in this chapter. The cartoon tiger and the caption above it reinforce the message about club's identity, pride and passion, which is dramatised by the 'starburst' effect of the white breaking into the orange at the top of the page, so that the tiger almost leaps out to the viewer, while also being strongly rooted in Hull City by the solid orange box below. The rattle, scarf and barrier to lean on were an almost spiritual trinity for many fans on the terraces in this period.

Another unusual feature of the programme is that has an advert for a prams/toys/nursery store, Babydom: childcare got little coverage in programmes those days. There is also an advert from a local company offering 'luxury tours' to destinations as exotic as Morecambe Illuminations, but mainly to Yorkshire resorts. Like the vast majority, if not all programmes of the time, it was produced by a local firm of printers: the money would have recirculated in the local economy.

Former Blackpool and England centre-forward Stan Mortensen, the First Division's top scorer in 1950/51, was leading the home side's attack that afternoon. It was his second and final season with Hull, before he moved to Southport and then Bath

City. Mortensen's hat-trick in the 1953 FA Cup Final never got the recognition it deserved because of the romance of Stanley Matthews winning the match. Indeed, 'Stanley Matthews Football Boots – Designed by the Master Himself', were advertised in the Hull programme, 'Obtainable from the Hull Co-operative Society Ltd.' The programme records how Mortensen had been injured after 30 minutes in the previous home game against Tranmere Rovers. Rochdale's manager was Harry Catterick, who, according to the programme, had brought in three players from Everton, his former club. Catterick returned to Goodison as manager from 1961 to 1973 and steered Everton to the league title in 1963 and FA Cup in 1966.

While tobacco adverts were from national brands, and tended to appear more in the programmes of bigger clubs, those for beers and stouts were often local at that time, though they were later taken over and put out of business by bigger companies. Cardiff City's 1955/56 programme had 'Rhymney and Crosswells Draught and Bottled Beers – On sale throughout Wales'. The company was taken over by the giant Whitbread in 1966, who proceeded to replace the local beers with their national brands, and then close and demolish the local brewery. The back page of Third Division (North) Grimsby Town's programme that same season advertised 'Hewitts Oatmeal Stout – Smooth! Strong!! Satisfying!!! The Greatest Sale of any Stout in North-East Lincolnshire', not exactly a claim to cosmopolitan fame and markets. This local brewery was taken over in 1961 by United Breweries Ltd. and closed in 1968.

In the Aston Villa programme for their match on 22 December 1956 against Manchester City (the game was postponed, so another inspired purchase by Euan), the second page proclaimed that 'After the Match There's no Match for Ansell's beer'. Again this was a local beer brewed in the Aston area of Birmingham. In 1961 Ansell's merged with Taylor Walker and Ind Coope to form Allied Breweries, which then closed the Aston plant in 1981, transferring production to their Burton-on-Trent site. In the Notts County programmes, it was Shipstone's 'The County's Favourite' from the Star Brewery, New Basford, Nottingham on page six. Home Ales, another local brewery, were on the back cover. In 1986 Home Ales was sold to Scottish and Newcastle as part of a deal that included 450 pubs across the UK, then the brewery was closed in 1996. Not until 2015 did brewing commence again in the old plant. Similarly, Shipstone's were an independent family business for over a century until they were bought out by Greenall's in 1978. In 1991 Greenall's ceased production in Nottingham. A local micro-brewery has now picked up the Shipstone's label.

Ipswich Town had an advert for Cobbold beers, Cliff Brewery, Ipswich, when they met Notts County in 1957. In 1977, the brewery was bought out by an investment arm of the notoriously secretive and mega-rich Barclay Brothers, who, at the time of writing, were owners of the *Daily Telegraph* and the *Sunday Telegraph*. They closed the Cliff Brewery in 1989. In the Leeds United programmes, Melbourne Ales were the 'best in Yorkshire'. Their story is by now familiar; bought out in 1960 by Tetley's, their brewery in Regent Street, Leeds, was demolished in 1973.

Thus, behind the mundane advertisements in these old football programmes there is the story of at least one of Britain's traditional industries. Breweries such as these were often established in the 19th century, and boomed as urban populations grew around them because the technologies of the day made it difficult to transport beer without losing quality and increasing the price. In general, UK brewers did not invest as much in the science and technology of brewing as did some continental counterparts. Then when the technologies did change, bigger, more efficient plants became possible able to serve national and even international markets with quality-assured products. UK brewing became controlled by six major companies, and standardisation replaced diversity in products, supported by a corresponding shift in marketing. Meanwhile, the old, now redundant breweries, because of their origins, often occupied valuable sites, which could attract speculative property developers. It was not until the 21st century that microbreweries and craft beers began to reshape the fringes of the industry. Control of a local economy, e.g. over the closure of a brewery that was a source of local jobs, pride and identity, was drained away, centralised and, as the case of the Barclay Brothers shows most clearly, was shifted towards a calculus of investment rather than a prime focus on product and place. Part of the nexus that bound together local communities, jobs, football clubs and businesses was weakened.

Often the breweries' adverts were accompanied by cartoon drawings that made a (tangential) link between the beer and football. Shipstone's, for example, had Ivor Thirst (get it?), a six-pointed star for his head atop a body in a Notts County kit in front of a sketch of a crowd and a six-strong back line of County players. Thirst was depicted kicking a pint glass of ale high into the air in the direction of the next page or a big centre-forward. In the Everton 1955/56 programme against Manchester United, a player has been flattened, his opponent is standing over him, and being admonished by a finger-wagging referee, while the script says, 'Sound Advice! Drink Bent's Ales and enjoy the Best!' On the following page there is a cartoon of a squat-looking man pushing open a door marked 'bar' alongside the instruction, 'Dart in for a Double Top Higson's Brown Ale.' Needless to say, Bent's was a Liverpool brewery, with 19th-century origins; Higson's were even older, another Liverpool business, and they took over Bent's in 1978, before eventually passing into the control of Whitbread in 1990, who subsequently closed the Liverpool brewery.

Appreciation of the link between a drinking culture and footballers' performances on the field was still some way off in the 1950s, though it seemed that there had been some progress. The Manchester City programme for their abandoned cup tie with Blackpool in 1956 (see Chapter 5) includes a half-page cartoon, 'It's a Fact'. It depicts a bearded, top-hatted man pouring liquid from a large jug into numerous cups. The accompanying text explains that from 1866 until 1871 Sheffield Wednesday gave players a beer allowance – a gallon (eight pints) to each member of a winning team, and half that to losers.

Lest it should appear that that football was solely beholden to fags and booze, there was at least one club doing its best to promote the cause of public health. The Queens Park Rangers programme for their Third Division (South) game with Watford on 30 November 1957 included a 'Welcome to the Butlin's Young Ladies', who were making a return visit. The young women from the popular chain of holiday camps were there to provide 'a demonstration of physical culture to music before the match'. Less tangentially to healthy living, the programme noted that there had been an enthusiastic response to the supporters' club's invitation to 'budding young footballers' to join their five-a-side teams.

Other entertainments were on offer. Grimsby Town's programme for their game with York City in March 1956 included not just a sketch map to help visiting supporters to locate places of interest in Grimsby and Cleethorpes, but also a crossword puzzle and a quiz. However, that programme also carries a reminder of the tensions in the professional game and the changes that were brewing. The Editor's Notes discussed 'the most momentous meeting of Football Legislators for many years' that was due to take place. It was the meeting that would lead to the replacement of the two 'old' Third Divisions by the new four-division set up. The editor explained Grimsby's concerns, 'It is the Third Northern that looks like being the

"Aunt Sally" in the battle for survival… if the proposal to make the 3rd Northern the 4th Division of the League comes off.' As noted earlier in this chapter, a more equitable compromise was reached, but it is possible to discern in this north/south clash, together with the soon-to-follow fate of the multitude of local breweries, an economic and geographical shift within the country that was hidden by the general rise in affluence and access to a previously unimaginable array of consumer goods.

- -

Programme Spotlights 22: A night on the (Grimsby) Town

Grimsby Town 2 York City 1, 3 March 1956. Football League Third Division (North)

The grey cover of this programme identifies the club with the town and its then dominant maritime industry. It displays nice vertical and horizontal contrasts, allowing prominence to be given to the match details on the top right of the page. As comparison with other programmes previously displayed shows, the use of an 'industrial' photo combined with this L-shaped cover layout, was rare, perhaps even unique. The other image is a sketch map which forms page 13 of the programme. It shows places of interest in Grimsby and Cleethorpes. To 21st-century metropolitans, the idea that there were places of interest in 1950s Grimsby may sound unlikely, but look again. The Blundell Park ground features prominently at the epicentre of the map, with four entrances highlighted. Four Grimsby cinemas are also picked out: the Gaumont, the Plaza, the Globe and the Regal, along with four hotels and the Conservative Club, and no fewer than three stations. Then to the bottom right there is Cleethorpes, a holiday resort, with its Wonderland, Pier Pavilion, Winter Gardens, bathing pool, and its own station, hotels and cafes. Did any York fans head off to the open air bathing pool on the Cleethorpes Lido after the match on that first Saturday in March?

- -

As aspiration took hold, the players were revolting. When England played Young England at Highbury on the eve of the 1960 FA Cup Final, George Eastham wore the number eight shirt for the junior team. The four-page match programme described him accurately as, 'A clever ball player whose speciality is the low through pass for the centre-forward to run on to,' and said that he was on the verge of international honours. That was far from the whole story. Eastham was in a bitter dispute with his club, and even after his transfer to Arsenal in October 1960 he persisted with, and won, a court case against Newcastle United. The ruling in his favour in 1963 meant the end for the retain and transfer system that had been introduced in 1893/94, and also for the restriction on the maximum wage for players which was agreed by the Football League in 1901.

At a time when Premier League players live in mansions, it may be hard to believe that housing was what triggered Eastham's acrimonious stand-off with Newcastle. Married players were often rented a 'club house' by their employer: rather like the tied cottage system in agricultural regions, this was something of a mixed blessing. On the one hand it helped a young couple get a house when houses were in chronically short supply, but the house was tied to the job. When a player's career ended he could lose the house as well, as had happened to an uncle of Eastham who had finished at Accrington Stanley.

When Eastham was going to get married, he pressed his employers to give him a house; they prevaricated and the newlyweds finished up living with the bride's parents. Eventually, when new manager Charlie Mitten declined the three-bedroom terraced house offered to him (did he still have money from his stay in Colombia? See Chapter 2), Eastham was offered it. However, it was in a mess, and again the club were slow to address their player's legitimate concerns.

Similarly, they never got round to finding him the part-time job he was pressing them for.

Eastham was not some fringe player. In 1959/60 he was an ever-present in Newcastle's first team, and scored 18 goals as they finished eighth in the First Division. A written transfer request, followed by an angry confrontation between Eastham and Mitten, resulted in the player refusing to go on the club's summer tour to Spain and Yugoslavia, which followed that England versus Young England showpiece game in May 1960. Instead he went with the England Under-23s to East Germany, Poland and Israel. In June 1960 he refused to sign a new contract with Newcastle, and the club turned down his transfer request and refused to pay him wages. Crucially the Magpies held his registration, meaning that they could prevent him from playing for anybody else under the 'retain and transfer' system. A wealthy family friend came up with a job in London as a cork salesman, paying more than his £20 a week as a professional footballer in the First Division. On 13 October 1960, Eastham and his advisors issued a writ against the Football Association, the Football League and the directors and manager of Newcastle United for restraint of trade, arguing also that the retain and transfer system was not legally binding. As my diary of the time records, Thursday, 17 November 1960, 'Newcastle and Arsenal agreed terms for George Eastham,' then the next day 'Eastham signed for Arsenal'. The fee was £47,500, the top end of the market in those days.

Eastham's treatment was a catalyst for wider action. By the end of 1960 the Professional Footballers' Association, under the leadership of Fulham's Jimmy Hill, had voted for strike action over the maximum wage. In January, with the strike imminent, the Football League admitted defeat. In taking industrial action to improve their wages and conditions, the players were part of a wider tide of change in industrial relations.

My 1961 diary, which recorded the calling-off of the footballers' strike on 18 January, also showed ways in which I had developed and my life had changed. There was still a lot of football and school in there, but the spelling was definitely better. Somehow, rather than leaving school to find a job at 16 like many of my contemporaries, I had made it into the sixth form, preparing for an unlikely combination of A-Levels in Geography, Geology and Spanish. I was listening to Radio Luxembourg, which broadcast pop music on 208 metres medium wave (though the signal would blur or fade), and *Saturday Club*, the pop music show on the Light Programme, which would often be playing on the coach radio while we were travelling to United's away matches. We still did not have a record player, but I was listing the hit parade number ones in the 'Gramophone Records' page at the back of the diary, though the 'Book List' pages remained conspicuously vacant. On 1 April, the diary tells me, I was kissed by a girl. Like the country, I had never had it so good.

Programmes cited in Chapter 6 that are in the collection:
- 25 August 1955, Notts County 2 Barnsley 2, Football League Second Division
- 14 September 1955, Everton 4 Manchester United 2, Football League First Division
- 10 December 1955, Portsmouth 3 Manchester United 2, Football League First Division
- 7 January 1956, Manchester City 1 Blackpool 1 (abandoned), FA Cup third round
- 14 January 1956, Cardiff City 4 Manchester City 1, Football League First Division
- 28 January 1956, Bristol Rovers 1 Doncaster Rovers 1, FA Cup fourth round
- 13 February 1956, Crystal Palace v. Rotherham United, friendly (result unknown)

- 3 March 1956, Grimsby Town 2 York City 1, Football League Third Division (North)
- 24 March 1956, Crystal Palace 1 Leyton Orient 2, Football League Third Division (South)
- 7 April 1956, Reading 3 Queens Park Rangers 1, Football League Third Division (South)
- 25 August 1956, Hull City 2 Rochdale 0, Football League Third Division (North)
- 29 August 1956, Leicester City 2 Huddersfield Town 2, Football League Second Division
- 15 September 1956, Accrington Stanley 1 Chesterfield 1, Football League Third Division (North)
- 22 December 1956, Aston Villa v. Manchester City (match postponed), Football League First Division
- 25 December 1956, Sunderland 1 Aston Villa 0, Football League First Division
- 19 January 1957, Sheffield Wednesday 2 Manchester United 1, Football League First Division
- 23 February 1957, Stoke City 8 Lincoln City 0, Football League Second Division
- 23 February 1957, Notts County 2 Sheffield United 2, Football League Second Division
- 25 March 1957, Manchester United 0 Bolton Wanderers 2, Football League First Division
- 7 September 1957, Ipswich Town 2 Notts County 1, Football League Second Division
- 23 November 1957, Newcastle United 2 Manchester United 1, Football League First Division
- 30 November 1957, Queens Park Rangers 3 Watford 0, Football League Third Division (South)
- 26 December 1957, Luton Town 2 Manchester United 2, Football League First Division
- 1 March 1958, West Bromwich Albion 2 Manchester United 2, FA Cup sixth round

- 30 April 1958, Chester 5 Accrington Stanley 1, Football League Third Division (North)
- 1 November 1958, Coventry City 2 York City 0, Football League Fourth Division
- 1 November 1958, Leeds United 1 Manchester United 2, Football League First Division
- 15 December 1958, Manchester City 0 Manchester United 4, FA Youth Cup third round
- 17 September 1960, Aston Villa 3 Manchester United 1, Football League First Division
- 19 August 1961, Manchester City 3 Leicester City 1, Football League First Division
- 28 April 1962, Fulham 2 Manchester United 0, Football League First Division

Chapter 7

Bovril or Boutiques?

PHILIP LARKIN'S poem, *Annus Mirabilis*, captures the exuberance of 1963, the year when 'life was never better'. The much quoted opening verse reads:

> *Sexual intercourse began*
> *In nineteen sixty-three*
> *(which was rather late for me) –*
> *Between the end of the 'Chatterley' ban*
> *And the Beatles' first LP.*

Something else happened that year which could easily have merited inclusion in Larkin's poem. George Best made his debut for Manchester United in September. More than anybody before him, or after him until David Beckham over 30 years later, Best fused the worlds of football, popular music and fashion. For a heady few years, and in an ill-managed way by today's standards, he became a brand, defined by being young, good-looking, fashion-leading and talented to the point of audacious, as well as by his collection of beauty queens that he kept in his bedroom. After his goals helped beat Benfica 5-1 in a famous 1966 European Cup game, for which Euan

20 years later purchased the frail, badly folded programme, Best was 'El Beatle'. Before Best the idea of a British footballer running a boutique would have been inconceivable; indeed the word 'boutique' would have been foreign in every way, even to the lads in fashionable Teddy Boy gear a decade earlier.

Programme Spotlights 23: A star is born

14 September 1963, Manchester United 1 West Bromwich Albion 0, Football League First Division

George Best's senior debut against West Bromwich Albion, on 14 September 1963, was the last but one match I was able to go to before heading off to university. In those days there was scant national media coverage of football. In particular, you always felt that the Reithian BBC rather disapproved of 'soccer'. You relied on a half-hour Light Programme broadcast at 12.30pm on a Saturday for that afternoon's team news. Before going to catch the bus to Old Trafford, I had heard Matt Busby extolling the qualities of the 17-year-old he had chosen to play on the right wing that day. As the team changes were read out, I scored out the name of another young hopeful, Ian Moir, and entered 'Best' instead. The 'With the Reserves and Juniors' page carried a report of the reserves' 1-1 draw with West Brom the previous Saturday. It described 'a pinpoint pass from Stiles which enabled Best to take it in his stride and beat Millington from close quarters'. Millington at that time already had three of his 21 Welsh international caps. Future World Cup winner Stiles was also a team change that afternoon, coming into the first team in place of the injured Denis Law.

The cover page is typical of United home programmes over a long period, with its excellent action photo from a recent game. There is an unused token sheet in the centre pages of my programme: being away at university meant I could no longer collect the requisite number of tokens to get priority in ticket purchase for big matches.

Regular readers of the Manchester United programme might first have become aware of George Best during a 2-0 home defeat by Birmingham City on 14 October 1961. It carried a report of a 'B' team game two weeks earlier. United's fourth-stringers had beaten Bury 'B' 5-1. 'A well-taken goal by Best' had opened the scoring after 30 minutes. Then in the second half, 'Gorman took a neat pass from Best to increase the lead.' Another of the goals came from 'a penalty for hands as Best looked certain to score'. Best was just a few months older than 15, and not playing in the United youth team of that season. He was, however, in the United 'B' team beaten by a Blackpool 'B' inspired by future World Cup winner Alan Ball in January 1962. The account in the United programme for the game with Cardiff City (3 February 1962) relates how Best gave United the lead against the run of play, by 'just beating Grayson to the ball to head home a Dunphy centre'.

The next home programme (for a goalless FA Cup fifth round tie with Sheffield Wednesday), two weeks later, tells readers that 'straight from the restart Best hit a great goal' in a 2-1 'B' team defeat against Oldham 'A', who presumably were a side including players three years or more older than Best. He featured regularly in 'B' team reports in 1961/62, sometimes scoring, or laying on a goal for others, and in a game against Rochdale 'A' completely mis-kicking to miss an open goal (programme of 24 March 1962)! A report in the United v. Birmingham City programme on 1 September 1962, of a 5-2 defeat by Burnley 'B', evocatively captures the qualities that soon would make Best a superstar, 'Best showing clever control to beat 3 men and finally rounded the keeper to shoot into the empty net'. Those of us who saw him in his pomp can easily conjure the image in our minds. Best's goal had put United 'B' 2-1 ahead, but he was then injured and the reporter observed that that 'changed the whole complex of the game'.

On debut, at home to West Brom, Best faced the experienced Welsh international left-back Graham Williams. To the growing frustration of the crowd, he spent the game trying unsuccessfully to dribble past his opponent. Then, in front of the Stretford End, he managed to leave Williams trailing, got to the byline and pulled a cross back for David Sadler, who was also in the youth team that season, to score. All was forgiven, and the 1960s really began.

That same year, 1963, was also the year that changed my life. It was the year when I got a girlfriend, Irene, who would become my wife. It was also when, directed by my headmaster, who told my parents what he was going to do with me, I became a student, studying Geography, funded and with full fees paid by a state scholarship and an exhibition from Magdalene College, Cambridge. Together these amounted to the equivalent of over £6,500 a year in 2021 money. I had to open a bank account in which to lodge my grant cheque. As the first member of my extended family to go to university, the grant was crucial for my path to social mobility. At the same time, Irene became a student at a teacher training college in Derbyshire. For bright young women from our generation and background, staying in education after 18 to become a teacher meant going beyond what was possible, or even conceivable, for their mothers. Many men of our parents' generation took the view that there was no point in girls lingering in education.

The welfare state had propelled a small minority of us into a very different world, one that was intimidating but also exciting. During term time, I was living a life very different from that back home. There were occasional weekends in London with Irene. Being students made such liaisons possible, small steps towards what soon became the 'permissive society'. Living away from home for the first time required cookery skills. These included heating up tins of baked beans and sausages; conjuring Angel Delight for desert by whisking the contents of a packet (preferably butterscotch flavour) into milk; and discovering that combining baked beans with tinned spaghetti makes a less appetising dish than anticipated. Dinner was usually taken in college in the candle-lit hall, where many of my contemporaries in the all-male college had come from England's best known private schools. I was addressed as 'sir' by middle-aged college servants, a disconcerting experience for a teenager.

It was tough at first. After a couple of weeks I was invited to lunch with the Master of the College, Sir Henry Willink, who had been the Conservative Minister of Health in the wartime coalition government. There were a couple of other new undergraduates present also, and as we chatted all went well until I went to use the pepper. I had never seen a pepper mill before. I shook it upside down, but no pepper came out. So I unscrewed the cap that held the top in place. At that point, the pepper mill came to pieces: the screw cap, the top, the main barrel and the base. While I reassembled the parts, the conversation continued around the table, discretely oblivious to my acts of deconstruction and reconstruction. Despite such occasional embarrassments, I knew how privileged I was. I was exposed to an open, critical and rigorous academic culture that shaped my later career and indeed my life. However, not all my former school pals who left home for university that autumn were so fortunate: one committed suicide in his first term at a northern university; some others had dropped out by Christmas.

Cambridge was not a football town; though its clubs were called United and City, neither was in the Football League. Coming from Manchester, I was a football snob, disdainful of these lower orders: the accent that marked me a poor relation in the junior common room, in my own mind defined me as football supporter aristocracy. However, transport connections from Cambridge to First Division grounds other than those in London were poor. It was a six-hour train journey back to Manchester; going home for a weekend was not an option. So during term times I was going to few matches. I only went to one game in Cambridge during my three years there, Cambridge City against Cheltenham in the Southern League (see Programme Spotlights 24). Furthermore, now that I had grown up a bit, I was no longer actively soliciting programmes from other clubs, though the collection remained in shoe boxes in a cupboard in my parents' home.

Programme Spotlights 24: Home killed meat
Cambridge City 1 Cheltenham 2, 10 October 1964,
Southern League

This was the only football game in Cambridge that I attended. After a morning spent dutifully studying in the college library, I cycled out on my rickety bike to Cambridge City's ground on the Milton Road. I stood on the terracing behind one of the goals, but I have no real recollection of what happened on the pitch: I retrieved the score from my diary.

What I do remember is that the ground was nothing like so packed as was depicted on the cover of the programme. Though misleading in that respect, the cover is actually rather good. The drawing conveys a sense of the drama and intensity of a game, with a spectator's view of 16 of the 22 players in frame in front of the crammed terraces. I also like the blue colour, though Cambridge's colours that day were white shirts and black shorts. One advert in the programme that catches the eye is for Adkins' 'Famous Pies and Sausages', 'The best home killed meat in the area'. Did they have planning permission to use their house as an abattoir?

My own football career in Cambridge got off to a bad start. I was chosen to make my debut for Magdalene College Second XI as the left-back against St John's College. Left-back is often a difficult pick, and must have been so in this case. Why else would you choose somebody for that position who had never played there before, could not kick with his left foot and needed to wear glasses to see the ball? We lost 10-1, after I had opened the scoring – by putting through my own goal after about five minutes. A low cross from the left hit me on the shins on the six-yard line as I tried to cover. At least I did enough to persuade the selectors never to play me at left-back again.

In these years of the early 1960s, popular culture, often led by people from working-class backgrounds and from the north of England, began to transform Britain. With my own background and new status as a student at a time when only about four per cent of my age group were going to university, I could identify with this. However, football trailed this wave of change rather than being at the forefront. The fact that George Best was compared to the Beatles, and like them had hair long enough to astound people over 30, simply affirms that it was music, not football, which set the pace, with film and theatre not far behind.

Some clubs did try to connect with the zeitgeist. The image on the front cover of Brentford's programme for their Third Division game against Luton Town on 8 February 1964 was a picture of Howard Sheppard, Ken Messenger, Miles Hamilton, Malcolm Franks, Dave Rogers and Lionel Baron. They were not footballers, club directors, or supporters. They were a rock group, The Bluebeats. Any baffled Griffin Park regular could find the explanation in bold type on page three. 'Today we add something new to your Saturday afternoon entertainment… Live music – and we do mean live! – will be played by the Bluebeats, a group we think will be going places in the "pop!" music scene.' The exclamation mark and apostrophes around 'pop' make it feel like a middle-aged uncle trying to sound cool. It went on to explain that the impact of the group at a recent club party was such that they had been booked for all the remaining home games that season, while adding in another revealing phrase, 'Of course, it won't be easy to create a ballroom atmosphere in the open air.' So here was the precursor for all those iconic rock concerts played in huge stadia – 18 months before the Beatles played Shea Stadium, The Bluebeats were rocking Griffin Park. Their record, 'Mary Marry Me' on the Pye label, did not make the charts.

I presume that the programme was bought by Euan on the basis that it was special, since Brentford's 6-2 defeat was the highest number of goals that they had ever conceded in a home match. Like so many, this programme defines its times. It gives an insight into how new products were changing the nature of housework – a Spinwasher, a De Luxe tumbler dryer and an Ezy-Press ironer were advertised. Even potato crisps were mutating: Smiths advertised 'two exciting new flavours' – cheese and onion, and hamburger. It may not have been what Bob Dylan had in mind that same year when recording 'The Times They Are A'Changing', but if so basic a part of British life as potato crisps were being reinvented then something was certainly stirring. Even chip shops were seeking new ways to attract customers. The Albany Fish Restaurant, '3 minutes walk from the ground', took space in that Brentford programme to advertise that they were now 'giving winning stamps', with a chance to win £5,000, a considerable sum of money in those days. However, the way to winning £5,000 was more indirect than it sounded. Buy chips, get a winning stamp, then when your book of stamps was full, you could exchange it for a £1 Premium Bond, which might eventually win you £5,000 in the monthly prize draw, or might not. Seven years earlier, Vance Packard's groundbreaking book, *The Hidden Persuaders*, had revealed the tricks advertisers were using to lure customers into buying their clients' products.

While the winning stamps was not the most sophisticated ruse, it is worth remembering that one of Packard's eight 'needs' was roots, and that by advertising products and services in football programmes, companies are tapping into that sense of shared identity.

In 1963, Britain's last National Servicemen were discharged. Two years later in October 1965, Notts County's programme against Torquay United carried an advertisement recruiting to the 'New All Regular Army' offering 'plenty of sport, adventure, travel, trade training'. It sounded fun, and there was no mention of the possibility of being drafted to what was then Aden (now Yemen) to put down a guerrilla uprising against the colonial power, a conflict that lasted until the British pulled out in 1967.

The Gillingham v. Doncaster Rovers programme for 22 February 1964 shows continuity with a world that was disappearing – Billy Bragg for Better Bicycles, Established 1923; The Army and Navy Hotel (Adjoining Town Hall, Chatham); the British Empire Cancer Campaign. Alongside these were harbingers of the new – ten pin bowling, which was a recent import from the USA, and, at a time when houses were cold and draughty (just like my room in Magdalene which was a damp, converted boathouse), there was an advert for heated towel rails.

British cuisine was also changing, again both for me and for my generation. While the food served up in the college hall (where you were required to eat at least five nights a week) was firmly in the tradition of British stodge, on the other two nights Cambridge restaurants offered more exotic options than anything I had known in inner Manchester, where we never ate out anyway. By the 1964/65 season, Peterborough United's programme was carrying an advertisement for the Great Wall Chinese restaurant, offering English and Chinese meals with accommodation for over 100. There had been substantial immigration from the Indian sub-continent into Blackburn, and the Rovers programme was carrying an advertisement for 'Indian Restaurant' at 18a Town Hall Street, 'We serve all English and Indian dishes.' Similarly, Bradford City v. Wrexham on 16 April 1966 has an advertisement for the East Pacific Restaurant in Manningham Lane, 'Indian dishes our speciality,' and also for the Fung Ying, which offered English and Chinese food. In contrast, Old Betty Plant's of Hanley, Stoke-on-Trent continued to buy space in the Port Vale programme v. Darlington in February 1966, to promote Betty's Herbal Cough Tablets: a confection with the tang of an England that was disappearing.

- -

Programme Spotlights 25: A Posh crowd
Peterborough United 0 Swansea Town 0, 20 February 1965, FA Cup fifth round

This purple-covered programme was acquired by Euan because it was Peterborough's record attendance, 30,096. The Posh had gained a reputation as cup giant-killers, but this was the first time they had reached the fifth round. They had made it to the fourth round in in 1956/57 while still a non-league club, and in 1960/61 when they went out 2-1 after a replay at Villa Park. In 1961/62 they had beaten Newcastle United at St James' Park, then in 1964/65 they had eliminated Arsenal 2-1.

Three names stand out from those playing. Derek Dougan wore number nine for the home team, and was the archetypal, physical British centre-forward. He had represented Northern Ireland at the 1958 World Cup finals and played in the First Division with Portsmouth, Blackburn Rovers and Aston Villa, where injuries set him back and he dropped to Third Division Peterborough before playing at the top level again with Wolves. In the 1970s, he became chair of the Professional Footballers' Association. The FA Cup tie with Swansea was goalless because 'The Doog' missed an open goal.

Behind him at right-half was another hard man, Welsh international Vic Crowe, who had recently joined Peterborough after a long career with Aston Villa. With these two on the park, it is no surprise that the game with Swansea was reported to be a fiercely contested affair. In goal for Swansea was Ronnie Briggs, a big red-haired Irishman. I was there when, as a 17-year-old third-team goalkeeper, he had culpably conceded seven goals to Sheffield Wednesday in an FA Cup replay at Old Trafford in 1961, leaving the field in tears.

The ethnic restaurants advertised by Bradford City, Blackburn Rovers and Peterborough United had no equivalent, for example in the Leicester City or West Midlands clubs' programmes, though these places also had growing Asian and Caribbean populations at the time. Similarly, The Bluebeats playing at Griffin Park was the exception not the rule: sometimes top-20 hits might have been played over the public address systems, but the staple pre-match entertainment was still the marching band. Flirtation with show business was limited to the occasional charity match – I still have the programme from such a game that I went to on 20 March 1960, in which a Showbiz XI featuring Sean Connery, Des O'Connor and Dave King beat a Sportwriters XI 1-0 in a game refereed by Manchester United's Dennis Viollet, and with Bobby Charlton fulfilling the duties of a linesman.

Changing social habits were directly discussed in an article by Cyril Chapman from the *Birmingham Post* in the programme for the FA Cup semi-final between Preston North End and Swansea City at Villa Park on 14 March, 1964 (see Programme Spotlights 27). 'The five day week has had its repercussions,' he wrote. 'When a man worked on Saturday morning it was a fairly easy transition from workshop to terrace. Now he has the whole of Saturday at his command for leisure... Football in England is faced with a very serious

- -

Programme Spotlights 26: 007 plays by the rules
Showbiz XI 1 Sportswriters XI 0, 20 March 1960,
charity match

The Showbiz XI played regular charity matches, while for their opponents this was a 'one-off' game, so the result may not have been the surprise it looks. Wally Barnes, an ex-Arsenal and Welsh international, was Showbiz because he was doing commentaries on BBC. Although, as the team changes I wrote in show, he did not play, Billy Wright was a former England captain, mentioned in previous chapters, and eligible because he was married to one of the Beverley Sisters who were recording stars in the 1950s. Singer Glen Mason had played professionally for Falkirk. Chas McDevitt at number nine was one of the leaders of British Skiffle, and had a good football pedigree as a schoolboy. The writers included ex-England internationals Len Shackleton and George Hardwick and the England amateur international Bob Hardisty. The only goalscorer was Dave King, who had several top-ten records as a crooner, and was described in the programme as 'The only British artiste ever to have his own live TV series in America.' Ronnie Carroll was also 'a firm entertainment favourite as a singer', as well as having been an Irish youth international footballer. This was the world of British popular music in 1960 that the Beatles, the Rolling Stones, The Who, The Animals and many others would disrupt from 1963 onwards. Sean Connery had played for Scottish Junior club Bonnyrigg Rose and was, according to the programme, 'one of Britain's most brilliant young actors'. At that stage of his career, he was not yet James Bond, so did not have a licence to kill, and had to abide by the laws of the game as laid down by the Football Association.

- -

challenge in its future prosperity.' As one who regularly does the shopping on Saturday morning and the ironing on Saturday afternoon, I have to wonder where it all went wrong. Mr Chapman's grasp of the dynamics of social change stopped some way short of the idea that women might go to football matches or have other ideas about how men might use Saturdays.

Chapman argued that after the ending of players' maximum wage 'the limit in wages has been reached'. At that time top players were probably earning no more than four to five times the national average wage. The sums of money that players were to earn in the 21st century would have been unimaginable to anyone writing in 1964, when the game was perceived to be in decline. Chapman anticipated that smaller clubs would cease to exist, and 'near neighbours' would amalgamate, 'Grounds that are left will need to become more in the nature of social centres, where the whole family can go in an afternoon or evening, not necessarily to watch football. More showmanship will have to be displayed in the presentation of matches.'

The same programme carries a fascinating article by Charles Harrold of the *Daily Mail* which was way ahead of its time in anticipating the advent of the kind of digital analytics that now have become commonplace in the professional game. Harrold explained that he was recording the number of shots by each side in a game. Revealingly, he stated that the title-winning Wolverhampton Wanderers team of the late 1950s were regularly having 30 or more shots in a game, though 'few teams have come anywhere near [that figure] in recent seasons'.

Harrold referenced the work of Wing Commander Charles Reeps, who had developed a form of shorthand to 'record every single thing that happened in a football match'. The results were then tabulated, and Reeps, perhaps not surprisingly an accountant, analysed over 500 games in this way, unearthing 'the secret of how best to score goals'. And the answer? A 'good side' needs nearly nine shots on average to score a goal, and the greatest number of shots and goals came from 'direct moves of three passes or less'. So much for tippy-tappy possession football!

Programme Spotlights 27: Repercussions of the five-day working week
Preston North End 2 Swansea Town 1, 14 March 1964, FA Cup semi-final

Programmes for semi-finals and finals generally are more expensive than those for less high-profile encounters, but the programmes themselves tend to be dull because they follow a set and neutral formula. The front cover of this one (see picture section) is not exciting. The small image of the rather ornate cup itself is rather discordant with the minimalist style of the rest of the page. The stripes in blue and orange reflected the colours of the shirts worn; blue for Preston and orange for Swansea.

What does make the programme more interesting is the article inside by a local journalist, which captures the sense of uncertainty of the time and the industry's discomfort with changes that were taking place in workplaces, inside and outside the game. In particular the rise of a five-day working week opened up new competition for Saturday afternoon leisure.

The game was played in a torrential downpour, and video footage gives a vivid picture of what it was like for those of us standing on uncovered terracing on days like this. I remember the rain that day as it was a day when I was travelling home from Cambridge, feeing lucky that I had decided to go by train rather than hitchhiking as I often often did at the end of term to save money.

Alex Dawson (see Chapters 3 and 5) scored Preston's equaliser from a penalty, before a long-range shot by centre-half Tony Singleton beat Tony Dwyer in the Swansea goal and also confounded the Pathé cameraman.

Harrold's comments about Wing Commander Reeps exposed a deeper truth about the relation between British football and society in the 1960s. Rather like the dog that did not bark in the famous Sherlock Holmes story, what stands out from the programmes is not so much a picture of rapid cultural change within football, rather the programmes inadvertently portray an industry either silent about such change, or even ill at ease with it. Thus Harrold in writing about Reeps's analytics was discussing the exception not the norm, an eccentric, not a prophet. Across our numerous 1960s programmes, published at a time when computers were beginning to be used in business, universities and even some branches of the public sector, there is no hint that the new technology could transform analysis of the game, or even the routine management of clubs (e.g. salary payments, databases for ticket sales, or player records).

It wasn't just the five-day working week that was a threat to the existing order, but also TV. The Wolves v. Blackpool programme of 3 September 1960 included speculative comments about the possibility of floodlit games being televised on a Saturday evening, but it would take decades for this to become a reality. Manchester United experimented with telecasts at Old Trafford of occasional away matches. On 3 March 1967, along with 28,422 others, I went to Old Trafford on a Friday night to watch a live black-and-white telecast on large screens of United's game against Arsenal at Highbury. United produced a 'Souvenir Programme' for the game, to celebrate 'The First Football League Match in Division One to be Televised on Closed Circuit TV'. In a small box at the bottom of page three, there was a note saying that the first CCTV relay of a league match had been Cardiff City v. Coventry City on 6 October 1965. The front cover of United's next home programme for the game against Leicester City on 18 March carried a photo of the Arsenal game on the big screens at Old Trafford. Then again on 23 April 1969, there was a telecast of the away first leg of United's 2-0 defeat by AC Milan in their European Cup semi-final. I did not go to this showing, as I was living in Scotland by then, but we do have a copy of the programme produced by Milan for their home leg, thanks to Euan's investing in programmes from United's away European games.

More generally, TV was seen as a threat, rather than an opportunity, and football, still steeped in Bovril rather than boutiques, was an industry in decline, mirroring the situation of other traditional sectors of the British economy. Attendances had fallen from those halcyon, entertainment-starved years after the end of the war, and there was no coherent response to new competition from those running the clubs. Football remained pre-modern; the way of playing, the way of managing and administering, the stadia, the presentation, all remained largely unchanged.

Programmes remained staunchly traditional, both in content and design. The paper was of a better quality than in the 1940s or early 1950s, but no programme in our collection has a psychedelic cover. Leeds United changed their strip from gold and blue to all white, hoping that some of the stardust from Real Madrid would stick to them, but generally changes were cosmetic rather than dramatic – a restyling of collars or sleeves perhaps. Supermarkets appeared on the high streets, but the way you consumed football remained unchanged – you passed through a turnstile on a Saturday afternoon and stood in your usual spot on the terrace; the half-time scores were displayed on the manually operated scoreboard, then there was a crush to get out and get the bus home. In part, innovation was blocked by legislation. Henry Ditton of the *News of the World* wrote in the Manchester United programme 11 September 1963 of the possibility of legislation being changed to make it possible to play games on a Sunday, an idea sure to provoke the wrath of the Lord's Day Observance

Society, a Sabbatarian campaigning group which had been founded in 1831, and continued to be active.

Ideas about gender were equally entrenched. On 13 October 1962, just hours before an American spy plane identified Soviet missile installations in Cuba, plunging us all into real fear of nuclear war, I went to watch Manchester United lose 3-0 at home to Blackburn Rovers. The programme includes a short article on 'Women' by Jack Clough, a former FA Cup Final and international referee. He opined, 'While the introduction of a "Sophia Loren" might infuse a degree of glamour, I hardly think the presence of women would improve the standard of the game.' Football, he asserted, was a 'man's game' and 'hardly a pastime in which ladies should be plunged'. He continued, 'The Football Association frown on the playing of football by women and will not listen to the question of affiliating these female teams with our own organisation.' The accompanying cartoon depicted a quaking number nine in the dressing room, with a coach explaining, 'Just heard that his mother-in-law is playing centre-half for our opponents.'

The 1966 World Cup created a degree of modernisation at some venues. Thus, Manchester United replaced the affectionately named 'Cowshed' where I used to stand under cover near the halfway line with a new seated cantilevered stand including a standing paddock in front. Fans in that part of the ground no longer had to crane their necks around stanchions to glimpse the action, though the cover did not protect from the rain if you were standing at the front of the paddock. In general such innovation was rare, and faced with investing in infrastructure or buying players, boards of directors put hopes of winning matches ahead of spectator comfort and safety. Notwithstanding a sequence of serious overcrowding events at Glasgow Rangers' Ibrox stadium (two fans were killed in a crush in 1961, eight injured in 1967, then

26 in 1969, before the disaster at the end of 1971 New Year meeting with Celtic saw 66 dead), it would take the tragedy of Hillsborough in 1989 (see Chapter 11) to force real change. At the big clubs, being crushed when a goal was scored, or on leaving the ground, was commonplace, something that we simply accepted; it was what would now be called 'the matchday experience'.

Despite such discomforts, there were many great days and memorable experiences, with the programmes of those times having a place in my life somewhat akin to that which relics from the Holy Land had in Medieval Europe. There were trips from Cambridge down to London to watch United. The first of these was to White Hart Lane in November 1963 for the European Cup Winners' Cup tie with Tottenham Hotspur, which was one of those familiar occasions where the fog rolled in and the game had to be postponed. So a week later I was there again to see Spurs win 2-0. The programme for the first game had 12 pages, while that for the rescheduled meeting was a single-sheet, four-page affair. After the game, I travelled back to Manchester on an overnight bus for the Christmas vacation: a sleepless, uncomfortable journey, but a cheap way to get home.

There was another memorable trip to White Hart Lane on an October Saturday in 1965. It all started so well: hitchhiking from Cambridge, I got a lift after just a couple of minutes that dropped me within walking distance of the stadium. However, Spurs won 5-1, with all their five forwards scoring. Scottish internationals Dave Mackay and Alan Gilzean dominated, but the goal of the match came from Jimmy Greaves, who dribbled past the United defence and goalkeeper then slid the ball into the empty net, in the way that modern day players of similar stature such as Eden Hazard or Lionel Messi do. To make matters worse, my hitching back to Cambridge came to a halt at the Hertfordshire village of Puckeridge, where I waited an hour and a quarter after darkness had fallen before

– yes! – getting my first ride in a Jaguar all the way back to college. The other bright spot that day was that I won three shillings on the traditional sweepstake among my friends for the first goalscorer – Gilzean.

There were also games I recall fondly which I saw during the vacations back in the north. The weekend after my overnight London to Manchester coach journey was the last time I saw Stanley Matthews, when he was just a couple of months short of his 49th birthday, appearing on Stoke's right wing in a game when an imperious Denis Law scored four. A year later, on 5 December 1964, I went to watch Leeds United at Old Trafford. The programme for the game is unremarkable, but the match itself is etched on my memory, because it revealed a new level of calculated cynicism. On a damp and misty afternoon United kicked off and swung the ball out to Best on the left: he was unceremoniously kicked up in the air by right-back Paul Reaney, setting a pattern for the rest of the game. This was the first time that I had seen a big centre-half (Jack Charlton) standing just about on the toes of the opposing goalkeeper at corners. Furthermore, Leeds's players seemed to spend much of the game talking to the referee and advising him on how to run things.

Bobby Collins (a crucial experienced component of manager Don Revie's team) scored for Leeds after about 55 minutes and from then on their defence, resolute but making liberal use of trips and kicks, held out, with play suspended after 79 minutes due to fog, only for the referee to restart it again ten minutes later. Ralph Finn, in what is now a much coveted book published in 1965, *Champions Again: Manchester United 1957 and 1965,* said of Leeds at that time, 'They lost a lot of support outside Leeds. Their football was dull, uninspiring and often irritating... they played the game as though it were a war.' It was calculated; it was effective; it was a new way of playing the game, which others began to follow.

Programme Spotlights 28: A fraught homecoming
Blackburn Rovers 0 Manchester United 5, 3 April 1965, Football League First Division

I remember this game both for the action itself, and for the circumstances surrounding my attending it. Somehow the match was goalless at half-time, then United's five goals came in 30 minutes beginning in the 48th. Bobby Charlton smashed a hat-trick between goals from David Herd and John Connelly, while Best was rampant on the left wing. United went on to win the league on goal difference from Leeds.

One of my former school pals, Mike Hill, was also home from university in London for the vacation. He had a 1937 Austin Seven car, probably the most popular economy car in the UK in the 1930s. Even back in 1965 there were not many of them left. Mike drove me and two other former school-mates to Ewood Park, where we revelled in the sunshine and the match.

The climb out of Blackburn on the way home proved too much for the geriatric vehicle and we ground to a halt, exultation giving way to anxiety, while Mike fiddled under the bonnet for the best part of half an hour. I was particularly on edge as I had tickets for myself and Irene, my girlfriend, for Harold Pinter's new play, *The Homecoming*, at the Opera House in the centre of Manchester, which started at 7.30pm. Understandably, Irene had been somewhat sceptical about my assessment of the logistics of getting back in time. In the end, we made it to our seats in the theatre with minutes to spare. Somewhat similar situations have recurred during our long marriage.

The programme's front cover has a slightly 'retro' look, as befits the club's proud history. Their pre-World War I triumphs are memorialised in the box, while the player in the top left also looks to have come from a pre-1960s era, with short hair, buttoned shirt, long shorts, and boots and ball that look heavy. The depiction of the ground highlights the floodlights, but also gives a good impression of what most grounds looked like in those days; they were compact with a large open terrace behind one goal. That said, the grass was never as green as shown, and by April there were many bare patches through the middle.

Otherwise the programme is unremarkable in terms of style and content, though it did include an advert for an Indian restaurant, a small indicator of the ethnic and culinary changes taking place in the mid-1960s in this former cotton town.

- -

After graduating in 1966, I returned to Manchester to do a two-year, full-time post-graduate Diploma in Town and Country Planning at the university. In those days, local authorities were able to fund students, and while my undergraduate years had been funded by a state scholarship and by the college, now I had a bursary from Manchester Corporation Education Department equivalent to almost £3,500 in 2021, plus, of course, they paid all my tuition fees. So for the 1966/67 and 1967/68 seasons I was a regular at Old Trafford once more, a period that culminated in the European Cup Final at Wembley (see Programme Spotlights 29). Tucked inside our copy of the programme, I still have the stub from my ticket which had cost £2: North Terrace, Row 18, Seat 301. In those days there was no penalty shoot-out, rather a replay would be staged at Highbury two nights later. As the match went into extra time, I was facing the agonising choice of returning for the replay or taking some of my examinations to graduate. Nowadays few students would bat an eyelid at failing to present themselves for an examination and would simply go for the resit a few months later. But for my generation not turning up for an exam was almost unthinkable and unforgivable. Happily, extra time proved decisive.

It was an emotional night, and the programme is a treasured memento of the occasion. Inevitably, the spectre of the Munich crash hung over the game, the more so because of the coincidence that it had taken place ten years previously, and so 1968 seemed a special anniversary. Also there was a sense that this was perhaps Matt Busby's last chance to win the European Cup, which had become his Holy Grail. He would pass his 60th birthday that same month, at a time when life expectancy for men in England was 69, and he had suffered life-threatening injuries in the crash.

For those of us who watched United regularly, there was also a sense that the team was past its best. The two seasons of 1965/66 and 1966/67 had seen Law and Charlton at their magnificent peak and they had been joined by the astounding talent that was George Best. Law was my personal favourite – so fast with his change of pace and ability to spot a chance, and a phenomenal header of the ball for a man who was not particularly tall. However, in 1968 Law was plagued by a knee injury that saw him miss the European Cup semi-final and final. In 1966/67 he had scored 23 goals in 36 league appearances; in 1967/68 it was seven in 23 appearances.

Also Charlton's midfield partner was Paddy Crerand, a player who was more important to the attacking fluency of the team than was often realised. He was a great passer of the ball, but lacked high pace. As teams switched to playing 4-3-3 instead of the 4-2-4 United had favoured, Charlton and Crerand, who was approaching his 30s, were being outnumbered and closed down. Only Brian Kidd had really come through from the youth team to force himself into the first 11. There had been no stand-out signing like Law had been. For one balmy night at Wembley in late May 1968, none of this really mattered. United had won the European Cup and I had been there to see them do it. The back page of the match programme that warm evening was an advertisement for 'Bovril – hot favourite for the cup'.

Programme Spotlights 29: North Terrace, Row 18, Seat 301

Manchester United 4 Benfica 1 (after extra time), 29 May 1968, European Cup Final

A historic occasion: the first time an English team won the European Cup, though the outstanding Glasgow Celtic team, locally born and bred, had won it for Scotland the previous year. Charlton opened the scoring with a rare header, only for Jaime Graça to equalise with minutes remaining, though there was still enough time for the great Eusebio to be thwarted by keeper Stepney when he seemed sure to win it. Best's goal in extra time, picking up a flick-on from a Stepney clearance, dribbling past José Henrique in goal before passing into the net, was the turning point. Goals from youngster Brian Kidd and a second for Bobby Charlton, all in the first half of the additional period, made it a heady night. However the real star of the show was John Aston on the left wing and throughout the match he outpaced Adolfo, his similarly inexperienced marker, and was a constant threat. This was Aston's breakthrough game, but his career was ended a few months later by a badly broken leg.

Tucked inside the programme I still have my ticket stub – North Terrace, Row 18, Seat 301, which cost me £2. Programmes for big finals or internationals lack the sense of local place and passionate identity that make club programmes interesting. The text is usually bland and even-handed, and the advertisements are from national or international companies, so there are few quirks. This one is no exception, except the only text in Portuguese was the translation of the welcome from the president of UEFA, which was also translated into French. The bold colours and the dynamic shape of the pendants and central placing of the word 'Final' do impart a sense that this is something special.

Programmes cited in Chapter 7 that are in the collection:
- 3 September 1960, Wolverhampton Wanderers 1 Blackpool 0, Football League First Division
- 14 October 1961, Manchester United 0 Birmingham City 2, Football League First Division
- 3 February 1962, Manchester United 3 Cardiff City 0, Football League First Division
- 17 February 1962, Manchester United 0 Sheffield Wednesday 0, FA Cup fifth round
- 24 March 1962, Manchester United 1 Sheffield Wednesday 1, Football League First Division
- 1 September 1962, Manchester United 2 Birmingham City 0, Football League First Division
- 13 October 1962, Manchester United 0 Blackburn Rovers 3, Football League First Division
- 14 September 1963, Manchester United 1 West Bromwich Albion 0, Football League First Division
- 27 November 1963, Tottenham Hotspur v. Manchester United (postponed), European Cup Winners' Cup second round first leg
- 3 December 1963, Tottenham Hotspur 2 Manchester United 0, European Cup Winners' Cup second round first leg
- 7 December 1963, Manchester United 5 Stoke City 2, Football League First Division
- 8 February 1964, Brentford 2 Luton Town 6, Football League Third Division
- 22 February 1964, Gillingham 1 Doncaster Rovers 1, Football League Fourth Division
- 14 March 1964, Preston North End 2 Swansea Town 1, FA Cup semi-final
- 10 October 1964, Cambridge City 1 Cheltenham 2, Southern League
- 5 December 1964, Manchester United 0 Leeds United 1, Football League First Division

- 20 February 1965, Peterborough United 0 Swansea Town 0, FA Cup fifth round
- 3 April 1965, Blackburn Rovers 0 Manchester United 5, Football League First Division
- 16 October 1965, Tottenham Hotspur 5 Manchester United 1, Football League First Division
- 30 October 1965, Notts County 1 Torquay United 1, Football League Fourth Division
- 26 February 1966, Port Vale 3 Darlington 1, Football League Fourth Division
- 9 March 1966, Benfica 1 Manchester United 5, European Cup quarter-final
- 16 April 1966, Bradford City 8 Wrexham 2, Football League Fourth Division
- 3 March 1967, Arsenal 1 Manchester United 1, Football League First Division (Manchester United programme for closed-circuit TV live showing at Old Trafford)
- 18 March 1967, Manchester United 5 Leicester City 2, Football League First Division
- 29 May 1968, Benfica 1 Manchester United 4 (after extra time), European Cup Final
- 23 April 1969, AC Milan 2 Manchester United 0, European Cup semi-final first leg

Chapter 8

World Cup Winners

THROUGH THE 1950s, there was a shared delusion about Britain's economy, global standing and the status of its football. A gap existed between domestic perception and international reality. We may indeed have 'never had it so good', but annual growth rates in West Germany between 1950 and 1958 ran at almost eight per cent per annum, while Britain's stop-go economic trajectory saw growth never reaching six per cent in any year and in bad years scraping along at less than one per cent. Similarly, at school we uncritically celebrated Empire Day even as Britain's imperial role was well into its sunset.

So too with the football: Britain had given the game to the world, but in 1950 England's finest had been eliminated from the World Cup after losing 1-0 to the part-timers of the USA. The nation had watched on their first TV sets as West Germany upset the odds by beating Hungary in the 1954 final, England having gone out in the quarter-finals, losing 4-2 to Uruguay. Then in 1958 we had been mesmerised by the brilliance of the Brazilians and the emergence of teenager Pelé, after England had been dispatched 1-0 by the Soviet Union in a group stage play-off. There was less exposure to the 1962 finals in Chile: TV highlights were not shown until the day after the game, because of the five-hour time difference and reliance on film that had to be transported before being screened. Winners Brazil comfortably eliminated England 3-1 in the quarter-finals. Scotland had not deigned to send a team to the 1950 World Cup finals, despite qualifying as runners-up to England, and *because* they were runners-up to England; then four years later their squad for the finals in Switzerland amounted to just 13 players.

During my lifetime, the only time that any British nation could plausibly claim any sort of global superiority on the football field came in 1966. Alf Ramsey, on becoming England manager in 1963, had declared that his team would win the 1966 World Cup, but few believed him, certainly among my generation. So in the winter of 1965, when Irene and I planned our wedding date for soon after our graduations, we were not consulting the calendar for the World Cup that England would host that coming summer. Irene's mum had spoken to the local rent collector and managed to get us an unfurnished house to rent, just round the corner from where she lived. Our address, 1039–1041 Rochdale Road, might sound palatial, but 1039 was a two-up-two-down terrace on the main road, and 1041 was the one-room cellar with an earth floor, exactly the sort of cellar dwelling that Engels described in his 1845 classic *The Condition of the Working Class in England*. The property had been built in 1826, had an outside toilet in the back yard, no bathroom or hall, and was damp (water would gather in the cellar). The rent was 25 shillings a week, which was roughly equivalent to £25 in 2021.

So, for me, the build-up to England's Russian linesman-assisted triumph on 30 July 1966 was overshadowed by earning some money, acquiring second-hand furniture and carpets, and securing appointments for us with the Family Planning Association clinic on the other side of town, so Irene could be put on 'the pill', which had only become available on the NHS four years previously. GPs were still reluctant to prescribe it to younger women, especially those who were unmarried.

On 29 June 1966, I was able to watch the TV highlights of England's 6-1 warm-up win in Norway, after starting work that Wednesday morning driving a van selling Wall's ice cream and ice lollies around the streets of north Manchester. Sunday, 3 July saw England win 2-0 in Denmark, while I took £16, ten shillings and seven (old) pence from my ice cream round. This was almost double my takings the following Tuesday when England won again, 2-0 this time in Poland. My career as an ice cream salesman was the gig economy before the term was invented. You were self-employed, paid to hire the van and bought your ice cream wholesale at the depot then kept your takings. There were no environmental health checks on my sales methods, which would have ruled out my innovation of cutting a 'family block' of Neapolitan or raspberry ripple, which retailed at two shillings, into five slices which I sold as cornets or wafers for sixpence each, giving me a premium of sixpence on each block sold this way.

England's first World Cup group game was an arid goalless draw against Uruguay on Monday, 11 July, a day when despite my best endeavours the ice cream sales amounted to only £6, 16 shillings and nine pence; Mondays were usually slow days for trade. I did not see their next match, 2-0 over Mexico, the following Saturday – I had taken the day off to go to the leaving party at Irene's teacher training college in rural Derbyshire, precariously exiting via a bedroom window early the next morning. Wednesday, 20 July was England 2 France 0 and progress to the quarter-final; ice cream sales were only £8, 13 shillings. Though England were through, expectations remained muted. Apart from Bobby Charlton's spectacular drive against Mexico, their performances had been workmanlike rather than memorable. Ramsay's prediction still looked fanciful.

The meeting with Argentina on Saturday, 23 July changed the mood. It was won by a glancing header from Geoff Hurst, but was most memorable for the refusal of the hard-tackling Argentine defensive midfielder and captain Antonio Rattín to leave the field after being sent off by the German referee. The incident created an eight-minute stoppage in play. At the end, Ramsay called the Argentines 'animals' and stopped England players swapping shirts with their opponents. The path to the Falklands War in 1982 and Maradona's 'Hand of God' at the 1986 World Cup had been laid.

Argentinians had long bridled at smug English colonialism. The dismissal of their skipper after 35 minutes was proof that a conspiracy existed, not just against them but also against Uruguay, and so – why stop there? – the whole of South America, with West Germany England's co-conspirator and beneficiary in another quarter-final tie. Rattín explained it all many years later, when he was in his 70s, his bitterness unabated. The referees were fixed: an English one for Germany v. Uruguay, and a German for Argentina's tie with the host country. While he does not mention that he had been booked for an early foul, Rattín has a case in arguing that his sending-off was unjust. Film of the match shows he was far from the ball when the incident began. Rattín says that, as captain, he was merely asking for an interpreter so he could understand the decisions the referee was making in favour of England. Herr Kreitlein, the referee, said he sent off Rattín for 'violence of the tongue', though as Kreitlein spoke no Spanish and Rattín no German there must have been a doubt about just what was said to whom. In later life Rattín became a local councillor for the Partido Unidad Federalista, a right-wing party with an authoritarian line on law and order. On the July afternoon while all this was happening, I was taking part in a Labour Party Young Socialists speaking contest, so missed seeing events unreel live on TV.

Now that England were in the semi-final, like the rest of the nation, I had to take it seriously. I was determined not to miss the live screening of the game with Portugal the following Tuesday – after all, England getting to a World Cup Final was something I might never see again in my lifetime. The complication was that Tuesday happened to be our wedding day. Happily, my new wife was understanding, and so, along with others in the TV lounge of a bed and breakfast in Shrewsbury, on a small black and white TV, I watched Bobby Charlton score the goals in a 2-1 win. So to the final, still on honeymoon and again witnessed live in the TV lounge of a bed and breakfast, but now at Bangor on the North Wales coast: extra time, the 'Russian' linesman (who we now know was actually from Azerbaijan), and 'They think it's all over… it is now!' Irene spraining her ankle earlier in the day had not deprived me of the chance to watch the drama, though I had been considerate enough to go with her to a local hospital where the ankle was strapped up. In the circumstances, what more could have been expected of me?

The only programme we have from that epic month is that for the final (see Programme Spotlights 30). However, the careers of those men who wore the red shirts at Wembley on 30 July 1966 had begun in the 1950s, and can be traced in our programmes of that period.

Goalkeeper Gordon Banks had started his professional career at Chesterfield, where he made his first-team debut as a 20-year-old in November 1958. The following summer he moved to First Division Leicester City for a fee of £7,000. At first he was understudy to Dave Maclaren, who had been signed from Dundee in 1957. However, with Leicester regularly conceding three or more goals a game, and lingering in the relegation zone, it was not long before Banks was the first choice. Maclaren moved to Plymouth Argyle at the end of the season, perhaps recognising that he would never displace Banks.

- -

Programme Spotlights 30: Suck a Mintoe and think of England

30 July 1966, England 4 West Germany 2 (after extra time), World Cup Final

Ours is NOT the original match programme. It is most likely one of the reprints issued in 1970. The original programme front background is deep blue; ours is lilac. 'England v. West Germany' is black, the original was bluish, and on the back page the stripe on the cigarette packet advert for Cadets cigarettes is tangerine rather than the scarlet red of the original.

Much of the text inside the programme was in four languages, English, French, German and Spanish. There were line-ups and results from all the previous games in the finals, except for the third-place play-off.

The centre pages had individual photos of all the players in both squads, but left each 'Selected Team' to be hand written in. As usual, there were plenty of pages given over to advertising, particularly for beer and cigarettes, as well as for *The Black and White Minstrel Show*, complete with sketches of blacked-up singers. Tudor advertised their 'BIG new taste… delicious Cheese 'n' Onion crisps'. Overwhelmingly the adverts were for British products, including archetypically Nuttall's Mintoes. A couple are worth noting. The most exotic was perhaps for Carl Zeiss Jena, whose scientific instruments and cameras were one of very few products from the then eastern bloc that exported significantly to the west. Also the Leycroft Motor Company from St Albans invited readers, using Spanish and German, to 'Pay for your visit to England' by buying any make of new British or Continental automobile at factory or tax-free prices.

- -

Our earliest programme to mention Banks was on his sixth league appearance on 7 November 1959, in Leicester's 16th game of their First Division campaign, at home to Sheffield

Wednesday. The league table in the programme shows that Leicester were third from bottom with 11 points from 15 games. The future World Cup winner kept a clean sheet as City triumphed 2-0. His opposite number in the Wednesday goal that afternoon was Ron Springett who was the England reserve keeper at that time.

The following spring, Wolves were the visitors to Leicester's Filbert Street ground for an FA Cup sixth round tie on 19 March 1960.

The programme noted that this was only the second time that a quarter-final had been played in Leicester. Banks was now an ever-present, and had clocked up 22 first-team appearances. According to the match programme, since the end of the previous November Leicester had only once conceded three in a game, and had risen in the table to the point where manager Matt Gillies was able to write in his column, 'We can claim to be in a reasonably comfortable position.' Banks seems to have made a difference. However, their improved form was not enough to see them progress in the cup. Second-placed Wolves won 2-1 with the benefit of an own goal by right-back Len 'Chopper' Chalmers, who headed over Banks as the goalkeeper came out to collect a harmless flick from a Wolves forward. Leicester's centre-forward of the day, Ken Keyworth, described Chalmers as 'a tough-tackling full-back' – you get the picture. Wolves went on to win the cup, beating Blackburn Rovers 3-0 at Wembley, a game in which they again benefitted from an own goal.

Right-back George Cohen had joined Fulham from school in 1956 and was in the team for their Second Division away fixture at Brighton on 27 December 1958, which Brighton won 3-0 in front of a then record home attendance of 36,747. The Brighton programme did not provide comprehensive pen pictures of their opponents. Fulham's stars – Johnny Haynes, Jimmy Hill and Graham Leggatt – along with ex-Brighton players Jimmy Langley and Mike Johnson, were discussed in the Club Notes section, but there was no mention of the future World Cup winner. However, by 1960, Cohen's importance to the Fulham side was recognised. The programme for their home match against Manchester United on 26 March begins with an exuberant account of their game the previous week in which Fulham had held the all-conquering Tottenham Hotspur to a 1-1 draw at White Hart Lane. 'George Cohen tamed Welsh international winger Jones': this was no mean feat as Cliff Jones was an outstanding attacker, pacy and great in the air, and at the peak of his game in that season. The 'Cottage Crumbs' page also gave Cohen congratulations for his performance in the England Under-23s' recent 5-2 win over their Dutch counterparts. Then the programme for the 1962 FA Cup semi-final, where Fulham held the outstanding Burnley team to a 1-1 draw at Villa Park, records Cohen's 'distinguished schoolboy record', and characterised him as 'a powerful tackler, being difficult to pass' and noted that he was 'a reliable player' who had made many appearances for England Under-23s.

England's left-back was Ray Wilson, undoubtedly now and forever the only holder of a World Cup winner's medal to set up business as an undertaker in Huddersfield after retirement. Huddersfield Town was his first club, though he did not sign as a professional until after completing his National Service. He made his debut at Old Trafford on 22 October 1955, though as a debutant he was not included in the 'Welcome to Huddersfield Town' page of player profiles.

Wilson soon settled in to the Huddersfield first team under legendary manager Bill Shankly. By the time they visited Derby County on 2 April 1960, he was the vice-captain and making his 78th consecutive appearance in the Second Division. According to the 'Our Visitors' review in that match programme, Wilson was 'on the fringe of international honours, having turned out for the F.A. and the Football League in recent times'. Though Derby triumphed 3-2 that day, the observation was prescient, as Ray Wilson won his first cap later that month, against Scotland at Hampden Park.

Programme Spotlights 31: From 5-0 in the reserves to a World Cup winner
22 October 1955, Manchester United 3 Huddersfield Town 0, Football League First Division

This match marked Ray Wilson's debut, at left-back against Manchester United. The programme contains a report on the previous week's meeting of the two clubs' reserve sides. Wilson had played at left-half in a side that went down 5-0: Huddersfield had been 'unable to hold our forwards and Bobby Charlton scored a grand hat-trick'. Eddie Colman, Liam Whelan and Albert Scanlon were among the other Busby Babes who had lined up alongside Charlton, so the future England left-back could scarcely be blamed for the drubbing. His return to Old Trafford a week later again saw him on the losing side against that season's league champions. I had written the team changes (and half-time scores) in one of the wonders of the age – red biro. Note the misspelling of 'Viollett'. The other team change saw Jack Crompton (see Chapter 2) play in goal.

I used to see Nobby Stiles on the bus. He was a couple of years older than me, and lived at 263 Rochdale Road, which the buses from Moston and Harpurhey passed on their way into the city centre. His autobiography, *After the Ball*, describes many places very familiar to me, including Newton Heath Loco (see Chapter 3) and the Essoldo cinema, whose reputation as a 'fleapit' never deterred me from patronising it. Stiles's book recounts his schooldays at St Patrick's, and their matches on the red blaize surface at Monsal Rec'. Stiles won his first England cap in 1965, but was a controversial selection right through to the World Cup Final. He was no stylist and could look clumsy but played with 100 per cent endeavour, and his main strength was in breaking up the play and man-marking opponents in an age when fierce tackling was still an integral part of the game. His celebratory jig as England paraded the trophy was the 1966 equivalent of 'going viral'.

On 18 September 1957, Manchester United hosted a Blackpool team that included Jimmy Armfield, Stanley Matthews and Ernie Taylor; the latter would join United months later as an emergency signing after the Munich disaster (see Chapter 5). Tom Jackson, who would be a victim in the plane crash, wrote his usual 'United Topics' page in the programme. This week he made reference to a recent schoolboy international, 'One of the latest youngsters to start on the first rungs at Old Trafford is Norbert Stiles.' Jackson noted that the lad had captained Manchester Boys the previous season and was five times an England schoolboy international, where he featured at inside-forward and at wing-half. Now he was 'combining his soccer apprenticeship with duties as an office boy with the club'. His first game in United's colours had been a couple of weeks previously, with the Juniors, in effect the fifth team. They had won 25-0! A dozen years later, journalist Brian Glanville, writing in the England v. Scotland programme, recalled seeing Stiles in a schoolboy international against Wales at Wembley, 'He was unquestionably the best player on the field, encouraged rather than daunted by the stirring cacophony of 90,000 cheering boys.'

On 19 October 1957, Stiles got a mention in the United programme (v. Portsmouth) again, scoring a hat-trick from inside right (his older brother Charlie was the right-winger) as the Juniors beat Brunswick United 7-1. By the 1959/60 season, Nobby was a key member of the United youth team and the one-sheet/four-page programmes of their FA Youth Cup games said of him, 'Made rapid progress through the junior sides and now commands a regular place in Central League side,' meaning the reserves. It also noted that he had won England youth honours. He had played in that 4-0 FA Youth Cup third round game against Manchester City in which Oakes and Wagstaffe were among his opponents (see Chapter 6). He made his first-team debut at Bolton on 1 October 1960; I had written him in as a 'team change' for right-half Maurice Setters in the programme. The first away programme to feature him in the pen portraits of visiting players was Arsenal's on 29 October 1960, which noted, 'This youngster made an immediate impact when he was first brought into the team at the beginning of the month.' It noted that he had retained his place for the friendly against the all-conquering Real Madrid side, 'a match in which he did as well as any', and went on to comment on 'his abounding energy'. The United programme the previous week (v. Newcastle United, 22 October 1960) recorded that Stiles had excelled himself in the 3-2 defeat by the European champions, who were on a £60 a man win bonus, 'not exactly chicken feed' as journalist David Meek wrote in that same edition. As his career developed, one feature of Stiles often remarked upon was that he wore contact lenses, a sufficiently rare occurrence in those days to merit comment.

Centre-half Jack Charlton was perhaps the least glamorous member of the World Cup-winning 11. The Manchester City programme for their home game against Leeds United on 29 March 1958 listed him under his actual name as John Charlton, and simply said of him, 'Born at Ashington, Co. Durham – therefore it is understandable that he comes from a famous soccer family, with uncles Jack, George, Jim and Stan Milburn. Began his league career in 1953 when 17.' Jackie Milburn was the legendary centre-forward for Newcastle United and an England international (see Chapter 4). In fairness, the City programmes in those days tended to be similarly brief when describing their opponents, usually noting little more than their position, birthplace, former club, and any transfer fees. The Manchester United programme for their home game with Leeds early that season had added that John Charlton was 'Our Bobby's elder brother and a six footer who took over at centre-half when John Charles moved into the Leeds attack', but again despite the mention of his debut at 17 and previous experience in north-east junior football, there was no reference to his particular prowess or promise; in contrast, outside-left Jack Overfield was hailed as Leeds' 'best left-winger since the war'. The visit to Old Trafford did not end happily for brother John; United won 5-0 with centre-forward Tommy Taylor, the man Charlton was marking, scoring twice.

Jack Charlton's unglamorous qualities were what endeared him to England's manager. A no-nonsense, pragmatic professional, it made sense to play him at the heart of the defence when his partner there was Bobby Moore, a more talented and stylish player, whose confidence and ambition could leave openings for opponents. Moore first appears in my programme collection as the number five in the England youth team who played West Germany at Bolton's Burnden Park on 12 March 1958. The match programme described him as 'Splendidly built for a centre-half. Strong in the air and a keen tackler. Has played at home and abroad for the youth team this season.'

Although the opponents were 'Germany', they should have been described more accurately as West Germany. However, this youth international was no prequel to the World Cup Final eight years later. Although all those representing their countries that Wednesday night in Bolton in 1958 would have been in the 25/26 age range, and so close to their peak, by the time England hosted the finals of the World Cup, of the 22 listed on the team sheet only Moore would make it to Wembley '66. On the German side, Günther Herrmann did win nine caps between 1960 and 1967, and was a member of West Germany's 1962 World Cup squad while playing for Karlsruher SC, and Friedel Rausch managed to play 195 times for Schalke 04 without becoming a full international. A professional career at the highest level is elusive, even for the most talented youngsters. The stepping stones from youth international to full international are slippery.

Moore made his debut for West Ham six months after that night, on 8 September 1958, in a home game against Manchester United. A couple of weeks later he was listed in the West Ham team in the match programme for the return game at Old Trafford on 17 September, though he was replaced by Bill Landsdown who had been a regular the previous season. However, Moore had done enough to get a pen portrait in the 'Welcome to West Ham United' page, even if it did conclude with the curt statement, 'No League appearances up to May 1958.' His record 17 England youth appearances were commented upon, along with his captaincy of that team in 1958, when they were runners-up to Italy in the European Youth Tournament. However, for me personally, that game against West Ham was memorable not for the mention of the future World Cup captain in the programme, but because it was the first time I had gone to a match wearing glasses, and so was able to stand at the Stretford End and clearly see the play at the Scoreboard End.

Alan Ball could scarcely have dreamed of being a World Cup winner when he was released as a teenager by first Wolverhampton Wanderers and then Bolton Wanderers. He went to Blackpool, and on 27 January 1962 played for their 'B' team away at Manchester United. The following week's Manchester United home programme for their game against Cardiff City noted the young Ball's impact on the game. As Blackpool dominated the early stages, 'A good header from Ball was only just wide and the same player started a good move which gave Thompson an easy chance, but he shot hurriedly past the post. Jones then made a flying save to turn away another good effort by Ball.' In the second half, Ball was again name-checked for setting up a goal in a 3-2 win for the young Seasiders.

Ball's breakthrough came when he made his debut as a 17-year-old at the start of the 1962/63 season. He had become a first team regular at inside-right by the time Blackpool, lying 17th in the First Division table with nine games to play, visited Old Trafford in March 1965. The résumé of the Blackpool team in the programme that day gives no indication of the greatness that Ball would soon achieve. It simply records that he was born in nearby Farnworth, and had signed for the Tangerines on leaving school in September 1961, becoming a full-time pro on his 17th birthday. He had England Under-23 honours and 'played for the Football League at Hampden Park last Wednesday'. On the field that day Ball was upstaged by another inside-forward, Denis Law who scored both goals in a 2-0 win for United.

Bobby Charlton was at the very heart of England's World Cup campaign, a graceful yet commanding figure in central midfield, whose two goals in the semi-final against Portugal had taken England into the final. Of course, like brother Jack, he shared the illustrious Milburn family background. However, unlike his sibling, Bobby had enjoyed a stellar schoolboy career. As he says in his autobiography, *My Manchester United Years*, 'By the time I was picked for England Schoolboys there was no doubt I would get the chance to join my uncles and Jackie Milburn in the professional ranks.' Eighteen clubs made offers of a career to the 15-year-old.

The earliest programme in my collection to feature him was the United v. Wolverhampton Wanderers game on 6 March 1954. He is listed as the inside-left and goalscorer for United Colts in a 3-2 win over Duckinfield Town at the Ashton United ground, in a game played on 13 February. Under floodlights at United's training ground, The Cliff, four days later he had again been part of a 3-2 Colts win over Hulme Lads Club, then he scored in a 5-0 win over Hulme Celtic, in a game played on the pitches at Heaton Mersey, where I would myself appear in 1967, putting in an ineffective performance on the left wing for Manchester University's Department of Town Planning. Last but not least, he had scored four of the Colts' ten in the return game against Duckinfield a fortnight after the first encounter.

Programme Spotlights 32: Opportunity knocks
6 October 1956, Manchester United 4 Charlton Athletic 2, Football League First Division

This was the game in which Bobby Charlton made his first-team debut, and announced himself with two first-half goals. The front cover features photos of the recent 10-0 rout of Anderlecht in the European Cup (see Chapter 4). From top-left and in anti-clockwise order they show Tommy Taylor about to net goal number six, the despondent defenders just after Dennis Viollet had taken the tally to eight, then John Berry's effort that made it nine.

Charlton was listed at number nine in the line-up across the centre pages. However, Charlton was also mentioned on page 11 in the report on the reserves' 1-1 draw with Manchester City on 22 September. He was part of 'a good move that looked dangerous' before 'Scanlon's high centre fell behind the line'. More pertinently, the report records that Charlton was injured in the 60th minute, leaving his team to play out the rest of the game with ten men. While still in some pain, he eagerly assured manager Matt Busby that he was fully fit when offered the chance of stepping into the number nine shirt two weeks later. Charlton's chance came because Tommy Taylor was playing for England against Northern Ireland in Belfast. United were also without captain Roger Byrne and also Duncan Edwards for the same reason, while Jackie Blanchflower was centre-half for the Irish side. Such absences were the norm when home internationals were played on a Saturday.

The following season he was the leading scorer for the 'B' team (i.e. fourth team) with 36 goals by the time the programme was printed for the United v. West Bromwich Albion game staged on 16 April 1955. He got a game in the reserves that season, and was part of the United youth team who went on tour to Germany and Switzerland at the end of it. The youths won ten out of their 11 tour games and Charlton hit a hat-trick in the final game, reported Alf Clarke in the United v. Aston Villa programme the following February. He started 1955/56 with a hat-trick for the 'A' team in their 9-2 victory over Bury 'A' in the opening game, a feat reported in the programme for the First Division match against West Bromwich Albion on 27 August 1955. The rest of that season was spent in the reserves, who won the Central League at a canter, with the future World Cup star contributing 37 of their 112 goals in his 37 appearances, according to the programme for the first team's final game of the season at home to Portsmouth.

He was injured in a reserve game against Manchester City on 22 September 1956, having sustained his regular scoring feats in the new season. He missed the Champions v. The Rest reserve match the following week, and then the Army fixture at Everton on the next Wednesday. Still not fully fit, but smart enough not to reveal it to his manager, he played at centre-forward on his first team debut against Charlton Athletic two weeks later on 6 October 1956 (see Programme Spotlights 32). His goals came in the 32nd and 37th minutes, the latter a volley. The programme for that historic day records that the full band of the Grenadier Guards would be performing that afternoon, quite a step up from the Beswick Prize Band, who had the regular gig: a routine 4-2 win for the champions but a special game all round. The entry about him in the FA Cup Final programme that season commented on his debut and on his decisive goal in the semi-final against Birmingham, just

60 seconds after John Berry had opened the scoring. As the programme said, 'What an entry into big football!' Charlton played in that final, replacing Viollet on the teams printed in the programme.

Martin Peters, scorer of the 77th-minute goal that put England 2-1 ahead against West Germany in the World Cup Final, appeared in the England v. Scotland schools international at Derby County's Baseball Ground on 4 April 1959 (see Programme Spotlights 33). He is listed in the programme for that game as 'Martin Peters (Dagenham) left-back. Plays for London and Essex. Captain of Dagenham Boys. Sound tackler and good distribution. 5ft 9in. 10st. 4lb.' Peters joined West Ham United that summer, and by 1962/63 had established himself in the first team, though he did not play in the FA Cup Final and was not mentioned in the programme for that match. However, on 19 May 1965, he was at Wembley wearing the number four shirt in the West Ham team that beat TSV München 1860 2-0 in what was only the fifth European Cup Winners' Cup Final. Now bigger and stronger at six feet tall and weighing 11st 6oz (70kg), he was described in the programme as 'one of the top creative wing halves in the game'.

More than any other player, it was Peters who enabled manager Alf Ramsey to reshape the England formation to 4-1-3-2, the 'wingless wonders'. Peters was not selected for the opening group match, and won only his fourth cap in the next game against Mexico. His skill, stamina, pace, passing ability and eye for a goal made him the embodiment of what would become a new type of midfielder, in his case on the left of a narrow three.

In contrast to the way that Stiles, Moore, Bobby Charlton and Peters progressed from stand-out schoolboys to first-team teenagers, Roger Hunt's path to World Cup glory was much less predictable. Hunt was three times with Warrington non-

----

Programme Spotlights 33: From Base One to a Home Run

4 April 1959, England Schools 2 Scotland Schools 3, schools international.

Martin Peters from Dagenham was the left-back for this England Schoolboys team. Several others who played that day went on to have good careers. Centre-half Christopher Lawler (Liverpool) was England's captain, a 'cool player of exceptional positional sense' who possessed 'all the confidence of a mature player', according to the notes in the programme. He went on to win four England caps and was a regular right-back in Bill Shankly's title-winning Liverpool teams. John Sleeuwenhoek, son of a Dutch paratrooper, though listed at inside-right for the game at the Baseball Ground, was a centre-half for Staffordshire and made his name as a defender at Aston Villa, and reached Under-23 level with England. Brian Dear, the schoolboy outside-left, went on to a career with West Ham, and left-half George Sharples went to Everton, then Blackburn Rovers before finishing with Southport. Their Scottish opponents included a young Bobby Hope ('Typical Scottish inside-forward with a strong shot in both feet. His inch-perfect passes open up the game'). Hope became a mainstay at West Bromwich Albion and won two Scotland caps. His left-wing partner, from Caldercruix Secondary School, was William Henderson, 'A very fast winger of the traditional Scottish type, he is courageous and very tricky.' Henderson made his Glasgow Rangers debut the following year and went on to win 29 caps, a figure that would have been more but for the brilliance of Celtic's Jimmy Johnstone, who also played on the right wing.

----

league club Stockton Heath, interspersed by spells at Bury and Devizes Town, before signing for Liverpool at the age of 20 in 1958, having completed his National Service. The

Liverpool programme for their Second Division game against Ipswich Town on 18 April 1959 (which only drew a crowd of 16,415) lists 37 players alphabetically in a table of appearances and goalscorers. The most eminent among them was Liddell W.B. Now nearing the end of his illustrious career, Billy Liddell had played 16 games in the Football League that season, scoring 12 goals, but also made a dozen appearances for the reserves, scoring four times. Jimmy Melia was the leading scorer with 18. 'Hunt R. (Amateur)' had managed just one outing for the Central League side, in which he also scored. He was the only one with 'Amateur' after his name. As with a number of his future international team-mates, there was nothing at this stage of his career to suggest the greatness that lay ahead. Hunt made his first-team debut, and scored, against Scunthorpe United at Anfield in the following September.

By the time Liverpool hosted Manchester United in an FA Cup fourth round tie on the last Saturday in January 1960, the programme (now putting players' initials before, rather than after their surnames, a gesture to a nascent less formal era) revealed that Melia was still the leading scorer with 13, Liddell had still managed to score four times in six appearances, and the no-longer amateur Hunt had 12 goals from 21 appearances in the Second Division, plus another seven in five reserve matches. The edition also recorded that Hunt had 'headed in a centre from Alan A'Court' to give them a 2-0 lead before half-time in the home game against Sheffield United a fortnight earlier, and continued, 'Our third goal was obtained by Roger Hunt with a terrific shot after a through lob from Gerry Byrne.' The 'From the Boardroom' page continued with a round-up of Liverpool's 3-3 draw at Middlesbrough that came between the Sheffield United game and the cup tie. An early goal by Brian Clough had set Liverpool back, but by half-time they led 3-1. Hunt had 'added the third, one of the best goals seen for some time'. Sadly this superlative is not supported by further details, with the next paragraph recording Clough's second goal and a late penalty for the home side's equaliser.

Sir Geoffrey Charles Hurst was a talented sportsman, good enough to make an appearance for Essex in a County Championship cricket match in 1962, although he did not trouble the scorers. His flirtation with the summer game reflected the fact that although he had joined West Ham United when he left school at 15, as a 20-year-old at the end of the 1960/61 season he had made only nine first-team appearances. Part of his problem was that he was in competition for the left-half position with Bobby Moore. Buried away in the lower half of an inside page of West Ham's programme v. Manchester United for the 11am Good Friday kick-off in 1960 is the unremarkable statement that would presage a most remarkable day at Wembley six years later. Reporting on the Southern Floodlight Cup semi-final at Highbury on Tuesday, 5 April, it says, 'We took the opportunity to include John Cartwright at inside-right for his second First Team game of the season and also had Geoff Hurst at inside-left for the first time in the senior side. Cartwright made the most of his opportunity' – he scored twice, had a part in a third Hammers goal and 'fulfilled a useful role with attacking play'. However, no further comment was offered on the presumably less impressive performance of the man who would go on to score a hat-trick in the World Cup Final.

In the goalscorers list, opposite the team sheet, G. Hurst had scored twice for the reserves in the Football Combination First Division, up to and including 9 April. When the teams met again at Old Trafford on Easter Monday, West Ham announced nine team changes from the side printed in the programme that had gone to press the previous week. Since the visit to Manchester was their third game in four days (they had been at Blackburn on the Saturday), this was perhaps no surprise. Moore moved from right-half to centre-half and Andy Smillie dropped back from inside-right to play at left-half, with Cartwright being selected to fill the inside-right berth. Even in this much reshuffled line up, there was no place for Hurst, as Ron Brett took the place of Welsh international Phil Woosnam at number ten, and made one of his 13 first team appearances during his three seasons with the Hammers. Geoff Hurst was no overnight sensation.

All these men had grown up in that post-war world sketched in the previous chapters of this book. Their earnings as professional footballers would have made them able to purchase the TVs and other consumer goods advertised in the programmes of the 1950s, but not to become property developers or to move stratospherically out of their modest social origins. Most of them had endured the boredom of doing National Service, and while playing in services teams was no doubt enjoyable and a way of keeping fit, that experience could hardly match the science-driven preparation that is lavished on today's young hopefuls.

All of them had been good footballers, of course, but only Stiles, Moore, Bobby Charlton and Peters had made a smooth transition from schoolboy stardom to the pinnacle of the professional game, sparkling from an early age at top clubs. The vast majority of those who appeared alongside them in schoolboy internationals either disappeared without trace or had modest professional careers, replicating the story of Joe Dean described in Chapter 3. The others who collected World Cup winner's medals had much less illustrious pedigrees as youngsters, and persevered despite setbacks that would have destroyed the self-belief of many. What did Roger Hunt feel when he returned to Stockton Heath for the third time? How could his strike partner Geoff Hurst, after being eclipsed by John Cartwright in that first outing at inside-left, have imagined scoring a Wembley hat-trick? Jack Charlton grew up knowing he wasn't even the best player in his family, as his younger brother was a far more gifted player than he was. What did Ray Wilson feel as he was part of the Huddersfield Town Reserves side beaten 5-0 by Manchester United Reserves, then losing 3-0 in his league debut the following week?

At a time when the 'big teams' would have been Manchester United, Wolverhampton Wanderers, Tottenham Hotspur and Arsenal, most of the future England team built their careers with less exalted clubs. Liverpool and Leeds would only become leading clubs in the mid-1960s; when Hunt and Jack Charlton signed for them, they were in the Second Division, as were George Cohen's Fulham. Banks's career began at Third Division Chesterfield. Though Ball and Wilson moved as fame kicked in, and others did so only as they approached retirement, nine of the 11 stayed loyal to their first club throughout the main part of their careers, despite the removal of the limitation on maximum wages in 1961 (see Chapter 6). But by the time England faced West Germany that famous July afternoon, Britain was already changing, and even the way that British football was played was entering a new era.

On the field, the great achievement of Alf Ramsey as a coach was to effect that transformation – from a craft anchored in tradition to a machine-like 'industrialised' process. Players became more efficient. Wingers, notoriously capricious characters often languishing metaphorically and physically on the edge of a game, were dispensed with. They were the equivalent of hand-stitched leather seats in cars, or artisan-made furniture in an age of assembly lines and mass production. Dilettanti wingers gave way to overlapping full-backs and energetic midfielders, as teams shifted to 4-3-3 line-ups. It did not always make for entertainment, but

England had won the World Cup (with a bit of help from a linesman).

Programmes cited in Chapter 8 that are in the collection:

- 6 March 1954, Manchester United 1 Wolverhampton Wanderers 0, Football League First Division
- 16 April 1955, Manchester United 3 West Bromwich Albion 0, Football League First Division
- 27 August 1955, Manchester United 3 West Bromwich Albion 1, Football League First Division
- 22 October 1955, Manchester United 3 Huddersfield Town 0, Football League First Division
- 25 February 1956, Manchester United 2 Aston Villa 1, Football League First Division
- 21 April 1956, Manchester United 1 Portsmouth 0, Football League First Division
- 6 October 1956, Manchester United 4 Charlton Athletic 2, Football League First Division
- 4 May 1957, Aston Villa 2 Manchester United 1, FA Cup Final
- 7 September 1957, Manchester United 5 Leeds United 0, Football League First Division
- 18 September 1957, Manchester United 1 Blackpool 2, Football League First Division
- 19 October 1957, Manchester United 0 Portsmouth 3, Football League First Division.
- 12 March 1958, England 1 (West) Germany 2, youth international
- 29 March 1958, Manchester City 1 Leeds United 0, Football League First Division
- 17 September 1958, Manchester United 4 West Ham United 1, Football League First Division
- 15 December 1958, Manchester City Youth 0 Manchester United Youth 4, FA Youth Cup third round

- 27 December 1958, Brighton & Hove Albion 3 Fulham 0, Football League Second Division
- 4 April 1959, England Schools 2 Scotland Schools 3, schoolboy international
- 18 April 1959, Liverpool 3 Ipswich Town 1, Football League Second Division
- 7 November 1959, Leicester City 2 Sheffield Wednesday 0, Football League First Division
- 30 January 1960, Liverpool 1 Manchester United 3, FA Cup fourth round
- 12 March 1960, Leicester City 1 Wolverhampton Wanderers 2, FA Cup quarter-final
- 26 March 1960, Fulham 0 Manchester United 5, Football League First Division
- 2 April 1960, Derby County 3 Huddersfield Town 2, Football League Second Division
- 15 April 1960, West Ham United 2 Manchester United 1, Football League First Division
- 18 April 1960, Manchester United 5 West Ham United 3, Football League First Division
- 1 October 1960, Bolton Wanderers 1 Manchester United 1, Football League First Division
- 13 October 1960, Manchester United 2 Real Madrid 3, friendly
- 22 October 1960, Manchester United 3 Newcastle United 2, Football League First Division
- 29 October 1960, Arsenal 2 Manchester United, Football League First Division
- 3 February 1962, Manchester United 3 Cardiff City 0, Football League First Division
- 31 March 1962, Burnley 1 Fulham 1, FA Cup semi-final
- 2 May 1964, Preston North End 2 West Ham United 3, FA Cup Final
- 22 March 1955, Manchester United 2 Blackpool 0, Football League First Division

- 19 May 1965, TSV München 1860 0 West Ham United 2, European Cup Winners' Cup Final
- 30 July 1966, England 4 West Germany 2 (after extra time), World Cup Final
- 10 May, 1969, England 4 Scotland 1, Home International

Chapter 9

Scotland

I COMPLETED my post-graduate Diploma in Town Planning at Manchester University in the summer of 1968, and we moved to Scotland. I accepted a job as a planning assistant with Glasgow Corporation. I was attracted by the scale of Glasgow and its redevelopment programme. In January 1968, many buildings had been badly damaged by a severe storm and roofs were still patched up with tarpaulin. Arriving through the East End felt like stepping back 20 years to a townscape still scarred by war damage and poverty. However, there was also excitement; Scotland was an exotic place defined by its dramatic landscapes, romantic history, staple diet of Tunnock's Teacakes and Irn Bru, 'heavy' beer, and an amazing array of bank notes bearing unfamiliar names like the British Linen Bank.

My first professional assignment was to analyse and report on the future of a derelict dockyard on the Clyde. So, on a sunny August afternoon, I headed out of the council office in the city centre to visit the site. Walking through the back streets, I was bemused by the graffiti, 'Remember 1690 FTP' or 'FKB'. This was just before the civil conflict in Northern Ireland burst into UK news. When I got back to the office, naively I asked colleagues what the cryptic messages meant, and was enlightened about the Battle of the Boyne, King Billy and the Pope. While Manchester had a large population of Irish extraction and segregated 'non-denominational' and Catholic schools, the sectarianism in the west of Scotland was new to me.

Glasgow in 1968 was steeped in football. There was saturation coverage in the local newspapers, dominated of course by Rangers and Celtic, and an unmistakable buzz about the city when a big match was on, as fans with their scarves and songs thronged the streets and public transport for hours before kick-off. In 1967, Celtic had thrilled millions by beating Inter Milan 2-1 after conceding the first goal, to win the European Cup with a team of locally born players, the never-to-be-forgotten Lisbon Lions. Rangers had reached the final of the Cup Winners' Cup that same season, losing 1-0 in extra time to Franz Beckenbauer's Bayern Munich, giving the Bavarians their first European trophy. It was the first time that two clubs from the same city had contested the major European finals in the same season. In addition, Kilmarnock had faced the powerful Leeds United side in the semi-final of the Inter-Cities Fairs Cup, the precursor to the UEFA Cup.

Just as famously, Scotland had recorded an epic 3-2 victory over Alf Ramsey's World Cup winners at Wembley, with Denis Law at his incisive best and Jim Baxter ensuring legendary status by playing keepy-uppy, while Jack Charlton hobbled with a broken toe as there were still no substitutes in Home Internationals, even then. The eminent journalist Brian Glanville, writing in the programme, had anticipated an upset, 'The intriguing thing about England-Scotland matches is that form plays so little part.' He noted how England had comfortably beaten Ireland and Wales, while Scotland had 'outplayed Wales in Cardiff but only drew, then made awfully heavy weather of beating an Irish team deprived of George Best... None of this will matter today.'

So, excited and still new to the city, on a pleasant September Saturday afternoon in 1968, with my Geordie friend and fellow town planner Hugh Martin, I made my first visit to Celtic Park. We had got tickets through a technician working in the Planning Department, who was arrested a few weeks later for taking bribes to try to influence planning permissions. In a pulsating game Rangers beat Celtic 4-2, with the outcome only settled by a goal from the visitors in the 89th minute. Travelling across the city, all the programmes had gone by the time we got to the ground, and we squeezed in to the packed terrace in front of the main stand. Although I was well familiar with big games, this was something else. The police presence was greater than anything I had seen before, and the fans around me had beer in one hand and whisky in the other, keeping themselves refreshed throughout the afternoon. The tickets had been shared 50/50, so the noise and the passion never dropped as fortunes ebbed and flowed.

Exhilarated by this raucous, high-octane spectacle, I went to another top-division game the following Saturday, Clyde v. Raith Rovers at Shawfield (see Programme Spotlights 34). It was one of those blessed and indolent early autumn days in Scotland, between the disappointing rains of July and August and the cold, damp, short daylight hours of onrushing winter. I was able to park my second-hand Austin Mini in a nearby street, stroll to the turnstile, buy a programme and select a spot on the terrace. Thumbing the programme revealed an advertisement for Dunsade, a brew manufactured by Joseph Dunn (Bottlers) of Glasgow, and promoted by a picture of a full bottle and the words, 'If you're heading for health and vigour try the fruitiest full sugar drink.' On the opposite page was another exhortation, 'Buy Walkers Sugar – Produced in Scotland.' Scotland's health statistics are not sufficiently disaggregated to identify data for a cohort of late-1960s Clyde fans, but as the programme also contained an advert for Coca-Cola (bottled in Glasgow), one for Schweppes tonic water (no such thing as 'lite' back then), four for beer, and one for whisky, it was easy to fear the worst.

- -

Programme Spotlights 34: A win for the Bully Wee, but not for public health

21 September 1968, Clyde 3 Raith Rovers 2, Scottish League First Division

The plain, black-and-white eight-page programme befits the restrained atmosphere at this meeting of clubs playing in the same league as Celtic and Rangers, but much smaller and poorer.

The club badge celebrates Clyde's formation in 1877, as a private members' club. More than a decade before Glasgow Celtic emerged in the East End of the Second City of the Empire, Clyde were there in the Bridgeton area, close to the river from which the club takes its name. They shared the ground with a club with the unlikely name of Albatross, which perhaps predictably soon folded. Clyde moved across the river to Shawfield in 1898, then relocated again in 1994 to Cumbernauld New Town.

Clyde's nickname is the Bully Wee, though nobody seems sure why. The most plausible explanation is 'bully' was a Victorian word meaning good, and the club were, and still are, wee. Their glory days were in the 1950s, when they twice won the Scottish Cup and were twice beaten finalists.

Harry Hood was in the Clyde team that beat the team from Kirkcaldy, and he scored one of their goals. This was a few months before his £40,000 transfer to Celtic (a considerable sum in those days) where he enjoyed a decent career. The programme is remarkable for the heavy sugar content in the products advertised, and the claimed connection between 'health' and a 'full sugar drink'.

- -

The game itself was a huge comedown after the previous week's Old Firm thriller. Though I didn't realise it at the time, most of the players were part-time professionals, and the game lacked pace. The terraces around the dog racing track were sparsely populated: the East End of Glasgow and neighbouring Rutherglen, the core areas of Clyde's fan base, were emptying as they underwent the kind comprehensive redevelopment that I had gone to Glasgow to work on. People were being scattered to new flats with bathrooms and central heating, but far and wide from their previous home, and Clyde never recovered the level of support that they had enjoyed previously. It was a pleasant enough afternoon but weak beer for somebody who had grown up with regular visits to the big Manchester clubs: it was inconceivable to me that these teams were in the same league as Clyde's Glasgow neighbours whose dramatic encounter had entranced me just a week before.

A few weeks later I made my first of many visits to Hampden Park, for Scotland v. Austria (see Programme Spotlights 35) in a qualifier for the 1970 World Cup. This was my first full international and another overwhelming experience, made even more intense by being under floodlights. Hugh and I went straight from the city centre council office where we worked, and partook of another staple of the Scottish urban diet, feasting at one of the many chip shops in the vicinity of the ground, and then, as we approached the stadium, breathing in the aroma from the vans selling hamburgers, pies and meat puddings in a variety of colours I had not known in meat puddings. Having passed through the turnstiles, I walked along a tunnel that led to the terrace opposite the main stand. I gazed down, down, far down to the pitch below. Then I turned around and saw that the terrace not only continued upwards, but was also topped by a rickety-looking stand. Hampden was awe-inspiring, yet it seemed to be from another era: parts of the terraces were ash, not concrete, recalling my visits to Newton Heath Loco (see Chapter 3). Scotland fans to the right of me, at the 'Rangers End', sang lustily as the band of the First Battalion of the Black Watch played 'God save the Queen', while the Scotland fans on the open terrace behind the other goal, the 'Celtic End', booed and whistled. This was another new, very place-specific experience.

Programme Spotlights 35: Law changes
**6 November 1968, Scotland 2 Austria 1, World
Championship qualifying group**

My first visit to Hampden. The design of the front cover, reproduced by permission of the SFA, with the stylised drawing of players, was used for internationals and cup finals at Hampden, though the actual image changed from game to game. The eight pages are densely packed with text, with the only advertisement being on the back page, which in this case was for Capstan cigarettes which 'reflects the trend to a natural taste'.

The programme carried information about important rule changes. Two substitutes per team were now allowed at any time, with five subs to be named before the start. Thus after 75 minutes Alan Gilzean of Spurs, another outstanding header of a ball, replaced Law, who had opened the scoring. The second rule change had in fact been introduced in 1967, but was 'even yet… not generally understood'. It concerned the previous restriction that goalkeepers could not take more than four steps 'while holding, bouncing or throwing the ball in the air and catching it again without releasing it'. Infringement would be penalised by an indirect free kick. The rule had now been changed to allow keepers to dribble the ball 'before, during or after taking the four steps' but 'he may not take it into his hands again, before another player has played it'.

Austria opened the scoring from a long range shot after just a couple of minutes. Then Law equalised with an imperious back-post header squeezed in after a corner from the left, and the stadium erupted into a swaying sea of celebration. Scotland went on to win 2-1, with Billy Bremner scrambling the ball in from close range after the Austrian goalkeeper collided with one of his defenders and spilled a John Greig cross from the left.

The programme is a reminder of the quality of players at Scotland's disposal. Goalkeeper Ronnie Simpson was a European Cup winner with Celtic, as was right-back Tommy Gemmell, whose attacking had thrilled those who watched that triumph in Lisbon. His partner on the left was Eddie McCreadie of Chelsea. The half-backs were Leeds United's tenacious captain Billy Bremner, then the Rangers stalwarts Ronnie McKinnon and John Greig. Then how about this as a forward line: Jimmy Johnstone, Charlie Cook, Denis Law, Bobby Lennox and John Hughes? Three of them were from Celtic's European champions, including Johnstone who was a supreme dribbler; Cook was the star man at Chelsea; and, of course, the incomparable Denis Law, quite simply in the view of many Scotland's greatest ever player.

It was Scotland's misfortune to be in the same qualification group as West Germany, along with Austria and Cyprus, from which only one team could go through. Unlike the Scots, the Germans had never failed to qualify for the World Cup finals and that was not about to change for Mexico 1970 where they would reach the semi-final, eliminating holders England along the way. For the visit of West Germany on 16 April 1969, the Hampden programme had grown from eight to 12 pages, though the price was still one shilling. The visitors' team sheet suggests that a 1-1 draw that evening was no disgrace to the Scots. Arch goalscorer Gerd Müller had characteristically stabbed the visitors ahead in the first half, before a memorable 20-yard 'screamer' from Celtic's Bobby Murdoch equalised, which was pictured in the England v. Scotland programme a month later.

The Germans had class throughout their side. Schnellinger played for Milan, had been to three World Cups and was the best left-back in Europe. Other 1966 World Cup finalists were Höttges, the outstanding Beckenbauer, centre-half Willi Schultz, inside-forwards Haller of Juventus and Overath, and Siggi Held. A point of interest in the programme is that, although the teams were set out in the conventional 2-3-5 pattern, there was a note beneath the Scottish listing announcing that the team would play in 4-2-4 formation. If the Germans were unsure of the shape of their opponents, they only needed to buy a programme to find out. The edition also explained that the Germans received no payment for their time with the national team, only daily expenses.

The programme of the Scotland v. England game in April 1970 (a drab 0-0 draw) included a half-page advert that reminded readers that Hampden held 134,000 fans, and added that 'every day Lees make enough chocolate snowballs to supply every one of them'. Another sugary blow for Scotland's health statistics! The half-page above it carried a generous tribute from Dr Wilfried Gerhardt from the West German FA to the Scotland team. It opened, 'As we prepare to take part in the 1970 Mexico World Cup Finals' – ouch! – and went on to say that they had never been closer to defeat than in the decisive game against Scotland in Hamburg the previous October. Dr Gerhardt opined that Scotland were a stronger team than 'quite a few' of those going to Mexico, and he was right. After a couple of year's residence, I had become attuned to the leitmotif of gallant failure that was to become a haunting theme in Scottish football identity for the remainder of the 20th century. During the game, Geordie friend Hugh and I muted our accents as we stood on the terrace amid the frustrated home fans. Despite the 134,000 capacity, the attendance for the England match was put at 137,438.

There were many memorable nights at Hampden. Two in particular stand out. In April 1970, I was one of 136,505 privileged to see Celtic beat Leeds United 2-1 in the second leg of the European Cup semi-final to reach the final. As the programme rightly predicted, 'Tonight will be an all-time record for an attendance at a European Cup match ... and is unlikely to be beaten. The venue had been switched because Celtic Park could 'only' hold 80,000. Celtic had a 1-0 lead from the first leg, but Bremner cancelled that out before half-time with a magnificent shot curled into the top corner from outside the penalty area. Early in the second half the Celtic pressure told. Roared on by a passionate crowd, they equalised when John Hughes, normally a left-winger but playing at centre-forward, headed home from six yards an in-swinging cross whipped in by Bertie Auld with his left foot after a short corner from the right. Then Jimmy Johnstone, socks round his ankles, dribbled into the area, pulled the ball back and Bobby Murdoch struck it home with his right foot from just inside the area.

Then there was the win over Czechoslovakia that took Scotland through to the 1974 World Cup finals. This time it was just a three-team group, and Scotland had beaten Denmark home and away, while Czechoslovakia had drawn in their away game with the Danes. A win now would ensure Scotland's qualification, regardless of the result in the return game three weeks later. The official attendance was 'only' 95,786. This was because the number of tickets for games at Hampden Park had been limited following the Ibrox disaster on 2 January 1971, when 66 Rangers fans had been crushed to death and over 200 more were injured on an exit stairway as late goals for each side created a dramatic but chaotic end to their game with Celtic. A dreadful bit of goalkeeping gifted Czechoslovakia the lead, but a few minutes before half-time, centre-half Jim Holton ('Six foot two, eyes of blue, big Jim Holton's after you') equalised with an imperious header from a left-wing corner. Leeds's Joe Jordan replaced Kenny Dalglish just after the hour. Still only 21 and having only made his international debut at the end of the previous season, the former Morton player was a relative unknown until the moment he electrified Hampden by heading home a deft cross from the outside of Willie Morgan's right foot.

The programme for England's 1970 visit provides a potent reminder of what this most iconic arena was like in its pomp. Hampden Park stadium occupied 16 and a half acres. The East Terrace (aka the 'Celtic End') itself officially accommodated 62,175, though the time-honoured practice of lifting youngsters over the turnstiles meant that there could be little doubt that number was exceeded on big occasions. Standing on the top of that terrace, as I did on occasions, you were 60ft above the playing surface, 385ft from the nearest goal and 903ft (275 metres) away from your opposite number on the top of the recently covered West Terrace, who would be crammed alongside 41,759 others. The North Stand Enclosure, where I had stood for the Austria game, could take 39,913; across from the South Stand Enclosure that could only take 5,644. Those who could afford to buy a seat in the North or South Stand numbered in total 14,530. This was a cathedral to mass, cheap, male working-class entertainment and culture. While the programme gave the figures for tunnels, turnstiles and crush barriers, it made no reference to toilet facilities, and many spectators on the terraces relied on in-situ solutions to needs brought on by continuous consumption of beer and lager.

In 1971, Euan, who would so augment the programme collection, arrived: Hearts 2 Dundee 2 in the Scottish League First Division in January 1978 was the first game I took him to. He was followed by his sisters Alice (1974), and twins Celia and Sophie (1978). We had moved to Edinburgh in 1971, by which time I was working as a lecturer in the Department of Town and Country Planning at Heriot-Watt University/Edinburgh College of Art. This hybrid institutional relationship assumed that free-spirited artists could be edged to think about functionality while engineers clasping their slide rules would come to appreciate aesthetics: suffice to say, neither did. One of my early students was a former professional footballer. Henry McLeish had been a Scottish youth international, and had been at Leeds United with other young Scots including Peter Lorimer and Eddie Gray, both of whom became stars in Don Revie's champion team. Henry, though, had returned home and played for East Fife. We have a programme of their League Cup defeat by Dundee (13 September 1967), in which Henry was listed as an ever-present and goalscorer in the early-season games. He was a good student, getting his BSc (Hons) in Town Planning, before becoming a Member of Parliament, junior minister, and then First Minister of Scotland in the devolved parliament. His passion for Scottish football remains undimmed, despite the disappointments of the first two decades of this century.

Football did not occupy such a dominant position in popular culture in Edinburgh as it did in Glasgow. However, in those early 1970s, Hibernian were an attractive and successful side, and I watched them regularly. John Brownlie was an outstanding attacking full-back who achieved international status until a broken leg effectively ended his career. Central defender John Blackley was also a class act. Another international, Pat Stanton, led the side from midfield, where Alex Edwards, though never far from a sending off, was a skilful and creative force. Until his big-money transfer to Arsenal, Alex Cropley sparkled and won international caps as an attacking midfielder, while up front the graceful Alan Gordon provided knock-downs and lay-offs for the under-rated Jimmy O'Rourke to plunder numerous goals.

On Saturday afternoons I often met up with some of my students on the main open terrace at Easter Road. There were views from there to the dramatic Salisbury Crags, a key element in Edinburgh's iconic landscape. Hibs' Easter Road home, set among the tenements and with its pitch sloping towards Leith, was an authentic football ground. Except when the Old Firm or Hearts were the visitors, the atmosphere at Easter Road in those days was less intense than I was used to, but still enjoyable. Applause would ripple round the ground in appreciation as Hibs weaved pretty patterns. However, the open terrace took on a Siberian character on dark winter days when east winds drove in sleet and snow.

As a schoolboy programme collector I had acquired a few Scottish programmes during the 1950s, mainly through responding to advertisements in *Charles Buchan's Football Monthly.* Among these were Hearts v. Rangers in the seventh round of the Scottish Cup on 3 March 1956. Notable comments in this programme for the meeting of the top two in the Scottish League that afternoon mentioned that every ticket had sold out within five hours of going on sale, and that Rangers, who had lost only one league game that season, had three part-time players in their first-team squad. The Hearts team that day included club legends, powerhouse wing-half Dave Mackay (later of Spurs and Derby County), Alex Young (fondly called the 'Golden Vision' in his time at Everton as a silky, ball-playing centre-forward), as well as Alfie Conn, Willie Bauld and Jimmy Wardhaugh at eight, nine and ten respectively. Hearts won 4-0.

The Aberdeen versus Clyde programme (Programme Spotlights 36) from that same 1955/56 season is in fragile condition. It was an early season game pitting the previous season's champions against cup winners. The sides had met in the 1954/55 semi-final, drawing the first game 2-2 at Hibs' Easter Road, with Clyde equalising in the last minute, then winning the replay 1-0, before drawing the final 1-1 with holders Celtic (after equalising direct from a corner on a windy day in Glasgow then triumphing 1-0 in the replay).

- -

Programme Spotlights 36: Should have been a red card

20 August 1955, Aberdeen 3 Clyde 2, Scottish League Cup qualifying round

The poor-quality paper makes this programme fragile. Printed red on white, the club colours, it is A5 in size and eight pages. The previous season Aberdeen had finished top of the A Division of the Scottish League, three points ahead of Celtic and eight clear of Rangers.

Inside there is a story about the Hibernian v. Aberdeen meeting the previous Saturday. The Dons' Paddy Buckley had 'outstripped the opposition and was racing towards [Hibs' goalkeeper] Younger. There was no chance of any defender stopping the Aberdeen centre, so he was promptly tripped up from behind… This desperate measure has been seen at most grounds (Including Pittodrie!) but we feel that all true sportsmen must look upon such tactics with disapproval.' There was no automatic red card in those days, but gentlemanly disapproval was noted. Indeed, there were no cards of any colour anywhere until the 1970s, and a fist fight was often the threshold required before a player would be sent off.

- -

Another early Scottish programme is a cup second round tie in February 1953 at Easter Road (see Programme Spotlights 37), where Hibernian faced Queen's Park, the historic amateur side, which, having formed in 1867, is the oldest senior football club. The Hibs line up that day featured the 'Famous Five' forward line: Gordon Smith, Bobby Johnstone, Lawrie Reilly, Eddie Turnbull and Willie Ormond. They defined Hibs' most successful decade and each of them scored more than 100 goals for the club. Hibs had been league champions in 1950/51 and 1951/52, and were top of the table again at the time they played Queen's Park. However, they failed to land a third successive title when a late Rangers equaliser at Queen of the South pipped them on goal average. Given Hibs' success, it is perhaps surprising that the crowd that day was less than 18,000. The programme contains a reminder of the playing conditions, and the way injuries were treated, 'Eddie Turnbull jarred his ankle badly when he crashed home that penalty at Brockville [Falkirk] last Saturday, and he's spent some time under the lamp at Easter Road, in an effort to get fit again. There was a Rugby flavour to the preparations for the kick, for a mark had almost to be "dug" in the spot so that Eddie could let rip at a stationary ball.'

Programme Spotlights 37: The big picture
7 February 1953, Hibernian 4 Queen's Park 2, Scottish Cup second round

This remains a handsome-looking programme on good-quality paper. Being larger than most of that era, albeit still only eight pages, allows space on the front to display an eye-catching action photo from the recent Hibernian v. Airdrieonians encounter. The winger crossing the ball is the legendary Hibs skipper Gordon Smith, who scored 125 goals for the club in 310 appearances between 1941 and 1959. There is a lovely symmetry between the sweep of the terrace and the pose of Smith and the Airdrie defender tracking him, which is then counterpointed by the rise of the tenements in the background to the right and the other Airdrie players in shot. The photo also gives a good impression of the open terrace from which I watched Hibs in the 1970s. It provided a beguiling vantage point in late summer but less so in bleak midwinter.

The use of green on the cover and in parts of the rest of the programme reflects the club colours, a graphic style that has always been widely popular. One downside with the size of the programme is that it was too big to slip easily into a pocket, as a horizontal fold across the middle testifies.

During the three seasons I was in the west of Scotland, I had mainly watched Celtic. However, I also attended games at the homes of the other Glasgow clubs – not just Clyde but also Rangers and Partick Thistle. Much to my regret I was not able to see Third Lanark, as they had gone bust before I arrived in Scotland.

As a football-daft boy in Manchester, Scottish football appeared exotic. Clubs had names that were every bit as extraordinary as Accrington Stanley or Sheffield Wednesday. Third Lanark had taken theirs from their 19th-century origins with the Third Lanarkshire Rifle Volunteers, but as a youngster I could not help but ponder what happened to First Lanark and Second Lanark.

Our oldest Third Lanark programme (see Programme Spotlights 38) is for their B Division home game against Morton on 10 March 1956. It was probably acquired from a programme shop that existed for a while in Edinburgh, near my workplace. Three of the four centre pages in the eight-page programme that day were mainly filled by the 'Editor Talking', headed by a cute graphic of a bespectacled man, with his sleeves rolled up, bashing out 'HI-HI' (the club's nickname) on sheets from his old-style typewriter. Third Lanark had scored 48 of their 64 goals that season at home. These included some astounding romps – nine against Montrose, seven against Albion Rovers, six against both Hamilton Academical and Stranraer, and just the five against Stenhousemuir. However, 'today's visitors' had put six past them when Third Lanark had travelled to Greenock earlier in the season. With a flourish, the writer declared 'why the dynamite in their boots should suddenly prove a damp squib in away games is something that would puzzle the proverbial Philadelphia lawyer yet facts are chiels that winna ding'. That famous phrase from Burns's poem 'A Dream' was worth the threepenny bit that the programme cost the fans.

That same amount was, as the editor explained later in his column, the difference between the price of admission to a B Division (one shilling and nine pence) and the two shillings asked for an A Division game. 'Getting down to cold, hard facts, there are clubs in the B Division who haven't the slightest appeal to the public.' In contrast the previous week's Scottish Junior Cup clash between Petershill and Lanark Thistle had drawn a crowd of 11,000. Well over half a century later, that same contradiction still echoes through the Scottish game. Semi-professional Junior football still holds the promise of blood-curdling contests infused with a passionate identity for what are mainly small town or village teams, while outside a few teams from the few large cities, the senior clubs struggle to draw crowds.

While most of the adverts in that 1956 Third Lanark programme are typical of that time, a few add to the aura of difference that still envelopes the long-defunct club. The whole of the back cover is an advertisement for Carswells The Modern Man's Shop, which announced 'the opening of Glasgow's most modern barber's shop'. What qualified that establishment for the accolade is less clear, though the starred items mentioned were sterilised equipment, first-class service and expert attention, prompting thoughts of what were the norms in more traditional barbers in Glasgow in 1956? Meanwhile, straddling the top-middle of the centre pages there was an advert for Reid's restaurants in the city centre, which were proclaimed to be 'Two of Glasgow's nicer Restaurants', another genteel suggestion that some rival dining places might be somewhat unsavoury. Last, but not least, Eglington Surgical Stores displayed in more discreet type that they retailed Durex Surgical Rubber Ware, Rendell's, Gynomin and Ortho (i.e. foaming vaginal contraceptives). The stores offered a 'Confidential Mailing List' and a 'Planned Family Booklet' – but to 'Adults Only'.

Programme Spotlights 38: Hi-Hi
10 March 1956, Third Lanark v. Morton, Scottish League B Division

The front page of the eight-page programme alerts the reader to the club's eccentricity: the official programme is *HI-HI NEWS*. Why? Because the club's nickname was the Hi-Hi, and fans chanted Hi-Hi-Hi! Seemingly, this came from an incident in a game in the late 1890s when a defender kicked the ball 'high, high, high' and out of the ground. The programme is printed in shades of brown on a white background: an unusual, even unique colour choice. As well as a photo of their home ground, Cathkin Park, the front cover lists the two sides, in parallel columns, and numbered from one to 11. Listing of the sides on the front of a programme was extremely rare, and back in 1956 programme editors almost invariably laid out the two teams as facing each other on the page in a 2-3-5 line up, since that was the system that every British side was playing, the only exception being Manchester City with their Revie Plan (see Chapter 5), where the number nine played in midfield. The clue to the eventual demise of Third Lanark is the name W.C. Hiddelston, there in italics, as the person to correspond with regarding the programme, and so the innovations described above may have come from him.

By the time they reached the League Cup Final at Hampden on 24 October 1959, Third Lanark were on the up. We have the programme of that game, won 2-1 by Heart of Midlothian. The Hi Hi were managed by the recently retired George Young who, as the programme noted, had won numerous honours with Rangers and was 'feared and respected'. Standing 6ft 2in tall (188cm), Young was an imposing figure, the equivalent in Scotland in his day of a defender like Jaap Stam or Virgil van Dijk. Young was still in his post when they beat Hearts 1-0 at Cathkin Park on 17 March 1962, our only other Third

Lanark programme. The design of the programme had changed slightly; it was still the *Hi Hi News*, but now red on white, with the teams laid out in conventional opposing line-ups across the centre pages. The Eglington Surgical Store were no longer buying space in the programme, whereas the Army was seeking to attract boys between 15 and 16 and a half years old to join the Cameronians (Scottish Rifles) by offering 'Travel, Adventure, Companionship, Good Pay, Free Food and Accommodation': apart from girls, what more could these adolescents want? The editor's column beamed with satisfaction that the Hi Hi had been watched by 35,000 at Ibrox in the league, then by 42,500 at Parkhead in a cup fourth round tie against Celtic, where a 4-4 draw had brought a replay at Hampden with another large crowd, albeit in an unmentioned 4-0 defeat. Earlier in the year, 19,000 had turned up at Cathkin Park for the league game with Celtic. Significantly, in those egalitarian days gate receipts from a match were shared between the two clubs.

So what went wrong? Third Lanark played their last game on 28 April, 1967, suffering a 5-1 defeat at Dumbarton. The clue to their demise was on the front cover of that programme for the match against Morton in 1956. In between the names of the linesmen that day and the pithy 'Aitken's Beer – Just What I Want', is written in italics, 'All further correspondence regarding the programme should be addressed to W.C. Hiddelston, Cathkin Park.' On page three, the same W.C. Hiddelston is listed along with four other directors, but then below them, in bold type and capitals, lest there be any doubt who is in charge, is the title 'Director-Manager', and the name of the man holding that post, W.C. Hiddelston.

Bill Hiddelston, described as being well educated and well-spoken, a wholesale glass merchant, had become a shareholder and director in 1954 at the tender age of 28. He had become manager by 1956, but then left in February 1957, when his resignation was requested by the other directors on the grounds that he had allegedly carried out numerous unauthorised cash transactions, including the purchase of a player from Doncaster Rovers. Hiddelston's name does not appear in the programme of the game against Hearts in March 1962. However, he had been plotting his revenge by busily acquiring shares through means fair and foul, and later that year he became the majority shareholder, at which point manager George Young and his staff resigned, and the club was on the road to bankruptcy.

Players were sold, including future Scotland boss Ally MacLeod; crowds slumped. Money taken at the gate, from car parking, advertising, and from at least one transfer fee failed to find its way into company accounts. Hiddelston claimed to have used cash to pay bills incurred by the club: recipients were identified by names such as 'casual labour' or 'trialist'. Third Lanark were also paying £5 a week to the schoolgirl daughter of Hiddelston, and £20 a week to the man himself.

There are colourful stories of visiting teams bringing their own soap and lightbulbs to games at Cathkin Park as creditors closed in. A few years later I was at a party where I met Frank Coulson, a centre-forward of Partick Thistle, whose wife taught at the same school as my wife. His story was that Third Lanark players were under instruction to hoof the ball out of Cathkin Park as soon as possible; this was not to keep alive the legend of how the Hi Hi got their nickname, but because the club had only one ball of the required standard, which needed careful conservation to prevent wear. The final blow came from the contractors who had built a new stand for which they were owed, but not paid, £40,000. There were reports that Hiddelston wanted to sell the ground to house builders and relocate the club. In 1968, a damning Board of Trade enquiry following the club's collapse described it as an 'inefficient and unscrupulous one-man business'. Four fellow directors were convicted of breaches of the Companies Acts and fined, but Hiddelston was already dead, following a heart attack in Blackpool in November 1967.

When I became an employee of Glasgow Corporation in 1968, Bailie James F. Reilly was a renowned local Labour politician: a bailie was the Scottish equivalent of an alderman. Glasgow had been virtually a one-party state. Reilly was a solicitor, famous for his bowler hat and pin-striped trousers, and for taking bribes. He could find you a council house in a nice neighbourhood, or fix a liquor licence. In 1966, the Labour Party suspended its Glasgow branch when Reilly was jailed for 18 months and banned from public office for five years. He had been chairman of Third Lanark and Hiddelston's right-hand man, and was roundly criticised by the Board of Trade enquiry.

Hiddelston was a man ahead of his time. He was asset-stripping before the term was invented. How he would have loved a leveraged buy-out, such as that accomplished by the Glazer family in 2005 where the debt that enabled them to buy Manchester United was put on the club, not the family themselves. From his grave, how he must envy the way that the owners of West Ham were handed the Olympic Stadium with massive public subsidy. Building the stadium had cost over £400m and then converting it to a football stadium racked up another £323m according to Owen Gibson writing in *The Guardian* on 2 November 2016. According to Gibson, West Ham agreed to pay £15m towards the overall conversion costs, plus a basic £2.5m a year in rent which is reduced if the club falls out of the Premier League. Hiddelston had decades earlier hit on the potential of milking public money from Development Corporations by relocating Third Lanark to a new town. Had he lived longer, he would not have needed the help of a corrupt local councillor to prosper. A generous, legal donation to a political party and he could have been elevated to a peerage or knighthood.

From a 21st-century perspective Hiddelston's ambition and behaviour look trivial, even pathetic, from the fiver a week for his daughter down to dying in Blackpool, rather than Las Vegas or on a yacht off Nice. Rather than having Third Lanark registered in a tax haven, and declaring himself a 'non-dom' for tax purposes, Hiddelston was probably even paying taxes, although he might not have been declaring all his income. His sidekick, Bailie Reilly, knew how to get somebody a council tenancy, but ask him to set up a shell company and he would probably have headed to the nearest beach. Liquidation threatened Third Lanark before Russia's natural resources had been handed over to gangsters and cronies, so there were no super-rich oligarchs to launder money through the club. Abu Dhabi and Qatar were just poor British protectorates, so no saviours there either. A story in the *Glasgow Herald* claimed that the man who destroyed Third Lanark told an interviewer, 'Football is no longer a game. It's finance now.' Saying that in the mid-1950s marks Bill Hiddelston as more than a 'fit and proper person'; he was a visionary.

Programmes cited in Chapter 9 that are in the collection:

- 7 February 1953, Hibernian 4 Queens Park 2, Scottish Cup second round
- 20 August 1955, Aberdeen 3 Clyde 2, Scottish League Cup qualifying round
- 3 March 1956, Heart of Midlothian 4 Rangers 0, Scottish Cup seventh round
- 10 March 1956, Third Lanark v. Morton, Scottish League B Division (result unknown)
- 24 October 1959, Heart of Midlothian 2 Third Lanark 1, Scottish League Cup Final
- 17 March 1962, Third Lanark 1 Heart of Midlothian 0, Scottish League First Division

- 15 April 1967, England 2 Scotland 3, European Championship qualifying tie
- 13 September 1967, East Fife 0 Dundee 1, Scottish League Cup quarter-final
- 7 January 1968, Heart of Midlothian 2 Dundee 2, Scottish League First Division
- 21 September 1968, Clyde 3 Raith Rovers 2, Scottish League First Division
- 6 November 1968, Scotland 2 Austria 1, World Cup qualifying group
- 16 April 1969, Scotland 1 West Germany 1, World Cup qualifying group
- 10 May 1969, England 4 Scotland 1, Home International Championship
- 15 April 1970, Celtic 2 Leeds United 1, European Cup semi-final second leg
- 25 April 1970, Scotland 0 England 0, Home International Championship
- 26 September 1973, Scotland 2 Czechoslovakia 1, World Cup qualifying group

Chapter 10

Sponsors, Violence and Economic Crisis

DURING THE 1970s, Britain changed. The country ditched its pounds, shillings and pence for decimal currency, joined the European Common Market, experienced the most bitter industrial unrest since the 1920s, and, along with others, experienced 'Stagflation' as the oil-producing countries of the Middle East hiked the price, sending the cost of living soaring while simultaneously depressing the economy. Unemployment mounted and industries that had been the mainstay of towns and regions for generations began to close. The post-war consensus that had extended and sustained the welfare state fractured. The British Army was on the streets in Northern Ireland where a civil war had broken out, and bombs were exploding in English cities. The feminist movement came to the fore, but there was also a resurgence of fascism in the form of the National Front and the British Movement. The story of this turbulent decade that shaped the trajectory of the country for the rest of the 20th century and beyond is written in our collection of programmes.

Through the 1960s, the quality of programmes had improved considerably. In general, paper was glossier, there were more pages, more content, and more photos. However, the costs of producing them were increasing, anticipating the much wider problems of inflation that engulfed the game and the UK economy during the 1970s. Aston Villa increased the price from 5p in 1970/71 to 6p at the start of the following season – one new penny or 20 per cent whichever way you saw it. The club explained how they had absorbed a cost increase of 20 per cent over the previous season, but were facing a further 14 per cent increase in production and selling costs. West Ham kept the price to 5p, but no longer included colour photos. They cited 'the spiralling costs of raw materials, labour, overheads etc.' which were impacting on printing costs. Other clubs opted to restyle their programmes; Coventry City (who actually cut the cost) and Lincoln City were examples. An undated issue of *Football League Review* in the 1970/71 season (with lanky Welsh target man Wyn Davies, then of Manchester City, on the front cover) asked readers' views about charging ten new pence for a programme, as Hull City and Bournemouth and Boscombe Athletic had now done. Mr Hawkins of Bristol responded, 'To say that the equivalent of two shillings is not too much to pay for a programme suggests a rather cynical try-on… It highlights another facet of the "great decimal swindle".' Britain's switch to decimal currency in February 1971 was often blamed for price inflation at the time (see Programme Spotlights 39).

As the post-war growth economy began to falter, British football entered the new decade looking for fresh ways to sustain the old game. One of these was sponsorship. The 1970/71 season in England started with the Watney Cup, at a time when Watney's Red Barrel was probably Britain's most popular beer. The official programmes for the semi-final and final contained a 'message' from the chairman of brewers Watney Mann, describing it as the first sponsored football tournament. Eight clubs were invited to compete. These were the highest-scoring

----

Programme Spotlights 39: Decimal inflation

6 March 1971, Hibernian 1 Dundee 0, Scottish Cup fifth round

10 March 1971, Hibernian 2 Morton 4, Scottish League First Division

20 March 1971, Hibernian 1 St Johnstone 2, Scottish League First Division

22 September 1971, Hibernian 1 Falkirk 0, Scottish League Cup quarter-final

These four Hibernian programmes illustrate the change to decimal currency and the accompanying inflation. The game against Dundee was on 6 March 1971. Although 'decimal day' was 15 February, a couple of weeks later the Hibs programme was still priced at six (old) pence. For the visit of Morton four days later, the price was two and a half new pence, which was the official 'exchange rate' for six old pence. Ten days later came St Johnstone and the price had gone up to three new pence, then for the following season programmes cost five new pence, a doubling of the price from just a few months earlier, though the number of pages had increased from eight to 12. The price went up again from 5p in 1973/74 to 7p in 1974/75.

----

pair from each of the four divisions of the Football League. Drawn games were decided on penalties, and so the first penalty shoot-out was in the Hull City v. Manchester United semi-final, with George Best the first penalty taker and Denis Law the first player to miss, though his team still won. In the final they faced the other First Division side, Derby County, who hosted the match and won 4-1. Our programme from the semi-final at Hull is special because it is autographed by Matt Busby (see Programme Spotlights 40). Football League secretary Alan Hardaker wrote in the programme for the final, 'Responsible sponsorship can become one of football's major developments over the next decade.' This proved more robust prophesy than the statement on the opposite page that following the success of Brazil in the World Cup, 'More and more teams will be going out to attack, not just in the hope of keeping the other side out and "nicking" a goal on a breakaway.' The lure of scoring lots of goals to win a place in the Watney Cup provided resistible, and the competition was closed down after four seasons.

- -

Programme Spotlights 40: Don't trust a keeper to take a penalty

5 August 1970, Hull City 1 Manchester United 1 (after extra time, Manchester United won 4-3 on penalties), Watney Cup semi-final

Page three of the programme carries the message from the sponsors, but more importantly is autographed by Matt Busby, the legendary manager of Manchester United. The match was notable because it was the first time a penalty shoot-out had been staged in a professional game in Britain. The previous form of tie-breaker had been a toss of the coin.

Hull had led through a Chris Chilton left-footed volley after 11 minutes, only for Denis Law to equalise with a trademark header in the 78th minute. After a scoreless period of extra time, George Best took the first penalty and scored. The sequence of success continued for the next five penalties (Terry Neill for Hull, then Brian Kidd, Ian Butler, Bobby Charlton and Ken Houghton). Then Ian McKechnie saved Law's kick, only for Ken Wagstaff to shoot wide. Willie Morgan made it 4-3 for the visitors. Goalkeeper McKechnie (once an outside-left) took Hull's fifth, only to see his shot fisted over the bar by Alex Stepney.

- -

Both the final and the Hull City v. Manchester United semi-final programmes had features about the football coverage being provided by ITV. Brian Moore, on his way to becoming a legendary commentator, wrote about how he went about his job. There were also photos and comments from ITV's 'Soccer Panel': Jimmy Hill (see Chapters 6 and 8), Malcolm Allison, Bob McNab, Derek Dougan (see Chapter 7) and Pat Crerand (see Chapter 7).

Hill was best known as a player during his years with Fulham in the 1950s and had been chairman of the Professional Footballers' Association. From 1961 until 1967, he managed Coventry City, before developing his career in television, where he is credited as the person who invented the panel of former players to comment on games and analyse tactics. Allison had been the leading figure in the West Ham Academy, a group of players who would eat together after training, and round the lunch table bounce ideas about how to play the game. His fame, boosted by his flamboyant personality, came as co-manager of Manchester City (with Joe Mercer) in the late 1960s and early 1970s. Bob McNab was a first-team regular with Arsenal at left-back, before moving to play in the USA in the mid-1970s. Dougan at this time was at his professional peak as centre-forward for Wolves and for Northern Ireland, and also chairman of the PFA. His media career prospered during the 1970s. While appearing on the panel, Pat Crerand was also still playing at the top level as a midfielder with Manchester United. He had a difficult afternoon on the panel analysing their Watney Cup Final defeat at Derby.

The semi-final programme explained how the panel had been a major success during the World Cup, a further indication that the presentation of the game was changing. Television was changing too: the Plymouth Argyle v. Tranmere Rovers programme 15 August 1970 carried an advert invoking fans to 'Brighten your life with COLOUR television', while Westward TV, the local independent station, were also advertising in the programme.

The Texaco Cup was also introduced in 1970/71 for teams from the top divisions in England, Wales, Scotland,

Northern Ireland and the Republic of Ireland that were not involved in European competitions. The clubs taking part that season were Burnley, Stoke, Nottingham Forest, Tottenham, West Bromwich Albion, Wolverhampton Wanderers, Heart of Midlothian, Dundee, Dunfermline, Airdrieonians, Morton, Motherwell, Derry City, Ards, Shamrock Rovers and Limerick. All games had home and away legs, and the games were played in the same weeks as the European competitions. Derry's home ground was in what was at the time 'Free Derry', an epicentre of the renascent Irish Republican Army a year after The Troubles had erupted. The first Texaco Cup programme in our collection is from the first round, second leg meeting on 30 September 1970 in which Heart of Midlothian overcame a 3-1 defeat in the first leg to beat Burnley 4-1 (see Programme Spotlights 41).

The American oil giant Texaco put £100,000 in to the competition, equivalent to over £1.5m in 2021. This was not a philanthropic gesture: it was small feed for an oil company, and in 1956 Texaco had taken over a stake in the Regent Oil Company, which as part of the British Empire had extracted its oil from Trinidad.

As the page on 'TEXACO: A new name in British Sport' in the Hearts v. Burnley programme relates, 'In 1967, Texaco acquired full ownership of Regent, a household name in Britain for 30 years, and the third largest marketer of petroleum products in the United Kingdom. Two years ago the company began to change the brand name at service stations all over the U.K. to Texaco. By the end of the year this changeover will be complete.' It goes on to list Texaco's many other sponsorships in countries across the world. The programme thus reveals one step in what was to become a major restructuring of the UK economy, the takeover of long-established leading British companies by bigger international businesses and investors.

- -

Programme Spotlights 41: Big oil comes to town

30 September 1970, Heart of Midlothian 4 Burnley 1,
Texaco Cup first round second leg

Burnley were a First Division club at this time, though they had not won a league game that season by the time they visited Tynecastle. Tony Waiters kept goal for them that evening, a five-cap England international who had retired to coach at Liverpool then moved to Burnley as a player. Ralph Coates wore number eight: when Burnley were relegated at the end of that season, he moved to Spurs for £190,000, a very large fee in those days. Mick Docherty, son of ex-Scottish international and manager Tommy (see Chapter 5), played, while centre-forward and future Burnley manager Frank Casper scored their goal.

Hearts' star at the time was striker Donald Ford. Though he was not on the scoresheet that night, he had an 11-year career with the club, won three Scottish caps and was in their 1974 World Cup finals squad. Hearts' goalkeeper was Jim Cruickshank, who made almost 400 appearance for them between 1960 and 1977, and was also a Scottish international. Hearts finished the season in 11th position in the 18-team Scottish First Division.

- -

As an aside, the Hearts v. Burnley programme also carried the news that Roy Gowdie, organist at Hearts' social clubs, had left 'to try his luck in Germany'. One can only ponder how his career developed. Also, 'Singing star Robert Young has now made a record which could well prove a big hit.' It didn't.

For the First Texaco Cup final, between Heart of Midlothian and Wolverhampton Wanderers, both clubs produced a programme for their home leg. The Hearts edition included a letter from a fan expressing dismay that admission prices for juniors had been hiked for the final from 15p to 40p. Wolves' version had photos of their goals in their 3-1 victory in the first leg. Hearts had made their home leg all-ticket with a 44,000 capacity, though in the end the crowd was 26,000, the largest in the tournament at that stage, according to the programme for their next home game with Motherwell. Wolves won the final 3-2 on aggregate.

Alongside these official club programmes, a brochure was also produced by Texaco for both legs of that first final: the picture on the front of the first leg at Tynecastle was of an earlier tie involving Airdrieonians, whereas at Molineux the photo was of the teams emerging from the tunnel at Tynecastle, with 'Texaco' obscuring part of the Hearts badge above the tunnel. Otherwise the content of the Texaco-produced brochures was identical. Inside, the Wolves chairman was quoted as saying, 'Sponsorship in football is something new.' His Hearts counterpart observed, 'Fears about sponsorship held by certain legislators have now been dispelled.' The CEO of Texaco in the UK wrote that it was the first time that Texaco had sponsored a major international sporting event in the UK and Ireland. The back cover page of the eight-page publications is an advert for Texaco. The word 'Texaco' appears a further 15 times in the brochures. Texaco also produced *Texaco Grandstand*, a booklet featuring teams and fixtures (as well as adverts for Texaco) for that season's Scottish First Division. It devoted four pages to the Texaco Sports Shop, retailing sports items produced by Lillywhites, including improbably a choice of two croquet sets (one with shorter mallets). More pertinently, for each club there was a map of the location of nearby Texaco filling stations, which in those days before superstores and their discounting were still plentiful in the older parts of cities around the grounds.

The significance of the Watney and Texaco ventures is threefold. As noted above, it set British football on a new path, paving the way to sponsors' names on shirts, the sale of naming rights to stadia, and the sponsorship of mainstream competitions up to and including the FA Cup. The first FA

Cup game to be sponsored was Peterborough United v. Leeds United on 26 January 1974: the programme devotes a page to this, 'History is being made today by Brierleys Supermarkets.' By bringing new money to clubs, sponsorship inflated budgets, to the benefit of players, coaches and owners. The second dimension of the change was in the relation of big business to the game. As we have seen in previous chapters, the kind of advertising that clubs attracted was often from quite local sources, and/or targeted at a local market, as the Brierleys sponsorship shows. The engagement of businesses with clubs was still largely local, and often very individually specific – men like W.C. Hiddelston at Third Lanark, Louis Edwards at Manchester United or Bob Lord at Burnley, the latter pair both running local butcher businesses. Watney Mann, and even more so the international oil giant Texaco, were were corporate giants in comparison. Finally, the sponsorship of football was part of a way in which businesses redefined both their self-promotion to customers and to the general public. Rather than selling a product, they were promoting a brand – a set of positive ideas, images, and feelings about not just the product but the company itself and as a whole. By associating with, and projecting a narrative of beneficence towards Britain's most popular sport, they were seeking the generalised affections of millions of fans for their businesses as corporate entities.

Shirt sponsorship proved more controversial. Derek Dougan was chief executive of Southern League Kettering Town when they wore the moniker of Kettering Tyres on their shirts for the match against Bath City on 26 January 1976. This breached a ban imposed by the FA in 1972. Confronted by a fine of £1,000, Dougan backed down. But the stand had been made and a much wider rift was to become increasingly evident over the next decade, and not just in football. The old patrician culture of British institutions was being challenged by impatient, entrepreneurial people not prepared to let old-fashioned decencies and practices stand in the way of making money. The future of football and of the country would depend on the beneficence of business, and trust in brands rather than in public services or traditional loyalties.

Faced with pressure from clubs, the FA removed their prohibition on shirt sponsorship in 1977. The Football League limited the size of sponsors' names at a time when the BBC still had rules restricting commercial advertising in its broadcasts. Thus if you look through the photos in the programmes from the late 1970s, shirt advertising was little more than a discrete logo of the kit manufacturer: the club badge and traditional colours sufficed to define identity. Our Wimbledon v. Gillingham programme from 16 August 1977 (see Programme Spotlights 42) is the first one we have where a sponsor's logo is (just about) visible on the shirts in a black and white team photo of the Gillingham squad. On the left breast was the club emblem, the Kent horse, while at the top of the right breast, adjacent to the armpits of the players (all had crossed their arms), is a smidgen of white which would have been the name 'Bukta'. E.R. Buck and Sons had been founded in Stockport in 1879, doing a good trade in producing shorts for British soldiers in the First Boer War (1880–81). By 1884, the firm was producing kit for Nottingham Forest, and by the 1970s was long-established as a leading producer for many English and Scottish clubs.

The Wimbledon programme that day marks an historic occasion in that it was their first home game as a Football League club, having been elected to the league that summer with 27 votes, at the expense of Workington Town who received only 21 votes; the rest of the bottom four in the Fourth Division – Halifax Town, Southport and Hartlepool United – were all re-elected. Dave Bassett scored in Wimbledon's 3-1 win. Bassett became Wimbledon's manager in 1981 and by 1986/87 had taken the club into the top division. The programme includes an action picture of John Leslie scoring against Kettering Town at Plough Lane in a Southern League game near the end of the previous season. There was no Kettering Tyres sponsor blazoned on the visitors' shirts.

Programme Spotlights 42: The stripper skipper
20 August 1977, Wimbledon 3 Halifax Town 3, Football League Fourth Division

The programme for Wimbledon's first home game in the Football League. A crowd of 4,616 turned up, not far short of the Plough Lane ground's capacity, and what turned out to be their best home attendance of the season.

The cover picture is from their pre-season warm-up meeting with Colchester United. The logo on the dark shirts of Colchester was of Umbro, who, like Bukta, were a traditional English kit manufacturer based in the Manchester area. The company was taken over by Nike in 2007. Wimbledon's shirt sponsor was the German company Adidas. Their 'three stripes' logo in blue was placed discretely from the collar to the cuffs and down the side of the shorts.

Inside this programme there is a profile of Wimbledon's captain Dave Bassett. It relates an incident in a bar in Sorrento, Italy, where Bassett 'insisted on standing on a table and "treating" his patrons to an impromptu striptease'. This is testimony both to the 'Crazy Gang' tag that was given to Bassett's Wimbledon, and also to the activities of some British males abroad in the early period of package holidays.

The issue of shirt sponsorship was particularly tricky in Glasgow. The bitterness of their sectarian rivalry meant that Rangers and Celtic were not able to get sponsors until 1984, some years later than other clubs. A company backing one of the pair could expect no favours from fans of the other. In the end a Fife-based double-glazing firm, C.R. Smith, solved the problem by sponsoring them both.

The Anglo-Italian Cup was another innovative competition. It began in 1969, the idea of the leading Italian football intermediary of his day, Gigi Peronace, who had organised just about all the big transfers between British and Italian clubs at that time. The ostensible trigger was that Swindon Town, as League Cup winners, had been denied entry to the Inter-Cities Fairs Cup by UEFA because they were a Third Division side. The chance to provide games (and hence revenue) to clubs over the prolonged summer break due to the 1970 World Cup finals in Mexico was another factor. In that first season, the new competition featured six teams from each country. These were Middlesbrough, Sheffield Wednesday, Sunderland, Swindon Town, West Bromwich Albion and Wolverhampton Wanderers, and Fiorentina, Juventus, Lanerossi Vicenza, Lazio, Napoli and Roma. There were three groups of four teams each, two from England and two from Italy, playing each other home and away. As well as the then conventional points for winning (two) and drawing (one), points were also awarded for scoring goals. A more enduring innovation was that five substitutes could be named and two used.

The final involved the highest point-winners from each country, so Swindon travelled to Napoli for a 5pm kick-off on 28 March 1970 in front of a crowd of 55,000. The programme was in both languages and included a selective Anglo-Italian dictionary running alphabetically from 'Admission Prices – Biglietto D'Ingresso' to 'Trainer – Allenatore'. It did not include 'Abandoned – Abbandonato', 'Missiles – Missili' or 'Pitch Invasion – Invasione Del Campo'. When Swindon went 3-0 up in the 63rd minute, the Napoli fans responded with a fusillade of bottle and stones, which was enough for the local *polizia* to launch tear gas canisters. Wooden benches provided further ammunition for the disgruntled *tifosi*, who also managed two pitch invasions despite the moat that separated them from the pitch. After a linesman had been hit by a missile, in the 79th minute the Austrian referee, Paul Schiller, decided the game could no longer continue. Swindon, who still led 3-0, were awarded the trophy. Over 100 spectators were injured and 30 arrests were made. The Italian Football Federation sanctioned Napoli by closing their ground until the end of September.

By 1973, there was an official, 52-page well-illustrated *Anglo-Italian Cup Official Souvenir Handbook*, which we have a copy of. It includes an advert from British European Airways and Alitalia highlighting that there were 'over 288 flights between Britain and Italy every week' during the peak summer schedules, an indication of the booming package holiday industry as families from the UK indulged in Mediterranean sunshine rather than face the elements around the British shores. The president of the Football League, Len Shipman, wrote, 'With this country's entry to the Common Market, our links to the Continent are going to get stronger.'

As the 1970 final had demonstrated, reconciling the different football cultures was not so easy. Tellingly, the handbook also announced the inauguration of an award for good behaviour, 'The organisers will award a trophy and a large financial incentive to the club from each country which, in the opinion of a specially-formed committee has the best record of player and crowd behaviour.' It referenced 'the often disproportionate attention given to the rare examples of bad behaviour' in the three seasons of the competition. I have not been able to trace who won this new award, but it seems safe to say that it went neither to Hull City nor to Lazio. They met at Boothferry Park on 21 February 1973, where the home side won 2-1. The *Hull Daily Mail* reported that the game 'deteriorated into a rough and tumble that twice threatened to develop into a wholesale punch-up'. Police intervened after a fight broke out between a steward and Lazio's physio. The competition was abandoned after that season, although it had sporadic rebirths through to the mid-1990s.

Fan violence was impacting in Britain as well. The Motherwell v. Hearts programme on 12 December 1970 printed a letter from two young female Aberdeen supporters about crowd trouble they had suffered at away games. A few months later, when Hearts hosted Motherwell on 17 April 1971, there was a letter from a Hearts follower telling of how coins had been thrown at him and the windows of a bus had been smashed at away games.

Watching a match was becoming a threatening experience, especially for supporters of the visitors. West Ham's programme v. Everton on 16 February 1974 carried a formal warning from the FA, following 'the throwing of objects on to the field of play, during the match' against Hereford United on 5 January. Clubs were reacting, in particular by erecting fencing to prevent pitch invasions. The Manchester United home programme for their FA Cup third round tie with Middlesbrough in 1971 described how changes had been made to the Stretford End terrace because of fans throwing things. Nottingham Forest in their programme v. Carlisle United on 20 January 1973 noted, 'Our destructive friends (?) in the Trent End Stand were at it again last Tuesday evening when the railings, erected for their own protection and to afford comfort to all Trent End patrons, were damaged.' In most grounds, it was still possible to move from terraces at one end to the other, and there was no segregation of the fans: the Hearts v. Motherwell programme ahead of the Texaco Cup trip to Wolverhampton highlighted the fact that Molineux was a ground where such free movement was not possible.

Violence was not confined to the grounds. The *Football League Review* magazine, bound inside the Leeds United v. Derby County programme on 7 October 1972, quoted the leading article in an issue of the Everton programme by David Exall, the Merseyside club's promotions manager. It stated that 'the real "battles" take place on the way to and from matches', noting, 'Hooliganism and thuggery… two cancerous growths inside football's society, have reared their unsavoury heads again this season.' Exall's article reported that 'hundreds of pounds' worth of damage' had been done to the interior of the coach on which they were travelling from Birkenhead to the game at Norwich by 'a group of hooligans purporting to be supporters of Everton'. The vehicle had been rendered 'completely unserviceable'. He went on to predict prophetically that because standing on terraces 'give an anonymity that is ideal for the thugs… within the next decade we may be forced by legislation to provide seating only'. It was indeed a foretaste of things to come (see Chapter 13).

The mounting violence in Northern Ireland was much more serious, as the province descended into a form of civil war. The Troubles made their mark within football, with Northern Ireland playing their home game against England on 12 May 1973 at Goodison Park. In his message in the programme, the president of the Irish FA noted euphemistically that the match should have been played in Belfast, but had been switched 'due to the continuing unhappy circumstances in Northern Ireland'. The programme also contained action photos from Northern Ireland's 'home' World Cup encounter with Portugal two months earlier, which had been staged at Coventry City's ground, along with text noting that 'one of the newcomers, Martin O'Neill of Nottingham Forest had scored in the 1-1 draw'. O'Neill would go on to become a key part of Nottingham Forest's European Cup-winning side and also had a distinguished managerial career.

In contrast to Northern Ireland, Kilmarnock had gone out of their way to play in a country engulfed in a guerrilla war. There is a fleeting reference in the programme for their game against Hearts on 3 October 1970, 'The ball for today's game was donated by one of the many friends the football club made in Rhodesia... during the team's stay in Salisbury the players were accommodated in the homes of Scots people resident there.' Salisbury is now Harare, and the government of Southern Rhodesia had made its unilateral declaration of independence in 1965, with the intention of preserving rule by the white settlers. The Prime Minister was Ian Smith, the son of a Scottish settler. Economic sanctions had been imposed on the rebel state by the United Nations. Furthermore, the planned 1970 cricket tour to England by the whites-only team of apartheid South Africa had been cancelled due to the fear of demonstrations and disruptions. In this context, Kilmarnock's tour in the summer of 1970 could scarcely have been undertaken without some awareness of its political significance. The liberation war was being fought by two rival guerrilla movements, ZANU (backed by China) and ZAPU (supported by the USSR). Aside from the politics, Rhodesia was not a place to go for a holiday, yet Kilmarnock played eight matches on their trip.

Back in Great Britain, industrial conflict was impacting on football. The quadrupling of oil prices that came with the OPEC embargo after the Yom Kippur War in 1973 (from $3 a barrel to $12 by March 1974) was not anticipated when Esso were advertising the benefits of oil-fired central heating that came with Green Shield stamps on every gallon (a collection and cash redemption scheme popular at that time) in the Nottingham Forest v. Newcastle United programme in January 1971. The escalation in oil prices quickly ran through the economy, and trade unions responded by wage claims and threats of industrial action. In November 1973, the National Union of Mineworkers announced an overtime ban, which had the intended effect of reducing coal stocks. Coal-fired power stations were the major source of electricity in the UK at the time. The industrial action began on 12 November, and the Conservative government of Ted Heath immediately announced a national emergency to preserve coal supplies.

The impact on football was immediate in a way that would not be experienced again until the coronavirus shutdown of 2020. On Wednesday, 7 November Hibernian had played a goalless draw at home against Leeds United in the UEFA Cup, in the second leg of a second round tie, the teams having drawn 0-0 at Leeds. The match was played under the floodlights with a 7.45pm kick-off, and drew a crowd of over 36,000. It was refereed by Paul Schiller from Vienna, who had had the misfortune to officiate at the Napoli v. Swindon Town Anglo-Italian Cup Final. It again ended goalless after 120 minutes, with Leeds (at that stage unbeaten after 14 games in the English First Division) winning 5-4 on penalties. The outcome was controversial since, as the Hibernian programme for their next home game (against Dundee on 17 November 1973, kick-off 2pm) pointed out, Leeds manager Don Revie and coach Les Cocker were standing in the centre circle while the penalty kicks were being taken. UEFA dismissed Hibs' appeal. Fourteen days after Easter Road had been packed for their meeting with Leeds, Hibernian were kicking off against Rangers at 1.30pm in a home League Cup tie. Manager Eddie Turnbull began his column with, 'Everyone will find this an odd time to have a midweek match.' The following month, Prime Minister Edward Heath announced that from the new year commercial users of electricity would be restricted to three days' consecutive supply in any week. The lights were going out and the three-day week began on 1 January 1974.

In the Boxing Day programme for their home game with Sheffield United, Tommy Docherty, Manchester United's manager, commented, 'The economic troubles haven't helped football.' He went on to write, 'Playing during the week on an afternoon is a waste of time,' pointing to attendances of less than 20,000 at home games played by Arsenal and by Liverpool. A similar theme had been struck in the Hearts programme for the visit of Ayr United on 15 December. Manager Bob Seith began his column with, 'These are difficult times for football clubs. And with the extra problems of the weather causing havoc with fixtures and the power situation bringing the need for early kick-offs, in so many cases, it is very worrying.' Seith described how some clubs had managed to hire generators to power floodlights, and had enlisted people to clear pitches. However, the gates had slumped, 'under 3,000 at Motherwell on Wednesday and less than 4,000 at our own game at Methil [East Fife] last Saturday'. The Manchester United programme for the visit of Ipswich Town three days after Boxing Day was reduced from its usual 16 pages to eight 'due to current power restrictions'. It also notified fans that the government restrictions on lighting and heating meant that office hours would be pared back to 9.30am to 4.30pm. Similarly, when Manchester City met Stoke City at Maine Road on New Year's Day 1974, their programme had been reduced from the normal 24 pages to 16, 'Due to the power crisis and the necessary restrictions.'

Some clubs tried to cheer spirits with a joke or two. Nottingham Forest's Irish 'joke' in their programme v. Fulham on 10 November 1973 is indicative of the way that Irish people were routinely disparaged at a time when the British legacy within Ireland was being contested bloodily across the six counties of Northern Ireland and by bombs in London. 'Did you hear about the Irish referee who called the teams together and said "It looks as though it might get foggy later, so we will play extra time first"?' Forest had three players from Northern Ireland in their team that day: defender Liam O'Kane, and midfielders Tommy Jackson and Martin O'Neill. More bizarre is an item in our Peterborough United v. Leeds United cup tie programme from 26 January 1974 (see Programme Spotlights 43).

Programme Spotlights 43: More elastic needed

**26 January 1974, Peterborough United 1 Leeds United 4,
FA Cup fourth round**

This programme denotes a landmark in English football history as the first FA Cup game to have a sponsor. Perhaps not surprisingly that sponsor was a company whose entrepreneurialism and innovation also came with a touch of eccentricity. Frank Brierley started out as a barrow boy then grocer in Peterborough, and built a multi-million pound supermarket business. Key to his success was his introduction of what we now take for granted in supermarkets: checkouts with cashiers and electronically driven rubber belts. Before that, sales assistants stood behind counters and priced and packed the shopping in a time-consuming process. Checkouts existed in the USA, but the claim is made that Brierley introduced them to Britain. He would also address customers over a tannoy in his store in idiosyncratic fashion. Known as the 'pirate king', he flew the skull and crossbones above his stores.

The programme includes a page devoted to a competition devised by Brierley. Five pounds' worth of groceries for life were offered to the first person to fly across the River Nene from Brierley's store. Walter Cornelius is pictured as he 'plummeted into the water in front of 3,000 spectators' plus TV cameras and photographers. The programme tells of other stunts at the store, where 'girl pipers, fully grown elephants, chimpanzees and kangaroos' were listed as some of the attractions. In Brierley's Northampton store, an escapologist had got out of a straitjacket while suspended 30ft above traffic.

Just months after the cup tie, Brierley was in gaol for fiddling the books. After his death in 1999, his biographer, Richard Yates-Smith, said, 'He was a wide boy and a villain in the nicest possible way. He saw opportunities and took them.'

The wider 'economic troubles' came at a time when football clubs already had their own economic difficulties. West Ham made this clear to fans in their programme of 16 February 1974 v. Everton, 'Inflation of running costs, overheads, salaries etc. has made League soccer increasingly dependent on hard cash. There has been a vast change over the past decade.' The article went on to explain the financial link between ground advertising and TV coverage of games. The power cuts had ended floodlit games, which had become an important source of revenue from TV. It had also led to clubs experimenting by playing games on a Sunday afternoon, particularly in the lower leagues. For example, our programme for the Fourth Division clash between a relegation-threatened Workington Town and seventh-placed Torquay United has the details on the front cover, 'Sunday, 17 March 1974, Kick-Off 2.30pm'. It also mentioning the 'long and tedious journey' that their visitors had taken to the Borough Park ground from the Devonshire coast some 400 miles away.

There were silver linings in the clouds. Sunday football was a success. Bernard Halford, Manchester City's secretary, writing in their programme versus Derby County on 6 February 1974, began, 'Sunday soccer looks here to stay!' He added, 'The present emergency has brought something of a boom,' while suggesting the four-o'clock kick-offs could 'satisfy many factions, including the religious side'.

It had been 'the religious side' that was most forcefully opposed. The Lord's Day Observance Society was critical of the number of activities that over the decades invaded Sundays: cinemas, shopping, and sport including football. Halford's article sketched the kind of social changes (but also stereotypes) that were taking place and impacting on attendances, 'Fans have found it easier to go shopping with their wives, or stay indoors with a beer and an afternoon's sport on TV.' But it was more than a matter of couch potatoes. Men going shopping with their wives would indeed have seemed outlandish not that long before. The change reflected the growth of consumerism; more goods were affordable for more people, as reflected in the advertisements that programmes carried. In addition, gender roles were changing with the rise of feminism challenging male expectations about their leisure activities, and about their responsibilities within a household. Masculine understanding of dress and identity was also being redefined by the burgeoning fashion industry. Plymouth Argyle's programme against Tranmere Rovers at the start of the 1970/71 season carried a half-page advertisement in the back for Louis Boutique, 'Definitely Different...', with a large picture of a male mannequin displaying the autumn collection in their shop window.

Lifestyles were changing. Aspects of that transition are captured in the Nottingham Forest programmes in 1970/71 season. Our one for their fixture with West Ham United on 10 April 1971, for example (autographed incidentally by match referee Jim Finney, and somebody else whose signature is indecipherable), had a half-column advertisement for the Greater Nottingham Co-operative Society Ltd indicating where Rawhides, 'the leisure shoe for today's man', could be procured. The Co-op was still the go-to retailer for the many, many working-class households, though it was not branded as being for 'today's man'. So continuity and change there, but more interesting is the full-page spread on the first inside page. A company called Oak Tree Holdings with a Nottingham address offered in bold, black, capital letters, 'Confidential Cash, Bank Loans, Personal Overdrafts' to 'property owners with or without existing mortgage... or if you possess a life or endowment policy in operation over 2 years'. Money from £200 to £10,000 could be repaid monthly over periods of three, five or seven years. Borrow £200 over three years and you paid back £279. The temptation was pitched, 'Get a car at no deposit terms…. Use the money as you wish, no restrictions. Holiday, car, caravan – you name it you can have it. Don't waste time saving – it takes too long.' Hire purchase was already in wide use to purchase consumer goods on credit, and Barclaycard had been introduced into Britain in 1966, though at first not many outlets accepted credit cards. However, there was clearly a gap in the market, as the adverts in the Forest programmes show. 'Don't waste time saving' was the clarion call to a new age, rejecting not just the financial habits of mine and previous generations, but also many of their fundamental values, such as caution, deference, self-denial and a collective sense of modesty. It was an essential complement to the ascendency of brands and a culture rooted in relations to money, rather than to class or place. Those of us brought up in working-class households during the period of post-war austerity (see Chapter 2) had been taught, 'If you take care of the pennies, the pounds will take care of themselves.' We had an education, both formal and through daily experience, that imbued survival skills for a life of making do. Those skills were now not just redundant, but barriers to be erased.

Everton v. Blackpool towards the end of that same season had an advert offering 'everything for the DIY enthusiast' including sheds and garages. Even I, as a man who had not exactly excelled at woodwork in my school days (nothing ever seemed quite level or to fit snugly), was drawn in to some of these endeavours: not a shed or a garage that might have been a life-threatening undertaking, but a bit of painting and decorating in the tenement flat we bought when we moved to Edinburgh in 1971.

Hibernian programmes in 1975/76 (e.g. for their UEFA Cup game with Liverpool – which was defender Chris Lawler's last game for the visitors before transferring to Portsmouth) had adverts for Mediterranean holidays; our first one was in 1972 to Lido di Jessolo near Venice. There was also a regular advert for the Americana Discotheque that was 'open 7 days per week' in Edinburgh's Fountainbridge. Like many couples in their early 30s at that time, we were trying to cope with two young children in 1975, and somewhat removed from what is now called the evening economy; so I cannot report personally on the Americana, but I imagine that it had a different ambience to the Gorton and Openshaw Men's Club where the Manchester United players had held their fundraising dance in 1953 (see Chapter 5). Going out dancing in a night club seven nights a week would have been seen as sinful by many residents of Bible-black Presbyterian Edinburgh in the 1950s. In Torquay United v. Rotherham United on 6 April 1974, Torbay's self-proclaimed 'Greatest Nightspot', The Mermaid Inn in Paignton, was offering 'For the Younger Set – Fabulous Disco', as well as a nightly cabaret that went on until 1am. This was well after the bedtime of young parents or people working long shifts in tiring jobs, although the family and employment profile of regular readers of Torquay United's programmes may have been atypical of those in other parts of the country.

In other respects, there were still strong continuities between the early 1970s and the early 1960s. For example, as shown in Chapter 6, in mining areas the National Coal Board (NCB) would seek to recruit to the industry through placing advertisements in football programmes. 'The goal is coal, coal and more coal,' said the NCB in the 1971 Nottingham Forest v. West Ham programme referred to previously; nobody had heard of climate change or carbon reduction. Four seasons later, after the miners' industrial actions had won big pay rises and contributed to the fall of Ted Heath's government, the NCB through the Forest programmes exhorted readers to 'Join THE Winning Team! JOIN THE MEN IN MODERN MINING', pointing up vacancies at most local collieries and offering apprenticeships for boys under 18. However, the advertising slot previously taken by the Co-op was now filled by a local kitchen and bathroom company. The Oak Tree Holdings advert had also gone.

It seemed that not much had changed for the smaller clubs. Their programmes were still filled largely with advertisements from local, consumer-oriented businesses; pubs, cafes, plumbers, car sales, coach companies and so forth. However, increased television coverage of the bigger teams, along with rising affluence and car ownership and the expanding network of motorways, was creating a new level of mobility among football followers. As a result, clubs' fanbases were becoming de-localised. As an issue of *Football League Review* in 1970/71 put it, 'Wandering Fans Worry the Smaller Clubs'. The article told how the linking of the M5 and M6 had created almost 200 miles of continuous motorway from South Wales almost to Carlisle. It quoted Walsall's general manager, 'I have been told that there are quite a number of Walsall people who regularly travel to Manchester, leave their wives in the city for shopping, and go on to Old Trafford or Maine Road. They can be there in less than two hours on the Motorway.' Similar concerns were expressed by Chesterfield, Doncaster Rovers and Port Vale. Conversely, the better connectivity made travel to away matches easier, though as mentioned earlier in the case of Everton's trip to Norwich, this could also lead to fan violence. Carlisle United, more protected by their remoteness, were reported to be developing extra car parks in the hope of extending their catchment to Lancaster once the extension of the M6 reached the border city. They also appreciated the reduction in travel time to away games.

Care of the health of players was also changing. 'Much greater emphasis is now being placed on hygiene in club dressing rooms than ever before,' wrote Ken Smailes, secretary and treasurer of Nottingham Forest, in their programme for the visit of Orient on 2 December 1972. He went on to give an example: the previous week most of the players and staff had received their flu vaccinations. A 'medical unit' of a doctor and two nurses had been in attendance. 'No longer is this the "jungle juice" injected through a big needle, but a modern spray gun is used.'

Another change within the game was the arrival of more foreign players. 'A Danish international in the Football League is indeed a rarity,' observed the Nottingham Forest programme on 16 January 1971, referring to Preben Arentoft, whom visitors Newcastle United had signed from Greenock Morton in 1969. At the start of the 1970s, professional football in the UK was a game played almost exclusively by white men born in the UK or Ireland. The managers and trainers were equally homogeneous. Some clubs throughout the Football League usually included in their programme a photograph of the visitors' squad with their manager and his assistants. Looking through our editions from 1972/73, Fourth Division Torquay United's programmes for their games against Portsmouth, Newport County, Gillingham and Doncaster Rovers showed a combined number of 85 visiting players and staff, all of whom were white, and where birthplaces were identified in the pen portraits pages, the most exotic of them were Rhymney and Drumcondra. However, Torquay themselves did have one player of mixed race, the Cornwall-born Mike Trebilcock, who had joined that summer on a free transfer from Portsmouth. A photograph of him taking a throw-in was on the front of the programme for the game against his former club.

In the Third Division, the Chesterfield programme for 24 February 1973 features 16 white men in the strip of Notts County, their opponents that Saturday afternoon. County's city rivals Nottingham Forest were playing in the Second Division that season. Their programmes usually included visitor squad photos: Swindon Town's shows 14 faces, all white, Orient 17, Carlisle United 21. The programmes also had a picture of the Forest squad in an advertisement seeking to recruit agents for the club's Development Association; the photographs showed 20 players, all of them white. The only sign of change would have been easy to miss among the detail of the facts and figures pages. By the time of the 20 January 1973 game against Carlisle, one Viv Anderson had made nine appearances for Forest's Midlands Intermediate League side, and was listed at left-back in their FA Youth Cup team that had lost a third round tie to Sheffield United on 27 December 1972. In 1978, Anderson became the first black player to play for England. Forest's youthful scorer in that defeat was another future England international and European Cup winner, Tony Woodcock.

The First Division was just as insular and white. The visits of Chelsea, Leeds United and Coventry City to Old Trafford saw team photos that in all included 57 men, all of whom were white. When Oxford United came for a League Cup tie in September 1972 their photo in the United programme again depicted an all-white group of 20. Norwich City at Arsenal on Boxing Day 1972, and Derby County at Leeds on 7 October both featured squad photos showing 15 white players. The Leeds United players listed in the FA Cup Final programme at the end of that season were born in Leeds (two), Huddersfield, Doncaster, London, Willenhall (West Midlands), Eighton Banks (Gateshead), Stirling, Dundee, Glasgow and Dublin. The birthplaces of their triumphant underdog opponents that afternoon at Wembley were Sunderland, Ryhope (a village on the edge of Sunderland), Newcastle (three), Annfeld Plain (a village in County Durham), Burton, Nottingham, Northampton, and towns in Scotland: Ayr, Alexandria, Coatbridge, and Dunfermline.

The most notable black player of this period was Clyde Best. Though he did not appear when Nottingham Forest hosted West Ham United on 10 April 1971, he was listed among the pen portraits of the visitors. He was 'born in Bermuda where he played for Somerset F.C. and Bermuda Youth. Played twice for Bermuda in qualifying series for the 1970 World Cup. Had half a season with the Hammers in youth and reserve team games before signing pro' in April 1969. Toured USA with the senior side in 1969 and made his League debut v. Arsenal in August 1969.' The West Ham United v. Manchester United programme on 2 September 1972 has photos of him scoring the Hammers' first goal of the season with a header against Coventry City (see Programme Spotlights 44).

Programme Spotlights 44: Young, gifted and black

2 September 1972, West Ham United 2 Manchester United 2, Football League First Division

The picture section shows action shots from the Hammers' first home game of the season, which were displayed on page 12 of this programme. They are remarkable for the time in showing a black player. Clyde Best, seen scoring the only goal of that game, was a strong and quick striker. He had arrived from Bermuda in 1968, aged 17. He made his-first team debut against Arsenal in August 1969, and he went on to make another 220 appearances for West Ham. In 1971/72, he had been an ever-present in the 42 First Division games, scoring 17 goals. He stayed at Upton Park until 1975 when he moved on to play in the USA.

The manager who gave him his chance at West Ham was Ron Greenwood, who as England boss selected Viv Anderson to be the first black player to represent the national team. In his autobiography, Best wrote, 'I think most English clubs back then were naive and scared to give black players a chance. Some of the best players in the world – like Pelé and Eusebio – were black but in England we didn't get the same opportunities as we do now.'

Also in the Nottingham Forest programme against West Ham was full-back John Charles, though like Best he did not play that day, and indeed had been injured most of the previous season. Charles's father was a merchant seaman from Grenada, his mother was a white woman living in London's docklands area (long before Canary Wharf), and he was one of nine children. Readers of the programme were told that Charles was born in West Ham, had joined the club from school and became a pro in 1962. He had been an England youth cap, and had skippered the West Ham team that won the FA Youth Cup in 1963. However, the programme did not make the point that he had been the first black player to represent England at Under-18 level, or the first black to captain a major English club team winning an FA competition. Meanwhile, the Middlesbrough programme for 24 September 1977 (v. Ipswich Town) carried an advertisement for a one-night-only appearance at Club Fiesta ('Cleveland's Top Nightspot') of *The Black and White Minstrel Show*. It involved white performers blacking up and acting out white stereotypes of black people. The fact that it ran on BBC television for 20 years until 1978 testified to its popularity, despite consistent criticism from anti-racist campaigners for most of that period. The shrill racism from the terraces that black players faced was underpinned by a set of cultural assumptions that were casually accepted.

Things were only slightly different elsewhere. A Borussia Mönchengladbach side boasting several classy players, including Bonhof, Heynckes, Netzer, Vogts and Wimmer, visited Aberdeen for a UEFA Cup first round tie in 1972/73. Again their team photo features only white faces, 24 of them. However, among their numbers were the Danish international Henning Jensen and an Israeli centre-back Shmuel Rosenthal. In contrast, in Portugal, which at that time still retained colonial power in Angola and in Mozambique, teams had players from more diverse ethnic backgrounds than those in the UK. Hibernian's Cup Winners Cup opponents on 27 September 1972 were Sporting Lisbon, who included in their squad the Brazilian Canothilo Wagner, Hector Yazalde from Argentina, and Carlos Manaca who had 'signed recently from Angola'. There was also the black, Portuguese-born striker Fernando Nelson, and Joaquim Dinis, another black player, who had been born in Luanda but was a Portuguese international. Sporting's manager was former England international Ronnie Allen, who hailed from Stoke-on-Trent, but was only in his job for that season before swapping life in Lisbon for Walsall. In the next round, Hibs faced FC Besa from Albania: the programme is conspicuous for the total absence of any information on the Albanian players except for a list of names. This is not surprising, since Albania was the most closed society in Europe, and it seems safe to assume that all their squad were natives of the country, and wise enough to swear eternal loyalty to Enver Hoxha, Albania's supreme leader from 1944 until his death in 1985.

John Charles, Clyde Best and the few other black players trying to make a career in the British game in the 1970s were regularly subjected to racist abuse from the terraces, and their courage and determination to succeed in a white man's work environment should be admired. Their numbers grew as the decade went on, and one game in particular was a watershed moment in establishing black players at the highest level of the English game. On 30 December 1978, I took my son Euan, then a seven-year old, to Old Trafford for the visit of West Bromwich Albion. It was a game we both remember vividly all these years later, and watching highlights on YouTube shows why.

Albion's 5-3 win was thoroughly deserved, and would have been more but for some brilliant saves by Gary Bailey in the United goal. Alongside a young Bryan Robson, the Albion team photo had three black players, who would become famous by the final whistle. They were right-back Brendon Batson, centre-forward Cyrille Regis and winger Laurie Cunningham. Despite being booed when he got the ball, Cunningham in particular illuminated that winter afternoon with his silky pace, dribbles and passes. The programme notes had given warning of what was to come, highlighting 'the exciting attacking skills of their coloured forwards'. The mention that they were 'coloured' highlighted the novelty of such players being stars. The trio, who became called the 'Three Degrees', had got in to top-level football the hard way. Regis had been born in French Guiana and was four when his family moved to London in 1962. In May 1977, he was signed from the Isthmian League club Hayes, on the recommendation of Ronnie Allen who by then was Albion's chief scout. Cunningham, born in London to a Jamaican family in 1956, had made it into the league side at Orient in 1974/75, signing for West Brom in 1977. Batson had been born in Grenada and arrived in England as a nine-year-old in 1962. He made ten appearances for the Gunners before being transferred to Cambridge United in 1974. Albion signed him four years later.

If football was becoming slightly more ethnically diverse, one thing that had not changed during the 1970s was its sexism. Everton's programme of 24 April 1971 against Blackpool carried a photo of Jessie Milne, secretary to the club's secretary. The caption told how the directors had given her a pearl necklace to mark 25 years' service. It noted that she joined straight from school and in those days had been one of the few women working with a league club. The 1973/74 Hearts home programmes included an advertisement headed in bold capital letters 'Men wanted for defence'. It was seeking volunteers for the Royal Army Medical Corps, to become 'Medical Assistants, Cooks, Technicians, Drivers, etc'. After providing further details, the last line adds, almost as an after-thought, 'Why not bring your girl-friend? She can join the Queen Alexandra's Royal Army Nursing Corps.' The programme for the postponed Halifax Town versus Doncaster Rovers meeting on 23 December 1978 carried an advertisement urging readers to 'Treat your wife to a day at Harvey's', which was 'Halifax's Leading Independent Department Store', offering 'Fashions, Fashion Accessories, Underwear, Corsets'. Come on, lass, get your coat on and I'll take you to buy a pair of corsets at Harvey's.

In summary, the decade saw British football adapting only slowly and with difficulty to wider changes. Going to a match, as I did regularly, now involved using decimal coins to buy a programme and taking a transistor radio to keep up with other scores, but was still an immersion in a world that was overwhelmingly male, white and British. The terraces, packed dangerously tight for big games and now behind security fences to prevent pitch invasions, belonged to working-class people, and in particular to adolescent boys and young men who might be attracted by advertisements to buy Watney's beer and cigarettes and to seek a career in mining or to join the armed forces, despite the risks to their health or of getting shot or blown up while serving in Northern Ireland.

In the same stadia where previous generations had stood to support their local team, I could still recognise my younger self from the late 1950s among the crowd, though the new generation were watching players with extravagantly permed hair, and were now more fashion-conscious, more violent, and living in households that had colour TVs and other home comforts and even owned cars, usually being paid for through hire purchase schemes. Companies like Oak Park Holdings had grasped the current of change and were about to capitalise upon it.

A new kind of figure was emerging. Within football, or attached to it, were men like Derek Dougan or Frank Brierley who had made money by being entrepreneurial, and were prepared to disregard the rules set down for them by bureaucrats or other traditional figures of authority. While racism and sexism remained entrenched and largely unchallenged within football, taboos such as saving up to buy something, or not playing on a Sunday, or forbidding shirt advertising, were being swept away. As Bill Hiddelston had realised years before, football was really a business, and business was about to assert itself in the culture and running of Britain.

Programmes cited in Chapter 10 that are in the collection:

- 28 March 1970, Napoli 0 Swindon Town 3 (match abandoned after 79 minutes), Anglo-Italian Cup Final
- 5 August 1970, Hull City 1 Manchester United 1 (after extra time, Manchester United won 4-3 on penalties), Watney Cup semi-final
- 8 August 1970, Derby County 4 Manchester United 1, Watney Cup Final
- 15 August 1970, Plymouth Argyle 0 Tranmere Rovers 1, Football League Third Division
- 3 October 1970, Kilmarnock 3 Heart of Midlothian 0, Scottish League First Division
- 12 December 1970, Motherwell 1 Heart of Midlothian 2, Scottish League First Division
- 2 January 1971, Manchester United 0 Middlesbrough 0, FA Cup third round
- 16 January 1971, Nottingham Forest 2 Newcastle United 1, Football League First Division
- 6 March 1971, Hibernian 1 Dundee 0, Scottish Cup fifth round
- 10 March 1971, Hibernian 2 Morton 4, Scottish League First Division
- 20 March 1971, Hibernian 1 St. Johnstone 2, Scottish League First Division

- 10 April 1971, Nottingham Forest 1 West Ham United 0, Football League First Division
- 14 April 1971, Heart of Midlothian 1 Wolverhampton Wanderers 3, Texaco Cup Final first leg
- 17 April 1971, Heart of Midlothian 0 Motherwell 1, Scottish League First Division
- 24 April 1971, Everton 0 Blackpool 0, Football League First Division
- 3 May 1971, Wolverhampton Wanderers 0 Heart of Midlothian 1, Texaco Cup Final second leg
- 22 September 1971, Hibernian 1 Falkirk 0, Scottish League Cup quarter-final
- 16 August 1972, Torquay United 1 Portsmouth 2, League Cup first round
- 30 August 1972, Manchester United 0 Chelsea 0, Football League First Division
- 2 September 1972, West Ham United 2 Manchester United 2, Football League First Division
- 9 September 1972, Manchester United 0 Coventry City 1, Football League First Division
- 9 September 1972, Torquay United 2 Newport County 2, Football League Fourth Division
- 12 September 1972, Manchester United 3 Oxford United 1, League Cup second round replay
- 13 September 1972, Aberdeen 2 Borussia Mönchengladbach 3, UEFA Cup first round first leg
- 27 September 1972, Hibernian 6 Sporting Lisbon 1, European Cup Winners' Cup first round second leg
- 7 October 1972, Torquay United 0 Gillingham 0, Football League Fourth Division
- 7 October 1972, Leeds United 5 Derby County 0, Football League First Division
- 11 October 1972, Torquay United 1 Doncaster Rovers 0, Football League Fourth Division

- 21 October 1972, Nottingham Forest 2 Swindon Town 2, Football League Second Division
- 25 October 1972, Hibernian 7 FC Besa 1, European Cup Winners' Cup second round first leg
- 2 December 1972, Nottingham Forest 2 Orient 1, Football League Second Division
- 23 December 1972, Manchester United 1 Leeds United 1, Football League First Division
- 26 December 1972, Arsenal 2 Norwich City 0, Football League First Division
- 20 January 1973, Nottingham Forest 2 Carlisle United 1, Football League Second Division
- 24 February 1973, Chesterfield 0 Notts County 2, Football League Third Division
- 5 May 1973, Leeds United 0 Sunderland 1, FA Cup Final
- 12 May 1973, Northern Ireland 1 England 2, Home International Championship
- 7 November 1973, Hibernian 0 Leeds United 0 (after extra time), Leeds won 5-4 on penalties, UEFA Cup second round second leg
- 10 November 1973, Nottingham Forest 3 Fulham 0, Football League Second Division
- 17 November, 1973, Hibernian 2 Dundee 1, Scottish League First Division
- 21 November 1973, Hibernian 0 Rangers 0, Scottish League Cup quarter-final second leg
- 15 December 1973, Heart of Midlothian 0 Ayr United 1, Scottish League First Division
- 26 December 1973 Manchester United 1 Sheffield United 2, Football League First Division
- 29 December 1973, Manchester United 2 Ipswich Town 0, Football League First Division
- 1 January 1974, Manchester City 0 Stoke City 0, Football League First Division

- 26 January 1974, Peterborough United 1 Leeds United 4, FA Cup fourth round
- 6 February 1974, Manchester City 1 Derby County 0, Football League First Division
- 16 February 1974, West Ham United 4 Everton 3, Football League First Division
- 17 March 1974, Workington Town 3 Torquay United 1, Football League Fourth Division
- 6 April 1974, Torquay United 3 Rotherham United 0, Football League Fourth Division
- 17 September 1975, Hibernian 1 Liverpool 0, UEFA Cup first round first leg
- 26 October 1974, Nottingham Forest 1 Bristol Rovers 0, Football League Second Division
- 16 August 1977, Wimbledon 3 Gillingham 1, League Cup first round second leg
- 20 August 1977, Wimbledon 3 Halifax Town 3, Football League Fourth Division
- 24 September 1977, Middlesbrough 1 Ipswich Town 1, Football League First Division
- 23 December 1978, Halifax Town v. Doncaster Rovers (postponed), Football League Fourth Division
- 30 December 1978, Manchester United 3 West Bromwich Albion 5, Football League First Division

Chapter 11

A Slum Game

THE 16-PAGE programme for Scunthorpe United's home Fourth Division game against York City on 10 March 1979 speaks of a Britain that would have been familiar in any previous decade covered by this book. The cover page in the then-red and white club colours has an image of two players competing for a header, the club badge (a shield with a white five-link chain horizontal across the middle of the plain red background), and in the top right-corner 'The Iron'. Similar to several other clubs, that nickname reflected the town's economic base. The origins of the iron and steel industry, and the growth of the town in what was a rural area, lay back in the mid-19th century. By the time of York's visit, three main iron and steel works had been nationalised and consolidated, as part of the British Steel Corporation. Some 20,000 people earned their living in these Scunthorpe furnaces.

The advertisers in the match programme, while not including a local candlestick maker, did have a family butcher offering 'the BEST in Quality Meats at Reasonable Prices', and Cyril Smith whose shops provided 'Home Baking and Provisions'. There were also the usual local hotels, petrol stations, printers, and a wince-inducing pun, 'See Naples and

Die – C. Nottingham and Buy at Ashby and Scunthorpe Markets', though just what was C. Nottingham's line of business was not disclosed. Scunthorpe Borough Council had a half-page advertising their Baths Ballroom, where 'Monday Night is Cabaret Night', an enticing prospect for an otherwise quiet night of the week.

You have to look carefully at the small print on the back page to see what makes this programme a harbinger of political, economic, social and cultural change that would restructure Britain, and football too. Under the listing of the teams, the referee and the names of the linesmen, and above the space in which to write in the score, scorers and attendance it simply says, 'Match Ball Donor: MICHAEL BROWN, Prospective Conservative Candidate'.

The Brigg and Scunthorpe constituency was a traditionally Labour seat. The sitting Labour MP had a majority of 6,742. A few weeks after the York City game, in the May 1979 General Election and after three recounts, Michael Brown captured the seat for the Conservatives, with a majority of 486. At 27, he was the youngest MP in Westminster. He was the first Conservative to represent Scunthorpe since Sir Berkeley Sheffield, the great grandfather of Samantha Cameron (wife of David Cameron, Prime Minister from 2010 to 2016) and 6th Baronet of Normanby Hall, who had lost the seat in 1929.

Intriguingly, a Cyril Nottingham, Mayor of Scunthorpe, standing as Democratic Labour after being expelled from the Labour Party, polled 2,042, while M. Nottingham (Independent) polled 123. The relation between these two candidates, and between Cyril and the 'See Naples and Die' advert is unknown to me. What is known is that Democratic Labour was formed after Dick Tavern, the pro-Europe Labour MP for Lincoln, was asked to stand down by his constituency party. Lincoln was the only other seat contested by Democratic Labour, but their formation anticipated the split in the

Labour Party that came when the Social Democratic Party was founded in 1981. Much more significant was Brown's victory, the kind of result that put Margaret Thatcher into 10 Downing Street with a majority of 43 seats.

Some of Scunthorpe's steel workers would have been on the terraces for that game against York in March: by December they were on strike. British Steel had decided to shut down plants and sack workers across the UK. Two of the three Scunthorpe plants were to close. The strike lasted for three months and was followed by the closures, with 10,000 people made redundant in a single day. Unemployment in the town reached 25 per cent. Brown was certain that there was 'no alternative', as he later wrote in *The Independent* on 8 April 2013. He was an ardent Thatcherite, an unswerving supporter of the apartheid government in South Africa, and a vocal Eurosceptic. With changes in constituencies and their boundaries, he continued to be an MP until the 1997 General Election. He endured scandal when the *News of the World* in May 1994 published pictures of him on holiday in Barbados with a 20-year-old gay man. He subsequently 'came out', but was also later exposed as a paid lobbyist for tobacco interests. In 2019, he joined the Brexit Party.

Might Michael Brown's ball sponsorship have helped him win a few votes? That small item in the Scunthorpe United programme from all those years ago can be extrapolated and projected to much wider events that followed. In its small way, that match ball set rolling not just a game of Fourth Division football, but the history of the next 40 years and more. The post-1945 Britain discussed in previous chapters, which was fraying in the 1970s as Chapter 10 showed, was swept away. An ideology previously seen to be extreme became normalised, and with it the economic geography of Great Britain (which was written in the location of Football League and Scottish League clubs) was changed fundamentally, as

London prospered as a global finance hub while coal mines, steel works and factories closed.

Programme Spotlights 45: The Falklands War Cup Final

22 May 1982, Queens Park Rangers 1 Tottenham Hotspur 1 (after extra time), FA Cup Final

The programme for the 101st FA Cup Final is a handsome 64-page production with plenty of coloured photos of players and match action. The game was the fourth all-London final in 15 years, and Spurs became the first club to reach the finals of both the League Cup and the FA Cup in the same season. It was QPR's first FA Cup Final.

The game was goalless at 90 minutes before Glenn Hoddle put Spurs ahead and Terry Fenwick equalised. Spurs won the replay 1-0, through a Hoddle penalty after six minutes.

This was the Falklands War Cup Final. British troops had landed on East Falkland on 21 May. Although Ossie Ardiles had returned to Argentina, his compatriot Ricardo Villa was listed in the Spurs starting 11 in the programme to wear the number seven shirt. However, Villa decided not to play because of the war. Villa was not listed in the team sheet in the programme for the replay the following Thursday, though the reason for his absence was not explained.

Britain captured the Falkland Islands from Argentina in 1833 and made them a British colony in 1892. Argentina invaded the islands on 2 April 1982, the day before the FA Cup semi-final between Tottenham Hotspur and Leicester City at Villa Park. Britain assembled a fleet of 30 warships to retake the islands, a task finally completed on 14 June 1982.

The Argentine internationals Ossie Ardiles and Ricardo Villa had joined Spurs in 1978, after Argentina's triumph in the World Cup of that year, and became cult figures after helping the club to win the FA Cup in 1981. While a banner at Villa Park read 'Argentina can keep the Falklands, we'll keep Ossie', the tide of revanchist English nationalism unleashed by the war ensured that Spurs' Argentinian stars were given a hostile reception, including from some of their own fans. The highlights on YouTube show Ardiles being booed from the moment he entered the field and every time he touched the ball. Ardiles had an assist for Spurs first goal in a 2-0 victory. The next day he returned to Argentina, ostensibly for pre-World Cup training. The 1982 FA Cup Final programme (see Programme Spotlights 45) had him in the team photo, but not in the profiles of players. The feature article about the Spurs team referred to Ardiles's return to his homeland and commented, 'Spurs were left wondering whether he would be back for the climax to their season... whether, indeed he would ever play for them again. Was that little wave, as he left the field on semi-final day, his sad farewell to British football? Let us hope not.' Ardiles went on loan to Paris Saint-Germain for 1982/83, but when Dundee United hosted Spurs in a testimonial for goalkeeper Hamish McAlpine on 17 August 1983, Ossie was back, with the match programme merely noting that he had returned after 'a spell' with the French club.

The cultural and political significance of the Falklands War has resonated through the decades that have followed. The ambience of retreat from Empire and of national decline with which I had grown up, and which was made stark by Hungary's 6-3 and 7-1 demolitions of England in 1953/54 (Chapter 4), was rolled back. I could only stare in disbelief at TV news footage of bishops blessing gunboats ready to sail to the South Atlantic, the sort of thing that might have been a sketch in *Monty Python's Flying Circus* a decade earlier. Though Argentina's military were relatively less formidable opponents than their footballers, the victory rekindled a sense of national superiority over 'foreigners'. What had started as a debacle with the arrival of Argentinian salvage workers on the undefended South Georgia Island, and the consequent resignation of the UK Foreign Secretary, ended in triumph for the Conservative government of Margaret Thatcher, with a resounding victory in the 1983 General Election.

Football soon became part of a wide-ranging assault on the institutions, identity and culture of working-class people. By March 1985 Britain's striking coal miners, like the Argentinian occupation of the Falklands, had been defeated. A couple of months later, a *Sunday Times* editorial described football as 'a slum sport watched by slum people in slum stadiums'. On 16 May 1985, Chelsea played Glasgow Rangers in a hastily arranged friendly to raise funds for victims of the fire at the Bradford City v. Lincoln City Third Division match the previous Saturday. It attracted fewer than 8,000 spectators. The eight-page programme, printed with a black cover page, says, 'By attending this match and buying a programme, you have proved that the spirit of goodwill exists still in a sport that has suffered more than its fair share of bad publicity in recent months.' Discussing 'the tragedy at Bradford City last Saturday', it reported soberly that 'people are still missing and it seems certain that the number of dead will rise as the days go by'. In the end, 56 fans lost their lives.

A public inquiry into the fire was hastily convened the following month, presided over by a High Court judge, Sir Oliver Popplewell. No lawyers represented the families of the victims. Andrew Collins QC, counsel for the inquiry, pointed the finger of blame at the fans who allegedly failed to move quickly from the stand when instructed by the police to do so. The inquiry was not told that there had been at least eight fires in premises owned by, or related to, the then Bradford City chairman, Stafford Heginbotham. The cause of the fire was attributed to an accident, a dropped cigarette, though that has been challenged. The West Yorkshire police did not investigate the possibility of criminality.

Popplewell also considered the question of seating. His report observed that football fans 'wish to stand, apparently, because there is for them a special atmosphere associated with being on the terraces. If seating is provided for them they may well tip back the seats and stand in front of them; then stand on the seats; and finally rip up the seats and use them as weapons.' This indicates how officialdom viewed those of us who were on the terraces in the 1980s. Things were about to get worse.

On 29 May 1985, between the fire and the public inquiry, Liverpool faced Juventus in the 30th European Cup Final at the Heysel Stadium in Brussels, when 39 people lost their lives and 600 were injured. The multi-lingual programme for the match noted that the stadium had hosted many high-profile encounters. 'To ensure that the cup final proceeds in an atmosphere worthy of the occasion,' the programme appealed to fans not to bring bottles into the stadium, throw any objects, or encroach upon the pitch at any time. Supporters were asked to 'keep their expressions of joy or disappointment within the limits of normal good sporting behaviour, help the stadium security officials in carrying out their duties', and 'prevent an unruly minority from spoiling the enjoyment of the majority'. There was no mention of the fact that the stadium was 55 years old, had been poorly maintained and was in a dilapidated condition. The crumbling venue provided a ready supply of stones to use as missiles: many Juve supporters were in an enclosure for Belgians separated from Liverpool fans only by chicken wire. When some Liverpool fans broke through, the Juve followers were pushed up against a wall which collapsed. The game was eventually played and decided by a Michel Platini penalty.

That evening I was in Bratislava, nearing the end of a two-week cultural exchange visit organised by the British Council, which had enabled me to visit urban planners in Prague and Brno and then in Slovakia. A thunderstorm raged as I returned to my official guest house just in time for the kick-off. On black-and-white television and with a commentary in Czech, I could scarcely comprehend the images I saw. Instead of football, there was turmoil and tragedy. It was clear that there was a serious situation. Late in the night the game was finally played, though it was only when I got home a couple of days later that the full scale of the tragedy became known to me: English language news was not accessible in the Warsaw Pact countries in those days and even telephoning was difficult.

Prime Minister Margaret Thatcher told the Football Association to withdraw English clubs from European competitions and two days later UEFA banned them anyway. The Charity Shield programme for the showpiece pre-season meeting of league champions Everton, bolstered by new signing Gary Lineker, and FA Cup winners Manchester United, made no reference to the events at the Heysel, nor to the ban that prevented both clubs from competing in the new season's European competitions.

Further tragedy was to follow. The 1987 FA Cup semi-final between Coventry City and Leeds United was played at Hillsborough. In the match programme, Sheffield Wednesday's chairman Herbert McGee, waxed lyrical about the improvements that he and his board of directors had made to the ground, making it what he claimed was a 'Perfect Setting' for the big occasion. He boasted how, since he joined the board in 1973, they had toiled to make improvements, 'Even in our terrible times we never neglected it.' A roof had been constructed over the Kop end, an event so grand that the Queen had attended to unveil a plaque at its opening. Below his article, and spread across two pages, was a pitch-level colour picture showing part of a seated stand and part of the covered Kop, complete with its crush barriers and metal fencing to stop fans on the terrace getting on to the pitch. In contrast, there was no metal fence in front of the stand. The last words at the bottom of the back page of the programme were 'Have a Safe Journey Home'.

Events on this occasion should have alerted the authorities to the dangers that would bring tragedy when Liverpool met Nottingham Forest there two years later. The Leeds fans were allocated the Leppings Lane End, Coventry the Kop end. The game was played on a Sunday and scheduled to kick-off at 12.15pm; however congestion at the turnstiles resulted in a 15-minute delay. The South Yorkshire Police blamed fans turning up late, so they could maximise drinking time before entering the ground. Once inside, the Leeds fans headed for the tunnel leading to the central pens behind the goal, which were already tightly packed. There were surges, crushing and no escape from the pens unless you could be lifted over the fence and on to the track behind the goal, or for those at the back to climb up to the seating above the packed pens. It was a rehearsal for a disaster.

In an exciting game, in which Leeds led, then Coventry, before a Leeds equaliser and extra time, Cyrille Regis (see Chapter 10) played a significant role in the winning goal, taking the Midlands club to Wembley after a 3-2 scoreline. The extra time prolonged the squeeze. South Yorkshire Police's report after the game did not mention the overcrowding: there were only plans for monitoring overcrowding at the Kop end. Two years later, 96 Liverpool fans were killed and over 700 injured in the Leppings Lane End at the semi-final with Nottingham Forest at Hillsborough. While the blame for the disaster would be contested for decades, there was immediate recognition that the practice of fencing spectators in had contributed to the crushing that killed so many.

The next Saturday, 22 April 1989, my son Euan and I went to watch Heart of Midlothian play Aberdeen in a Scottish

Premier League game, standing as usual on the open terrace behind metal fences separating us from the pitch, though there were no pens dividing the terrace into sections. Fans hung their scarves on this fence in a tribute to those who had died at Hillsborough, and as a gesture of solidarity. In his column in the programme, Hearts chairman Wallace Mercer mourned the loss of life, while reassuring readers that 'safety measures are operated as standard practice – this does not seem to have been the case in Sheffield'. Mercer expressed a wish to see 'a further reduction in fences at Tynecastle'. The same programme carried a one-page feature on 'The caring face of football', promoting the work of the Football Grounds Improvement Trust 'to provide modern facilities and comfort for all football spectators'.

New technology was introduced to manage crowd behaviour. In the summer of 1988, Mrs Thatcher told the FA and Football League that a compulsory scheme would be introduced from the start of the 1989/90 season that would require away fans to carry identity cards and present these to gain admission to matches. It would require computer technology which the clubs would have to pay for. In the end the idea was dropped when the Taylor Report into the Hillsborough tragedy argued that ID cards, by extending the time it took to pass through turnstiles, could cause more problems than they would solve.

The Queens Park Rangers programme for their FA Cup fifth round second replay with Blackpool on 26 February 1990 has a short feature on closed-circuit television, informing readers that CCTV was now installed in every Football League ground, and at more than 110 British grounds in all. 'The cameras have a range of 150 metres and immediate close-up prints can be produced. Within minutes of an incident offenders can be identified and arrested with film made available as evidence in court.' This step towards intensive surveillance of football fans was made possible by money from The Football Trust, which in turn got its money from Spot the Ball competitions run by the big football pools companies.

Millwall's programme for the visit of Manchester City on 7 April 1990 even demonstrated the use of CCTV. Reproducing photographs courtesy of *The Times*, highlighting in a circle miscreants in a crowd, the programme explained, 'Three minutes before the interval, a bottle was thrown towards the opposing side's goalkeeper. The incident was captured by the CCTV system and 57 seconds later the police had arrested the offender. By the half-time whistle, he had been led away for questioning, charged and subsequently pleaded guilty at the court hearing.'

While stadia and facilities may have been allowed to deteriorate, and then given intensive security measures, programmes were being given a makeover to fit into the emergent consumer society. They became big and glossy, with more pictures and colour, and they cost more. From 1954 until 1962, the year in which Spurs retained the trophy by overcoming Burnley, FA Cup Final programmes had 20 pages, only two pages more than in the days of paper rationing. Then from 1963 until 1975 they were 24 pages with the exception of the Leeds v. Sunderland final of 1973 which was 32 pages. Manchester United v. Southampton in 1976 ran to 28 pages, but the following year for United v. Liverpool, and for the next two seasons, the programme was 48 pages. Arsenal v. West Ham in 1980 was 52 pages, and by the following season the programme was 64 pages. It stayed at 64 until 1985 when it was scaled back to 60 pages, though the pages were much larger, and the price reached £1 for the first time (in 1984, the programme had cost 80 pence). That format lasted until 1988 when Liverpool v. Wimbledon was only 52 pages. That game was notable for the first time a penalty had been missed in an FA Cup Final; John Aldridge had his shot saved by Dave Beasant. However the price for the 1986 Everton v. Liverpool game was £1.50, and then the Coventry City v. Spurs programme in 1987 was £2, and there was an 'Official Match Day Magazine' for another £1.50. Then came the escalation – 1989's final between Everton and Liverpool had a 128-page programme costing £3; Crystal Palace v. Manchester United in 1990 was 116 pages, and still £3. In real terms, the one shilling charged in 1962 would have amounted to about 45 pence, allowing for the general rate of inflation in the UK over that period. Thus the £3 charged amounted to a steep price increase, though part of that would have reflected the better quality and greater length. See Programme Spotlights 46.

Programme Spotlights 46: Place branding
5 May 1962, Burnley 1 Tottenham Hotspur 3, FA Cup Final
12 May 1990, Crystal Palace 3 Manchester United 3 (after extra time), FA Cup Final

The design, structure and number of pages (20) of FA Cup Final programmes remained unchanged from 1954 through to this 1962 edition. Major changes came in the 1980s. The programme for this 1990 final was 116 pages, all in glossy colour. The size of the programme was transformed. The 1962 one measured 23.5cm (9.25in in those days) by 15.25cm (6in). The 1990 one is 29.85cm by 20.95cm. The size and bulk of the 1990 programme makes it effectively impossible to fold and put in a pocket: it requires a briefcase to carry it around! The centre pages with the team sheets fold out to provide a near double-page team photo of each squad. There are more articles of course, but also many more pages of advertisements.

Another notable change is that the Empire Stadium had become 'Wembley – Venue of Legends', whereas for the 1982 final (see Programme Spotlights 45) it was just 'Wembley Stadium'. This transition signifies both the demise of empire and a more sophisticated approach to marketing, with the branding of the stadium as a place defined by historic events and enduring memories. In 1962 the 'Final Tie' suggests one more in a long sequence of games, but by connecting it to those preceding it the uniqueness is diluted. By 1990, the words 'Cup Final' stand out: this is an occasion, a drama to remember. To this end the image of the cup itself is used, the antique silverware reinforcing the message of history being made that very day, by linking it to the dramatic photos of the four players, two of whom are captured as if lifting the trophy, another iconic image of past cup finals. The black background heightens the visual impact of the words and pictures. The verticality of the design also fits with the dimensions of this large programme.

Through the programme you become part of the story, and part of the brand. In contrast the 1962 edition, with its three horizontal bands and aerial view of the stadium, keeps the reader at a distance, inviting only awe at the scale of Wembley, but stripping out any sense of engagement with players, trophy or place. It defines a more hierarchical relationship between an organisation and fans, rather than between a company/brand and customers/brand followers. Football, and the FA Cup Final in particular, had become a part of the nascent 'experience economy'.

The changing composition of the First Division over the 1980s mirrored the changes in England's economic geography during that decade as the industrial areas and mining towns of the north suffered serious declines in well-paid jobs, while London and the south-east boomed on the back of the de-regulation of the financial industry. In 1979/80, 14 of the 22 clubs in the top division were from the north or the Midlands. These were the four from Liverpool and Manchester plus Bolton Wanderers, four from the West Midlands (Aston Villa, Coventry City, Wolverhampton Wanderers and West Bromwich Albion), Nottingham Forest and Derby County from the East Midlands, then Stoke City, Middlesbrough and Leeds United. London had only three representatives: Tottenham, Arsenal and Crystal Palace. The remainder were scattered across the south: Bristol City, Southampton, Brighton and Hove Albion, Ipswich Town and Norwich City. A decade later, the top division had been reduced to 20 teams, and had eight London sides, the previous three having been joined by Queens Park Rangers, West Ham United, Millwall, Charlton Athletic and Chelsea. Southampton and Norwich were still there and had been joined by Luton Town. There were no First Division clubs north of Manchester, and while Sheffield Wednesday were there, Bolton, Stoke, Leeds, Middlesbrough, Wolverhampton and West Brom had all been relegated.

Perhaps the clearest indication of the direction that football and Britain's economy and society had travelled in the 1980s is to be found in the Scotland v. Argentina programme from 28 March 1990, a match played under the lights at Hampden, which had changed little from my first visit in 1968. An advertisement from the Training Agency urged readers to 'Get your business in shape for a brighter future'. It went on to ask about 'the challenges of the 1990s', which included 'How to recruit staff when there are fewer school leavers?' Even more telling was an advert in the same programme for the Enterprise Allowance Scheme. It read, 'Be Your Own Boss. Unemployed? Want to be your own boss? On the Enterprise Allowance Scheme you get £40 a week on top of what you earn in the business. To qualify you must: be receiving unemployment benefit or income support; be unemployed for at least 8 weeks; raise £1000 to invest in your business (a loan or overdraft will do).' Similarly, the Employment Training Group advertised in the Heart of Midlothian programmes in 1989/90 offering 'training that matches the job you want', below a sketch of a strong-looking stonemason with heavy hammer and chisel. Fortunately, I had a job, as I would not have made much of a fist of becoming a stonemason.

Sheffield was particularly hard hit by industrial closures. England's fourth-largest city had traditionally enjoyed unemployment rates below the national average, with well-paying jobs in coal and steel industries. In 1978, unemployment in the city was four per cent, but by 1981 it was over 11 per cent and above the national average, and by 1984 it had soared to 16 per cent. 'Unemployed? Employ yourself' exhorted an advertisement for the Enterprise Allowance Scheme in Sheffield Wednesday's programme for their FA Cup third round tie with Torquay United on 7 January 1989. With unemployment benefit at that time running at just over £30 a week, there must have been a question mark over whether the long-term unemployed would be able to pay 80 pence for the Wednesday programme. It is also perhaps significant that Sheffield Wednesday's shirt sponsor was a local manufacturing company, VT Plastics, while other First Division sides had international companies, particularly in the growing electronics and IT sector. Examples include JVC with Arsenal, Commodore with Chelsea, Holsten with Spurs, Carlsberg at Wimbledon, KLM for Queens Park Rangers, Avco for West Ham, Candy for Liverpool, and Sharp for Manchester United.

Despite the evident distaste for football at the highest levels of government, major financial businesses began to be closely associated with the game. Barclays Bank became sponsors of the Football League in 1987, and by 1989/90 they were placing full-page advertisements in the programmes of several clubs – examples in our collection include Crystal Palace, Millwall, Tottenham Hotspur, Leyton Orient, Fulham, Arsenal, Torquay United, Chelsea, Manchester City, Manchester United and Oldham Athletic. Northern Rock, then still a building society with strong roots in Tyneside, were advertising in Newcastle United's programme. The Bank of Scotland ran a regular advertisement in Hearts' programmes, along with others offering forms of financial services: Lints and Company (estate agents), Melville Harrison Associates (financial management), and Scott and Paterson (accountants).

The financialisation of the economy had indeed trickled down to take in spectators at the 'slum sport', but often advertisements were aimed at businesses. Debt recovery specialists IHJ Collection Ltd were match sponsors for the Hearts v. Dunfermline match on 10 February 1990. This, perhaps more than anything else, summarised the deep changes that had taken place in the UK during the 1980s. Bank lending had created demand, but also debt, with the boom peaking in 1990/91. The loss of jobs in manufacturing had been partly offset by growth in jobs in finance. The making of goods became secondary to the selling of credit. The exception was the rise of industries built on silicon chips. For example, the consumer electronics company Brother became the shirt sponsor for Manchester City, lifting their players to dizzy heights (in a forklift truck): see Programme Spotlights 47.

House purchase and the commodification of housing was a key part of the bubble of consumer debt during the 1980s. Edinburgh-based builders Miller's advertised in Hearts' programmes ('A Miller Home Everybody's Goal'), while the match sponsor for Hearts v. Morton (26 March 1988) was a building firm, Kelly & Steel Ltd, who took a full-page advertisement to promote a 'Luxury Development' of four semi-detached and two detached bungalows at Lasswade in Edinburgh's commuter belt. Since then just about all new houses have been promoted as 'luxury developments'.

In Hearts' local rivals Hibernian's programmes in 1987/88 there were advertisements from the Allied Irish Bank (who had also advertised in Hearts' editions the previous season) as well as the Bank of Scotland, and from two firms of solicitors/estate agents. One of them, McKay and Norwell, highlighted 'council house purchases' as among the services they offered to clients. This reflected the 'right to buy' that the UK government had given to tenants of public sector housing, perhaps the Thatcher government's most far-reaching domestic reform. To encourage potential purchasers, tenants were given discounts on the market valuation of their house, starting at 33 per cent (for tenancies up to three years) but increasing by one per cent for each additional year, up to a maximum of 50 per cent or £50,000.

- -

Programme Spotlights 47: The highest forklift truck in Europe

13 March 1988, Manchester City 0 Liverpool 4, FA Cup quarter-final

The City sponsor, shown on the cover page, was Brother. The centre-page spread of the programme has a sky blue background. Set on the top of the page are cigarette card-style images of six 'Stars of the City line-up' (Kenny Clements, John Gidman, Neil McNab, Imre Varadi, Paul Stewart and Andy Hinchcliffe), while on the bottom are images of four 'Stars of the Brother line-up' (a dot matrix printer, a 'hi-speed cooker' – i.e. a microwave – an electronic typewriter complete with TV monitor, and a knitting machine). The programme also includes a story of a visit made by players, staff and officials to the sponsor's premises in nearby Guide Bridge, which had 'strengthened the bond' between the two.

In one of the more bizarre spin-offs from sponsorship, one of the reported highlights of the visit was the highest forklift truck in Europe, lifting pallets to a height of 13 metres. 'Some of the players were given the opportunity to see if they had a head for heights... some were clearly not so keen.' The seven city players who took up the offer are pictured on their ascent.

- -

Enterprise Zones were another controversial policy introduced by Margaret Thatcher's first government. Local councils were invited to bid to declare such zones, within which there would be tax breaks and a simplified planning regime. Again, football programmes mark the adoption of this measure. Trafford Council took out a whole page in the Manchester United v. Charlton Athletic programme on 1 January 1988 to proclaim themselves to be 'Greater Manchester's Prestigious Area of Industrial and Commercial Opportunities'. Explaining why 'there's no better place than Trafford to build a business', the advertisements highlighted the 'three extensive areas within the Trafford Park Industrial Estate with full Enterprise Zone status – benefits include no rates payable until 1991, and 100 per cent Capital Allowances on investment in buildings'. It also pointed up the 'available pool of labour within easy reach of Trafford', including 'the high percentage of available female labour'.

Corporate clients were increasingly targeted through the programmes, perhaps indicating that the 'slum game' held a wider appeal than some imagined. In the Hearts programmes, Novafone was offering free car phones, 'Does your company meet our criteria? Dial 100.' Novafone sponsored Hearts v. Dundee on 30 March 1988, including a full-page advert for car phones (£499, equivalent to about £1,350 in 2021, plus VAT and installation and network charges). It showed Kenny Dalglish clutching a hefty mobile phone to his left ear while holding the steering wheel in his right hand and looking at the camera. A smaller advert featured Hearts chairman Wallace Mercer similarly encumbered, 'When the Chairman is buzzing around… His NOVAFONE is just the bizz.' In 1988, with four kids, I was barely able to afford a car (an old Peugeot 504 with the extra row of seats to reduce intra-sibling squabbling), let alone have that kind of money for a car phone, despite being at the top of the senior lecturer pay scale, and so in the higher income bands of those buying match programmes.

The executive box now became a familiar feature of the 'matchday experience'. Some wealthy people had probably always attended football, and though they may not have stood on the terraces they had been content to sit in the stands alongside regular fans. Similarly, as previous chapters have shown, it was not uncommon for local figures from the business world to take an active part in a club by advertising in the programme, or by sponsorship or directorships. By the late 1980s the business presence had become more corporate, sealed behind glass and pampered: the word 'exclusive' was often used to promote executive boxes.

The programme for the Mercantile Credit Football League Centenary Classic Football League v. The Rest of the World game at Wembley at the start of the 1987/88 season has a stapled four-page insert on yellow paper, slightly smaller than the main pages of the publication and on less glossy paper. It promotes the forthcoming England match with Turkey. One page is mainly given over to a 'menu' that reads, 'May we suggest the Scotch salmon – Welsh lamb – Italian ice-cream – and – French cheese. Followed by England v Turkey.' The play on nationalities and food is clever. The text below the 'menu' says, 'Now you can entertain in style at Wembley, by leasing one of our new executive boxes in the Stadium – available from early 1988 – or choosing from our hospitality packages available now for our major events.' By the time of that season's Liverpool v. Wimbledon FA Cup Final, there was a half-page advert listing the executive suite holders: Scandinavian Bank Group; Hi Tech Leasing plc; A.D.T.; UNISYS (an American IT company); Throgmorton Investment Management Limited; Independent Insurance Company Limited; General Portfolio Group PLC (selling pensions and investment plans, some of which subsequently proved worthless); National Car Parks; Blue Arrow PLC (an employment and recruitment agency); BET plc (an industrial conglomerate); Pentland Industries PLC (a rapidly growing company with interests in sports goods); Barclays Bank; Laing Homes; Tiphook plc (a transport services company that was on a debt-fuelled buying spree in the late 1980s before crashing a few years later); I.C.S. (unknown line of business) and The Spirit of Boston Company Limited. The listing hints at the kind of businesses whose ascendency came to define the 1980s.

The executive boxes signified the dispossession by corporate and financial interests of the slum people's slum game. Hearts chairman Wallace Mercer, who had made his fortune in property development after setting up his company by using part of the proceeds from selling his London home, enthused in the Hearts v. Morton programme on 26 March 1988 about how income from the Executive Club and the Business Club had made it possible to retain the services of Hearts' best players. He went on to describe season tickets for the following season as 'an excellent investment'. Like Michael Brown MP, Mercer was a strong supporter of Margaret Thatcher, a brave and lonely stance in Scotland by the late 1980s.

Set in the same late-1980s period, Irvine Welsh's novel *Trainspotting* was published in 1993, exposing the other face of Edinburgh, socially far removed from the executive boxes despite being close to them in the grounds at Tynecastle and Easter Road. Welsh's collection of vivid, heroin-addicted characters are Hibs fans, like their creator. *Trainspotting* has a chapter headed 'Victory on New Year's Day' in which Begbie, Renton and their friends attend the traditional New Year's Day Edinburgh derby. Fitting the Leithers' grim fate in the book, Hearts win 4-1. Presumably it was, or was inspired by, the 1991 game, actually played on 2 January. Euan, while reading the book, remembered being there, and we do have the programme. That world of rampant social disintegration and division was hinted at in the programmes of Hibs and of Hearts in the 1992/93 season with an AIDS awareness advert from the National AIDS Helpline. Its message 'It's time to TAKE CARE' linked to a diagrammatic wrist watch made no mention of the dangers to drug users of sharing needles. Rather it addressed only the risks from sex, and suggested celibacy, condoms or 'being faithful to a faithful partner' as ways to 'take care'.

At a more personal level, we entered the 1980s with four children under the age of nine. They dominated the lives of my wife and I, having gained numerical superiority over us when the twins, Celia and Sophie, were born. Amid struggles to cope at home as they grew up, while also surviving as an academic, football remained embedded in the life of the family. I would tow the twins on their tricycles to watch Euan play boys' club football on winter afternoons. There are also cherished memories of being on packed terraces at Old Trafford, St James' Park or Tynecastle with myself and their older siblings clinging on to Celia and Sophie who were perched on the crush barriers to see over the heads of the crowd. For the games in Manchester, our family group were laden with a generous supply of confections and sugary beverages from my mother, ever alert to the dangers of malnutrition striking down her grandchildren. Some three decades later, in the curtailed 2019/20 season, there would be a three-generational visit to watch Hearts play Aberdeen, involving Euan, his wife Carrie, and their daughters Isla and Esther.

One thing that connected family, work and football was that quintessential new entertainment technology of the 1980s, the video recorder. At the start of the decade I was teaching a project-based class that required my students to work in groups to make a community-based video. One of the finished products, on Edinburgh's Old Town, was entered into a national student video competition and won a prize, a new Betamax video recorder. Joy was not tempered by any anticipation of the subsequent demise of Betamax. As it was not feasible for the group of students to share the prize, the department bought it off them. So, on occasional weekends I was able to borrow the equipment, rent a film from the local video shop, and keep the four children content.

We could also record from the TV. Our recording of the 1983 FA Cup Final Replay in which Manchester United beat Brighton 4-0 was frequently replayed. The commentator's phrases, 'turns it in for Whiteside' (the 18-year-old prodigy's headed goal made it 2-0) and 'he scores with his left foot' (Mühren's penalty for the fourth goal) became 11-year-old Euan's catchphrases, a soundtrack to accompany carefully conceived ways of niggling nine-year-old sister Alice, to provoke the outraged response he sought.

While the success of my students had enabled the Hague family to be early adopters of the new video technology, by the end of the 1980s it seemed that everyone else actually owned their own machine, except us who still relied on my sporadic borrowing. Pressure to rectify this anomaly was ramped up insistently, and resisted with, though I say it myself, commendable fortitude. In the summer of 1990, I decide the time was right. Coincidently, the purchase of a VHS video cassette recorder was made just in time for the Germany v. England World Cup semi-final, which, in a spectacular piece of bad timing, happened to coincide with a parental visit night to the Girl Guides camping week in the Scottish Borders where Celia and Sophie were participants. Claims that my eventual purchase of our own VHS recorder were driven by self-interest were ill-founded, but have persisted over the subsequent decades. In contrast, the recording of the match was quickly erased.

As mentioned in Chapter 1, our collecting of programmes peaked in the 1980s, as Euan invested his earnings from his newspaper delivery round on programmes. He also subscribed to a magazine entitled *The Unexplained*, which chronicled bizarre occurrences. One such triggered Euan successfully to organise a petition among fellow pupils requesting

Boroughmuir High School to offer a Scottish Vocational Qualification in spontaneous human combustion. They didn't. The legacy of the surge of programme purchasing has stayed with us long after *The Unexplained* volumes were recycled. Well, I think they were. Surely they are not still up there in the attic, are they? So it is that our programme collection includes some surprising ones and some gems. Why, for example, do we have the programme from Bourne Town v. Northampton Spencer from 24 August 1976 (see Programme Spotlights 48)?

Programme Spotlights 48: The Wakes
24 August 1976, Bourne Town v. Northampton Spencer, Greene King Cup preliminary round
Bourne is a small market town in the south of Lincolnshire. The football club was formed in 1883. The clean, uncluttered cover page displays the club badge – knotted ropes over a shield – and the nickname, 'The Wakes'. I am unaware of the story behind either.

The outside of the eight-page programme is printed in blue and white, but the inside is on plain paper and looks to have been run off on one of the duplicating machines that were common in offices at that time. We learn that the United Counties League Knock Out Cup had now been renamed the Greene King United Counties Cup, following its sponsorship by the brewery. Could this 'first' explain Euan's purchase of this otherwise unremarkable programme? Among the numerous small local advertisements on the three other colour printed pages is one seeking 'Scrap Cars £8 each'. In the 1970s, cars reached the scrap stage quite quickly.

And the gems? Too many to mention, but how about the 1963 European Cup Final, which was played at Wembley? The programme has a rarity value, and some value because of the sense of occasion that any final carries, though the market value of our copy is reduced by having two holes punched in it for filing in a ring binder, which probably made it affordable to Euan all those years ago. The match is recognised as having marked a turning point in football's evolution. AC Milan's victory was the triumph of the defensive and counter-attacking catenaccio tactics, ending an age of innocence.

- -

Programme Spotlights 49: Did AC Milan train on Bovril?

22 May 1963, Benfica 1 AC Milan 2, European Cup Final

Wembley programmes before 1963 could be quite boring, but together with the FA Cup Final programme from the same year, this one shows more imagination in the cover design. The two-tone and fading effect between the royal blue and the white draws the eye, while the images of the trophy and the sketch of the stadium convey the sense of the final being rooted in the place, and contribute to the overall symmetry of the page. The red font and spacing of the text add to the sense of impending drama.

The back cover, as usual at Wembley, was an advertisement for Bovril. Quintessentially British, it proclaimed 'Why top footballers train on Bovril', though it requires a stretch of the imagination to envisage the players of Benfica and AC Milan, being so nourished, given the gastronomic traditions of Portugal and Italy. Similarly, the sketch in the advertisement is cast in British football of the 1950s. A goalkeeper stretches to catch a heavy-looking ball as a rugged forward in a striped shirt challenges him in the air. You can't help but feel that a split-second later the unfortunate keeper will be flat on his back. Both players are wearing what look like heavy-duty boots that covered the ankles, while in the background behind the stand there are what appear to be a factory and chimneys.

- -

The programme described Nereo Rocco, Milan's manager, as 'a bluff, heavy Tristino, who made bricks without straw as manager of Padova'. In the 1962 final Benfica had put five past Real Madrid (for whom the great Ferenc Puskás had scored a hat-trick). Faced with a Benfica side at the height of their attacking powers, Rocco made a decisive change from the team printed in the Wembley programme. Winger Paolo Barison, an Italian international who had scored twice with headers in Milan's home legs against Ipswich Town and Dundee on the way to the final, was left out. The team change brought in a player not even listed in the programme page devoted to pen pictures of 13 Milan players. Gino Pivatelli, a 30 year-old ex-forward, now used occasionally in a defensive role, replaced Barison. His job was to stop Mario Coluna. Like Eusébio, Coluna had been born in Mozambique when it was a Portuguese colony: the pair were the first world-class players from Africa. Coluna was described in the Benfica pen portraits as, 'Brilliant organiser and tactician of the Benfica side and also the national team.' Benfica led at half-time through a goal by Eusébio, finishing a move started by Coluna. Milan's Brazilian centre-forward Altafini equalised on 58 minutes. Then came Pivatelli's definitive intervention. As Coluna raced away from him into space inside the Milan half, Pivatelli cynically tripped him. Coluna tumbled, broke his foot, and with no substitutes allowed, was out of the match. Minutes later, with Benfica still going forward, a counter attack saw Altafini through on the goalkeeper to score what proved to be the winner. Others took heed of how Milan had won Europe's top prize, and the game began to change.

Some of our programmes evoke family memories, such as the 73 that we have of matches involving Torquay United. In his senior years at secondary school, Euan formed the Scottish Torquay United Supporters' Club. It was at a time when Torquay were struggling at the bottom of the Fourth

Division, and this, together with the distance between their home and Edinburgh, meant the eccentricity of the idea was irresistible. We found out on a parents' evening at the school, from a beleaguered teacher, that the day-to-day business of the supporters' club was mainly conducted during the physics class. The physics teacher pleaded with us to support his efforts to compete with the club for his students' attention, 'Euan will pass easily so it does not matter for him, but some of the others actually need to follow the lesson and do some work in class if they are to pass.'

The big day came on 28 November 1987, when Euan and four class-mates, members of the supporters' club, two boys and two girls, set off by train to Carlisle (see Programme Spotlights 50). The five made their way to the visiting supporters' end at Brunton Park, boosting the total number of Torquay fans there to 13, and swelling the overall attendance to 2,017. When the home side quickly strode to a 3-0 lead, embarrassment threatened: the trip had been much touted back at school, and humiliation awaited on the following Monday morning. To the delight and relief of the Edinburgh Five, the team from Devon staged a fightback and the game ended as a 3-3 draw.

Euan, all set for the trip to Carlisle United v. Torquay United game, November 1987.

Programme Spotlights 50: Scottish Torquay United Supporters' Club away day

28 November 1987, Carlisle United 3 Torquay United 3, Football League Fourth Division

Unremarkable to many, this programme has historic value within the limited confines of the Hague household. On a dull day at the end of November 1987, Euan led his contingent of recruits from class-mates at Boroughmuir High School on what would be the first of two away trips for the self-styled Scottish Torquay United Supporters' Club. The second such excursion, with depleted numbers but boosted by his younger twin sisters and one of their friends, and aided by free overnight accommodation with his grandma in Manchester, would be to witness a goalless draw at Stockport County in March 1989. Though only five in number, the contingent from Edinburgh made a significant and unexpected addition to the numbers gathered behind the goal at the away end at Carlisle's Brunton Park.

The programme highlighted Paul Dobson as Torquay's leading scorer, and recounted his 94th-minute equaliser against Crewe at the end of the previous season, and the saga of Bryn, the police dog. There is a table in the Carlisle programme of leading Fourth Division goalscorers, in which Dobson was fifth with 13. The leading pair would go on to become much better known. Steve Bull of Wolves had 20 and David Platt of Crewe had bagged 17; both became England internationals, with Bull's call-up coming at the end of the season in which he helped Wolves to promotion from the Third Division. The front cover of the programme promotes Carlisle as 'The County Team', reflecting its extensive hinterland as the only Football League club in Cumbria.

We have the programme for Torquay's record home attendance (21,908 against Huddersfield Town in the FA Cup fourth round in 1955), which could legitimately be called a collector's item, though it does have one page mysteriously cut out and liquid stains in the top corners. Many Gulls fans must have turned up early that day to make sure they got in, and would have bought the bumper 16-page programme for the visit of a First Division side while the hosts were in the lower half of the Third Division (South). One page is given over to the music programme performed by the band of the 1st Battalion of the Devonshire Regiment. The repertoire included singalong favourites of the time such as 'I Do Like to Be Beside the Seaside', 'End of the Road', 'She'll Be Coming Round the Mountain', 'I've Got a Lovely Bunch of Coconuts', and 'Pack Up Your Troubles in Your Old Kit-Bag' among others, concluding with 'Land of Hope and Glory' and then the traditional FA Cup Final hymn, 'Abide With Me'. Rock and roll it was not.

The programme for the Devon Professional Challenge Bowl Final in 1971, in which the Gulls overcame Plymouth Argyle (a single sheet, four-page edition in excellent condition) is perhaps less sought-after, but we do have it. Inexplicably, given its significance in our household at the time, we do not have the Torquay v. Crewe Alexandra programme from May 1987, when, as the clock ticked down towards 90 minutes and Torquay, 2-1 down, staring into the abyss of automatic relegation from the Football League, police dog Bryn came to their rescue. As Torquay full-back Jim McNichol went to take a throw in, Bryn bit him. This canine intervention meant four minutes were taken in attending to McNichol's wound. In a tense finale, Torquay equalised in the fourth minute of added time, so saving their status at the expense of Lincoln City. There is a film in there for the Disney Channel.

I had done some coaching while Euan was playing primary school football in Edinburgh in the early 1980s, and this led to my meeting one of my all-time idols, Denis Law. During the summer vacation I managed to get a week's employment as a coach at Denis Law Soccer Schools, which operated at Edinburgh University's Peffermill playing fields. My highlight of the week/decade was when Denis himself came to meet the kids. I was in charge of the youngest age group, who were about eight years old. So I had to give them a briefing about the great man, who had retired about the time they were born. Law did not disappoint. He engaged with the youngsters, signed autographs, then said he wanted to see them play, which they loved. I wasn't going to let the opportunity pass. I had taken with me my copy of the Manchester United v. West Bromwich Albion programme from 18 August 1962. That game was Law's United debut after signing that summer from Torino for the then-astronomical fee of £100,000. On the front of the programme, as was often the case for the first game of the season, was the squad photo, with Law sitting on the front row. I got him to sign it, and together we reminisced about the header he had scored that day.

The end of the 1980s also marked my own final 11-a-side game of football. In December 1989, we staged a staff v. students game as a fundraiser for a good cause that I cannot now remember. All the money was on the students sponsored to score. They included a first-year boy who had represented Liverpool Schools and played with a twinkle in his feet. The staff XI had been bolstered by the addition of Euan, who was home for Christmas from his gap year; one of our recent graduates who was now president of the Student Union; and a tall and skilful undergraduate generously loaned to us by the students, 'to even things up'. In an upset for the books, the staff won 3-1, largely thanks to the efforts of our three younger 'imports', including one goal from Euan. However, the goal of the match was the one that put the staff 3-0 up. Our right-winger received the ball just inside the opposition half, raced down the wing, looked up as he approached the edge of the penalty area and with no supporting player unmarked, he hit the ball with the outside of his right foot so that it soared then curved into the top corner beyond the goalkeeper's reach. Some said it was a freak, assisted by a gale-force wind that was driving sleet across the pitch, but it was no freak, because, reader, I scored that goal.

Programmes cited in Chapter 11 that are in the collection:

- 29 January 1955, Torquay United 0 Huddersfield Town 1, FA Cup fourth round
- 5 May 1962, Burnley 1 Tottenham Hotspur 3, FA Cup Final
- 18 August 1962, Manchester United 2 West Bromwich Albion 2, Football League First Division
- 22 May 1963, Benfica 1 AC Milan 2, European Cup Final
- 4 May 1971, Torquay United v. Plymouth Argyle, Devon Professional Shield Final
- 5 May 1973, Leeds United 0 Sunderland 1, FA Cup Final
- 1 May 1976, Manchester United 0 Southampton 1, FA Cup Final
- 24 August 1976, Bourne Town v. Northampton Spencer, Greene King Cup preliminary round (result unknown)
- 21 May 1977, Liverpool 1 Manchester United 2, FA Cup Final
- 10 March 1979, Scunthorpe United 2 York City 3, Football League Fourth Division
- 10 May 1980, Arsenal 0 West Ham United 1, FA Cup Final
- 22 May 1982, Queens Park Rangers 1 Tottenham Hotspur 1 (after extra time), FA Cup Final
- 27 May 1982, Queens Park Rangers 0 Tottenham Hotspur 1, FA Cup Final replay
- 17 August 1983, Dundee United 1 Tottenham Hotspur 1, Hamish McAlpine testimonial

- 26 May 1983, Brighton and Hove Albion 0 Manchester United 4, FA Cup Final replay
- 16 May 1985, Chelsea 3 Glasgow Rangers 2, benefit match for Bradford City Appeal Fund.
- 29 May 1985, Juventus 1 Liverpool 0, European Cup Final
- 10 August 1985, Everton 2 Manchester United 0, FA Charity Shield
- 10 May 1986, Everton 1 Liverpool 3, FA Cup Final
- 12 April 1987, Coventry City 3 Leeds United 2 (after extra time), FA Cup semi-final
- 16 May 1987, Coventry City 3 Tottenham Hotspur 2, FA Cup Final
- 8 August 1987, Football League 3 Rest of the World 0, Football League centenary friendly
- 28 November 1987, Carlisle United 3 Torquay United 3, Football League Fourth Division
- 1 January 1988, Manchester United 0 Charlton Athletic 0, Football League First Division
- 13 March 1988, Manchester City 0 Liverpool 4, FA Cup quarter-final
- 26 March 1988, Heart of Midlothian 2 Morton 0, Scottish Premier League
- 30 March 1988, Heart of Midlothian 2 Dundee 0, Scottish Premier League
- 14 May 1988, Liverpool 0 Wimbledon 1, FA Cup Final
- 7 January 1989, Sheffield Wednesday 5 Torquay United 1, FA Cup third round
- 22 April 1989. Heart of Midlothian 1 Aberdeen 0, Scottish Premier League
- 20 May 1989, Everton 2 Liverpool 3 (after extra time), FA Cup Final
- 10 February 1990, Heart of Midlothian 0 Dunfermline Athletic 2, Scottish Premier League

- 26 February 1990, Queens Park Rangers 3 Blackpool 0, FA Cup fifth round second replay
- 28 March 1990, Scotland 1 Argentina 0, friendly
- 7 April 1990, Millwall 1 Manchester City 1, Football League First Division
- 12 May 1990, Crystal Palace 3 Manchester United 3 (after extra time), FA Cup Final
- 2 January 1991, Hibernian 1 Heart of Midlothian 4, Scottish Premier League
- 29 December 2019, Heart of Midlothian 1 Aberdeen 1, Scottish Premiership

Chapter 12

Foreign Fields

IT WAS not until I was 23 years old that I went abroad for the first time. That was when I was at Manchester University and we were taken on a study visit to the Netherlands. So on a Sunday afternoon in April 1968, a group of us took the train to Delft to watch a football match. Xerxes were hosting Ajax, and although I did not manage to get a programme, I was able to watch a young player who would transform the status of Dutch football, Johan Cruyff. In contrast, the home club hit the skids. Formed in 1904 in Rotterdam, they had recently merged with a Delft club, and though they finished a creditable seventh in the 1967/68 top division, they went bankrupt and dropped out of the league.

By the 1980s, my life was becoming increasingly international. A European student exchange programme with the architecture school in Aarhus led to a friendship with a member of staff from there, which in turn saw us doing a house swap for the 1988 summer family holiday. Thus it was that we were able to see the Danish Fodbold First Division game between Silkeborg Idrætsforening (SIK) and Vejle. On a balmy July evening, there was an element of culture shock at experiencing a stadium where the two sets of fans could mingle together, and there were no fences penning in the supporters. As Chapter 11 showed, top grounds in England at this time caged fans in like animals. The biggest crowd at Silkeborg's previous five home games that season had been 7,945: the attendance the night we were there was 4,553.

The drive from Aarhus to Silkeborg was about 30 miles, and we arrived slightly late at the ground, so were unable to find a programme seller. This proved to be no problem. As the players trooped off at the final whistle, we went on the pitch and strolled after them in to the tunnel, and asked an official about the chance of buying a programme to add to our collection. We were taken up a short flight of stairs, and into a lounge where plates of sandwiches were laid out for the players, and there a spare programme was found and gifted to us. The 40-page edition is dominated by small adverts for local businesses. It does not include a team sheet, although it does have a short introduction to the visitors, including a list of their staff (professional and amateur). Among the pros who played that evening was Allan Simonsen, the only player to have scored in the European Cup, UEFA Cup and Cup Winners' Cup finals. After spells with Borussia Mönchengladbach, Barcelona and Charlton Athletic, he had returned in 1983 to Vejle, the club he had started with in 1971.

A few days later, when we were in Copenhagen, we agreed that Euan, now 16, could go by himself to watch Brøndby play, while the rest of us went to the famous Tivoli Gardens and amusement park. His experience in Silkeborg was to stand him in good stead. He had misread the information in the Danish newspaper and thought that Brøndby were the home club. Having navigated his way to the ground on public transport, he realised that things were strangely quiet. This was because Brøndby were actually playing away, but fortunately they were at another Copenhagen club, Brønshøj. A bit of inspired research, map-reading skills (he would go

----

Programme Spotlights 51: A Danish detour
24 July 1988, Brønshøj Boldklub v. Brøndby IF, Danish First Division

Thanks to Euan's diligence as a 16 year-old collector, we have five copies of this programme. It is an eight-page tabloid newspaper, displaying the club's yellow and black stripes and a cartoon wasp alongside the badge. The Wasps is Brønshøj's nickname.

The top half of page three has the Holdopstilling (line-ups) with Peter Schmeichel listed as number one for Brøndby: he is one of four players (two from either side) whose photo is shown next to the team sheets. Schmeichel's pictured team-mate is striker Torben Frank, who would also be a part of the Denmark side that won the 1992 European Championship, after gaining last-minute admission to the finals when war broke out in Yugoslavia.

On another page is a photo and story about a former Brønshøj midfielder, Preben Arentoft (see Chapter 10). He had left the club in 1965 to play in Scotland for Greenock Morton, before being transferred to Newcastle United in 1969, where he was a member of the team that won the Inter-Cities Fairs Cup, so becoming the first Dane to be a winner in a major European competition. By playing professionally in the UK he ceased to be eligible to add to his four international caps until 1971, as Denmark's national team was all amateur until that date. Brøndby would go on to win the league, while Brønshøj finished just above the two relegated clubs.

There are plenty of small advertisements in the programme from local businesses, but also one from Coopers and Lybrand for their auditing services, and a quarter-page one on the front page from the SDS Savings Bank, again hinting at the kind of coalescence with financial services during the 1980s discussed in Chapter 11 in respect of the UK.

----

on to become a Geography professor) and his Copenhagen public transport three-day travel card got him to the game, which, of course, had started when he reached the stadium. The turnstiles were closed, so the only way in was through the players' entrance, from where he emerged pitchside from the tunnel and then was able to duck under the railing and stand on the terrace. Again, this would have been unimaginable in a top division game in England or Scotland.

On that same holiday, we also went to see Aarhus Gymnastik Forening host Boldklub 1903 from Copenhagen. With zero knowledge of Danish it is not easy to construe the significance of the information in the shiny paper 64-page programme. It includes a photo of 16-year-old Trevor Francis in Birmingham City's boot room. Google Translate suggests that the Danish text below the photo says, 'He dreams of how many stoves he is going to slide up. It's been successful, just fine.' It could be that 'goals' might be a more appropriate translation than 'stoves', as I am not aware of any evidence that the young Francis was an obsessional stove slider, and even if he was it did not seem to hinder his subsequent career. However, by 1988 that career was winding down, and as the programme appears to explain, Francis had been transferred from Glasgow Rangers to Queens Park Rangers. QPR were to play Aarhus in a pre-season friendly a couple of weeks later.

Another former Glasgow Rangers player, Jan Bartram, was in the Brøndby line-up in the Brønshøj programme. His stay in Glasgow had been brief and recently curtailed, not long after an interview he had given to a Danish newspaper in which he referred to his manager, the normally placid Graeme Souness, as a 'beast' or a 'hooligan' depending on the translation.

Leading student study visits to look at urban planning and housing in the Netherlands in the late 1980s enabled me to add some Sparta Rotterdam programmes (see Programme Spotlights 52) to our collection. In 1986/87, they ran to 42 pages, but by the following season they had grown to 54 glossy pages. The Ajax team who were listed in the programme to line up for a cup third round game on 11 March 1987 included Frank Rijkaard and Marco van Basten. Not surprisingly, there

---

Programme Spotlights 52: A great Ajax side

11 March 1987, Sparta Rotterdam 0 Ajax Amsterdam 0 (Ajax won 4-3 on penalties), KNVB Cup third round

Sparta play second fiddle to Feyenoord in Rotterdam, and the 42-page programme conveys a homely feel, and a sense of historical continuity. The sketch of the player on the front cover looks like the red stripes have been hand-painted on, with a slight slip behind the left ear! There is no sponsor's name on the shirt, whereas at the time Sparta wore UNISYS across their chests. There are splashes of colour in some of the advertisements, but only the cover pages are glossy, and much of the text looks like it was written on an early home computer. At A5 size, it easily fits into a pocket.

This was the second great Ajax side: the first had won the European Cup consecutively in 1971, '72 and '73. The 1987 vintage included the peerless striker Marco van Basten, and defensive midfielder Frank Rijkaard, both of whom would soon move to join Ruud Gullit at AC Milan. Danny Blind was also in the team, and he would win all three European club trophies with Ajax, as well as 42 international caps. Other names of note listed in the Ajax squad that day were winger Johan van 't Schip, striker John Bosman, Jan Wouters who was a midfielder and became Dutch Footballer of the Year in 1989/90, and Arnold Mühren, a silky left-sided attacking midfielder who had returned to Ajax in 1985 after starring in England for Ipswich Town and then Manchester United (see Chapter 11). All these players were in the Netherlands squad that won the European Championship in 1988 and thrilled the continent with their verve and skills.

---

was a three-page feature on defender Danny Blind, signed by Ajax from Sparta the previous summer. Blind would go on to win all three European club trophies with Ajax, as well as 42 international caps for the Netherlands. Johan Cruyff was the technical director at Ajax. The game finished goalless, with Ajax going through on penalties and progressing to win the competition.

Reviewing the Ajax team, the programme noted that while van Basten was coveted by AC Milan, and money was important, it was not all important. Within months van Basten was a Milan player. There was also mention of a 17-year-old Dennis Bergkamp as one to watch for the future. He became one of the stars of Euro 1992, and moved to Inter Milan the following year, before joining Arsenal in 1995. Such was the distinction with which he performed for Arsenal that there is a statue of him at the Emirates Stadium. Famously, his father wanted to call him 'Denis' after Denis Law, but Dutch law at the time restricted names that could be used, and the baby boy had to be registered as Dennis.

Advertisers in the Sparta Rotterdam programmes from the late 1980s included estate agents (Zomerhof-Muys) and the ABN bank, as well as import/export and transport specialists; Heineken; a bingo hall and a range of car dealers and restaurants. UNISYS were the shirt sponsor. In the 1988/89 season, there were two notable additions. Nencini advertised their sweaters and sweatshirts with a half-page photo, mercifully in black and white, of seven young men posed wearing baggy sweaters with the kind of designs that would make you squeeze out a grunted 'thank you' if you got one for a birthday present. Then, in a small box on the top-right corner of page nine, next to a similar box promoting a Ford dealer, and above one for a florist, is an advertisement for *ROSIE – HET BESTE SEXBLAD VAN HEEL NEDERLAND*, the best sex magazine in the Netherlands.

On another visit to Amsterdam, I sat on a wooden bench on an open terrace to see Ajax take on Olympique Marseille at the stadium that had staged the 1928 Olympics. It was the second leg of the 1987/88 European Cup Winners' Cup semi-final, Ajax having a 3-0 lead from the game in France. The programme is big, glossy and colourful. It includes a feature article on foreigners who had played for Marseille; in those days there were sufficiently few to make it a story. One pictured was Laurie Cunningham (see Chapter 10) who had spent the 1984/ 85 season with the French club after leaving Real Madrid.

Ajax took a first-half lead, but then a defence-splitting pass put centre-forward Jean-Pierre Papin through one-on-one with the Ajax keeper, and the prolific French international slotted home with ease. Marseille won 2-1 with a last-minute goal, a spectacular long-range free kick by their big German centre-back Karlheinz Förster. My abiding memory of the game is the performance of Arnold Mühren, who was approaching 37 years of age. As I wrote in my monthly column in *Planning* (13 May 1988), I saw similarities in his style of play and my own. We both were one-footed, weak tacklers and not good headers; the difference was, 'With his left foot he hits unerring passes, long and short, through all sorts of angles, with great imagination.' The programme had a two-page feature on him, describing him as one of the great stars of the first leg.

Programmes from eastern Europe in the 1980s were much more basic and demonstrate the gap between the command economies and the commercialisation of lifestyles in the west. For Lech Poznań v. Bałtyk Gdynia on 15 June 1985, a routine Polish league fixture, the programme was a single sheet of cheap paper, folded vertically into three, creating six narrow pages which were not entirely symmetrical, with the back fold narrower than the front one. Far from glossy or colourful, and in an eye-straining small font size, it has just one (blurry) photo on the front, and one advert seeking to recruit school leavers into an engineering career. There is no listing of the likely line-ups, though it does have a slim box in which to write the 'Wynik Meczu', the match result, which was a surprise 2-0 win for the visitors, who were in danger of relegation.

From 1945 to 1989, the very name of many clubs in Soviet satellite states was loaded with a state-imposed meaning. Spartak Varna played Manchester United in the European Cup Winners' Cup in October 1983. The Bulgarian club was created by a merger of three existing clubs in 1945. 'Spartak' was a Soviet term for a sports society, commemorating the Spartacus Rebellion (73–71 BC), the most successful slave uprising during Rome's imperial period. The Spartak moniker was widely applied across the eastern bloc. Like that of Lech Poznań, the programme for United's visit was on non-glossy paper; the inside cover pages were blank, and there were no adverts at all. The blurry team photos showed the visitors easily winning any contest with the Bulgarians for length and amount of hair, with Remi Moses leading the way with his afro. The early 1980s were the period of peak perm among British footballers: within the Soviet sphere, a short back and sides was the regulation, and any hirsute display would suggest a dissident spirit. The game kicked off at 4.30pm local time. The venue was the Yuri Gagarin Stadium, which commemorated the name of the Soviet cosmonaut, who, in 1961 in the capsule Vostok 1, was the first human to travel into outer space.

Thus this simple programme from the Black Sea tells many stories: a gladiator-led rebellion in ancient Thrace; the appropriation of the name by the early USSR, and its post-war imprinting across the states that the Red Army had liberated from the Nazis then occupied; Russia's early lead in the space race; the contrasts in daily life between east and west during the Cold War; and, not least, football as a stepping stone to European integration.

Dukla Prague had been United's opponents in the previous round. They were the Czechoslovakian army club, though their players were unlikely to endure the full rigours of military life. The name commemorates the Battle of Dukla Pass, a bitter tank battle between the Nazis and the USSR that lasted through September and into October 1944 in the Carpathians, on the Poland-Slovakia border, and led to the Soviet breakthrough in the region. The club was formed in 1948 as ATK Praha (Armádní Tělovýchovný Klub – Army Physical Education Club), and the Dukla name was applied only from 1956. Their all-time star player was Josef Masopust, the Jim Baxter of Czechoslovakia, an imperious midfielder who carried his national team all the way to the 1962 World Cup Final. Their 1980s away colours of mustard and burgundy were famously celebrated by indie band Half Man Half Biscuit in their 1986 track 'All I Want for Xmas is a Dukla Prague Away Kit'.

Dukla's home game against Manchester United in the autumn of 1983 ended 2-2, with a long-range rocket from Bryan Robson and a powerful header by 18-year-old Norman Whiteside seeing the visitors progress on the away goals rule. The programme was properly printed on good paper with colour photos of both squads and a coloured front page. The hair style gap was narrower than in Varna, in part because Remi Moses had been shorn, leaving the blond Scott McGarvey as the standout individual winner by a distance. The advertisements were for state firms such as ČKD, which made trams and electrical equipment, and for ČSD seeking to attract people to work on the railways.

The programme for the first leg at Old Trafford commemorated the previous meeting of the clubs in 1957/58 in the European Cup (see Chapter 4). United had triumphed 3-0 in the first leg, with Dukla gaining some consolation from a 1-0 win in the return in Prague in front of a crowd largely composed of special duty soldiers. United's experience of that winter trip to central Europe would prove fateful. As journalist David Meek recorded in the programme for the 1983 meeting, fog had disrupted the travel home from Prague: the players got back through Amsterdam but the press did not arrive until the Friday after a 16-hour journey, the last leg of which was by rail from Birmingham. This disruption meant that the English champions decided to switch to a charter flight for their journey back from their quarter-final meeting with Red Star Belgrade, a trip that ended so tragically at Munich (see Chapter 5).

Another Dukla Prague home programme we have is for their meeting with Hearts in the first round of the 1986/87 UEFA Cup. A 1-0 win was enough to take the Czechoslovaks through on away goals after the first leg at Tynecastle had finished 3-2. One of the pages listed Dukla's record in European competitions, starting with that 3-0 defeat at Old Trafford in 1957. A measure of the strength of the club in the years that followed is that the sides that eliminated them in the European Cup knock-out ties were SC Vienna (1958/59), Tottenham Hotspur (1961/62), Sporting Lisbon (1962/63), Borussia Dortmund (1963/64), Real Madrid (1964/65) and Glasgow Celtic (1966/67).

What makes this Dukla programme unique in our collection is that it is perforated, so what should be an eight-page black and white production on poor quality, now-yellowing, paper folds out into one sheet. I am not sure whether this is how it was meant to be – a sort of DIY programme assembly, or if it is an anomaly. It is also surprising to find that the quality of the 1986 programme is inferior to that from 1983. Had the economy deteriorated or was the 1983 edition a special because Manchester United were the visitors? An enigma within a puzzle.

Throughout the 1980s I had been making research visits to Czechoslovakia. However, it was not until March 1994, when I was delivering training to Czech officials and politicians learning to transition to a market economy, that I actually got to attend one of Dukla's home games. Their Stadion Juliska was just a short walk from the Czech Technical University where I was based. Both the stadium and the university are in the Dejvice area of Prague 6, and in those days the station (originally named Leninova) was the terminus for Line A of the metro. Construction of the underground began in 1967. As my official Prague guidebook (1979) purchased on my first visit in 1981 tells it, 'In view of the important technical assistance rendered by the Soviet Union the underground railway is marked as a structure of Czechoslovak-Soviet co-operation.' The metro station (now called Dejvická) opened in 1978. It is not far from the International Hotel, which opened in 1956, and is one of those 'wedding cake' architecture buildings from the Stalin years with grim cavernous interiors. I had stayed there during one of my 1980s visits, when you felt sure your room was bugged.

- -

Programme Spotlights 53: Thoughts of Josef Münzberger

20 March 1994, Dukla Prague v. Baník Ostrava, Czech First League

The front cover from the game I attended in 1994. It was game week 17 of the first season of the Czech First League, following the split with Slovakia. At that point, Dukla's record was drawn three and lost 13, goals for 12, against 45. The player featured on the front cover is Josef Münzberger, and inside he answered questions about the team's 3-1 loss the previous week to Bohemians, another Prague club. Very roughly translated, he was sick as a parrot but thought that the lads would be over the moon if they could beat Baník Ostrava.

The programme evokes memories of my many visits to Prague, but also of the Busby Babes (Chapter 5) who met a more formidable Dukla side in 1957.

- -

When I went to watch Dukla in 1994, they hosted Baník Ostrava in the Czech First Division (see Programme Spotlights 53). Admission for a seat in the stand cost me 22 Czech Crowns (about £1). The crowd was sparse but the stadium was impressive, with a large stand built into a hillside giving a lop-sided feel. At that time, and like many central and eastern European clubs, Dukla remained a multi-sport club (until 1996). The pitch sat inside a running track, again a typical feature of grounds in that part of Europe from that era. Dukla's football team was in what proved to be terminal decline, and its link with the army was ending. In that 1993/94 season, the first of the new Czech league after the split from Slovakia, Dukla finished bottom with only ten points (two points for a win was still in operation) while their visitors from the provincial coal-mining town of Ostrava ended third and reached the cup semi-finals.

The eight-page unstapled programme from that cold and damp afternoon was on paper that remained of communist-era quality, though the advertisements from state enterprises had given way to a few from private businesses such as sports goods shops. There was also an advertisement for Hotel Praha, which proved, like Dukla, to be a doomed relic of the previous era. The height of communist luxury when it was completed in 1981, so much so that I was never accommodated there, the 136-room hotel with swimming pool, circular staircase and winter garden, was demolished in 2014 by its new plutocrat owner whose house it overlooked. So like my Spartak Varna programme from a decade earlier, this Dukla v. Ostrava programme carries a tangled history, but because I went to the match and had such a long involvement in Prague and in the Czech Republic more generally, it also evokes memories of a particular time in my life, of friendships, my many rides on the metro and in Ladas and Trabants (one of which stereotypically ground to a halt on the Czech-Moravian Highlands late one wet Sunday night), Czech beer, innumerable varieties of dumplings, and the streetscapes and neighbourhoods of Prague.

Instead of following Dukla when on research or training visits to Prague, I would catch the tram to the Vršovice district, walk through the seven- and eight-storey Stalinist grey blocks of flats on Vladivostocká and go to stand on the terraces to watch Slavia Praha in their nostalgic ramshackle stadium. Slavia were known to be the 'independent' side in the city, and their programmes from the early 1990s were altogether more imaginative in their design and lay-out than those of Dukla. For example, the 24 November 1996 programme for the match against FK Jablonec has 36 pages, and a glossy cover. Slavia's traditional shirts are red and white halves, with a tilted red star on the breast of the white half. This colour scheme defined the front and back covers; there were black and white action photos from recent games and the large font and use of red juxtaposed with black in the text pages made it attractive to look through, even though I did not know enough Czech to comprehend what was being said.

By 1992, Boris Korbel, a Czech-born American entrepreneur, owned Slavia, according to the programme for their UEFA Cup visit to play Heart of Midlothian (30 September 1992), an early example of big money buying up assets in the former Soviet bloc. His investment had enabled Slavia to purchase a few star players including Radim Nečas (from Baník Ostrava), Dragiša Binić (an experienced Yugoslav international, bought from Red Star Belgrade) and the Russian Vladimir Tartarcuk, as well as retaining some of their local stars such as Pavel Kuka and Jan Suchopárek, both of whom would be in Czechoslovakia's squad for the Euro 96 finals, where they were runners-up to Germany. TV commentator Archie Macpherson did not do sham neutrality during his match commentary, exerts of which are on YouTube. He mused on Slavia's new owner who, he said, was not only buying new players but also looking to sell players, 'Every time Slavia play, their players are in the shop window.' In that part of Europe in those years money could buy almost anything.

The Tynecastle match was a thriller with Gary Mackay's early goal for Hearts levelling the tie, only for the visitors to equalise, Hearts to go 3-1 up, be pulled back to 3-2 (so losing on away goals) and then get the winner with a long-range free kick from Glynn Snodin, formerly of Sheffield Wednesday and Leeds United, who spent that season with Hearts. Patrik Berger, later to star with Liverpool, was a late substitute for Slavia: the programme described him as 'tall and powerful, and an excellent passer' and said that the 19-year-old had been man of the match in the first leg in Prague. Berger was sold to Borussia Dortmund in 1995 for a reported £500,000. Pavel Kuka went to 1 FC Kaiserlautern in 1994; Suchopárek joined Strasburg after Euro '96.

It is also revealing to read in that same programme that Hearts 'completely misjudged the "corporate market" for the trip to Prague' for the away leg, and would have cancelled the plane they had chartered if that had not been 'financially embarrassing'. This lack of interest from UK businesses reflected what I observed as a regular visitor to Prague in those days; I saw the rapid arrival of German, Austrian and American companies, but little UK presence. Meanwhile, at the time of writing, Slavia are now owned by CITIC, one of China's biggest conglomerates, which I encountered in 2016 building a new town in Angola. The historic Prague club's journey from sports club through the Communist era to US ownership to part of CITIC's global portfolio is a parable of globalisation.

Our collection also includes an international match in Prague from 1976, in which Czechoslovakia beat Scotland 2-0 in a World Cup qualifying group game. It was played at Stadion Sparty, the home of Sparta Prague. The Czechs were the new European champions, a victory made famous by Panenka's decisive chipped penalty to win the shoot-out after the final in Belgrade with West Germany had ended 2-2 after extra time. The programme has pictures of that moment. Just as fascinating is the whole-page advertisement in Czech, on the first inside page, for the Prague-Moscow Review of Czechoslovakian and Soviet Co-operation in Culture, Science and Technology, no less. Beneath a photo of a high modernist building towering over a transport interchange, the text explains that the magazine focuses on the fight against anti-communism and anti-Sovietism: well it would do, wouldn't it, in Czechoslovakia in 1976, eight years after the Warsaw Pact troops crushed the liberalising Prague Spring? Its appeal to fans reading the programme would have been limited, I suspect.

We have the programme from another international, East Germany v. Hungary in Leipzig in July 1987. The 12-page programme had blank pages on the inside front and back covers, and carried no advertisements at all – just short articles, the team sheets (all players on both sides were with clubs in their own national leagues) and photos of football games in previous Sportfests since the inaugural event in 1954. The logo on the front is for the 40th Spartakiade, which was combined with the eighth Sportfest.

A Spartakiade was a regular event in the USSR and its satellite states. It was a display of mass gymnastics and callisthenics, where thousands of children and fit young men and women would be gathered from across the country to perform together rhythmic exercises to music. Displays were carefully choreographed, so that at key points the placing and coloured clothes of the performers would spell out appropriate political slogans. My 1979 Prague guidebook described the Spartakiade venue at Strahov as being a display area of

200m by 300m, able to accommodate 16,000 performers. A Spartakiade was like a low-budget version of the opening ceremony of the Olympics or the World Cup, but was also the event itself, not a prelude. I can still recall one rainy Saturday afternoon in 1980s Bratislava, when the Spartakiade was the only entertainment on the black and white TV in the guest house where I was accommodated.

Programme Spotlights 54: The first 'Panenka'
13 October 1976, Czechoslovakia 2 Scotland 0, World Cup qualifying group

In the final of the 1976 European Championship, Antonín Panenka achieved a kind of immortality by softly chipping the crucial penalty over the diving West German keeper Sepp Maier and into the centre of the goal to make it 5-3. Nobody had ever seen a penalty like that before and all such subsequent kicks have been known as 'Panenkas'. An inside page of this programme shows the pictures of that landmark event, the only major trophy won by Czechoslovakia. This was the first time a shoot-out had decided a European Championship Final, so was all the more dramatic at the time.

Panenka opened the scoring in the game with Scotland with a much more powerful shot from distance. Scotland went on to win the group and head to the finals in Argentina, having eliminated the newly crowned European champions.

September of 1989 saw me on a research visit to Hungary. On a sunny Saturday afternoon I plotted my way on the Budapest trams to watch Honved play a home league game. For me, the ghosts of the past hung over the game. I could not get a programme, but outside the ground modest memorabilia was on sale commemorating the great Ferenc Puskás, and the side that were the core of Hungary's legendary Golden Team of the early 1950s (see Chapter 4). Inside the ground, rather like fans in Scotland would consume gristly pies, the sprinkling of fans chewed pistachio nuts, and lamented to me that all the best Hungarian footballers were playing abroad. At that time, a few months before the fall of the Berlin Wall, Hungary was more open than any of the other states behind the Iron Curtain. After the final whistle, and thanks again to the public transport system, I dashed across Pest in time to watch the local derby between Újpest Dózsa and MTK which kicked off at 7pm, and where the crowd, the floodlights and the more compact stadium gave the game a much better atmosphere.

I got what I assumed to be the match programme, only to find it was not really a programme at all. Rather it was the 26-page magazine of the Újpest Dózsa multi-sports club, with a front-page photo of a young man who had won three gold medals at the European championships, though there was no guide to just what his sport was. Football did dominate the inside pages. The centre two pages reviewed the long history of meetings between Újpest and MTK going back to 1905. There was an article about forthcoming fixtures, starting with the MTK match, followed by Pécsi Munkás away the following Saturday, then Váci Izzó at home before, at the end of September, the visit to bitter rivals Ferencváros for another Pest derby. However, there were also sections on athletics, ice hockey, boxing and pentathlon.

The programme made extensive use of the club colour, purple, for headlines. It included black and white photos, all of which were rather too dark to reveal much, but one does seem to show a young man in dark glasses pointing a pistol at the camera. Was it a harbinger of things to come? On a visit a couple of years later, I was turned away from my favourite restaurant in the old square in Újpest by a well-upholstered man in a suit, every inch the Hollywood mobster, and parked on the paving of the pedestrianised square outside the restaurant door was a stretch limo with tinted windows and American number plates.

In contrast to East Germany or Czechoslovakia, Hungary had been given some leeway to follow its own path within communism. Thus the Újpest Dózsa v. MTK programme had five full-page advertisements. These included one for the Budapest Bank, and another advertising jobs in a local supermarket chain. Another was for Keravill, which looked to me like it was selling landline telephones. Unsure I sought help from my Hungarian friend Roland Láposi. He explained that Keravill was, 'The now defunct state enterprise providing household stuff such as fridges, TVs, radios, irons and so on. The name itself goes like this KER – kerékpár/bicycle; Ra – rádió/radio; VILL – villamossági/electric. According to my mother it started at around the 1950s and went into administration after the transition in 1989. So – "HOTLINE TO KERAVILL – Free delivery of items ordered via telephone from our brochure within Budapest. You buy and pay for while staying in your home. Please call 110-601."' For an even more bewildering advertisement in the programme see Programme Spotlights 55.

- -

Programme Spotlights 55: It's a gas
9 September 1989, Újpest Dózsa v. M.T.K., Hungarian League First Division

Go to the picture section, any guesses what this advertisement in the programme is about? My Hungarian friend Roland Láposi explains, 'It belongs to the gas infrastructure and service provider company the Fovárosi Gázmuvek which means the Gasworks Company of the Capital City. It is about detecting breaks in gas pipes either in the home or in public space. I do remember this. Here it goes, "GASWORKS COMPANY (van picture with detectors at the front over the road) – If you learned about / detected gas leaks report it immediately at 228-228 or 384-000."'

- -

The same programme carried an advertisement selling camping and garden furniture. This was accidentally apt, since the parks in Budapest in those late summer days of 1989 were full of 'tourists' from East Germany living in tents. Hungary's reformist Prime Minister Miklos Nemeth had decided to stop maintaining the barbed wire fence that marked the Iron Curtain dividing his country from Austria. The news had got out that it was possible to cross to the west, and I will always remember the Trabants trundling down the motorway through Czechoslovakia, as would-be emigrants from the Deutsche Demokratische Republik stuffed in as many of their belongings as the 600cc two-stroke engine could manage to carry.

The Berlin Wall came down a few weeks later. The Hampden Park friendly between Scotland and the German Democratic Republic on 25 April 1990, in which Gary McAllister made his international debut, was the last time that East Germany played in the UK. After this, they played two more games, both away, against Brazil and Belgium. The programme for the match in Glasgow rightly mused that German reunification would 'change the face of the game in the DDR at both club and international level'. It anticipated top East German clubs joining the Bundesliga and the merger to create just one national team. At the time East and West Germany had been drawn in the same qualifying group for the 1992 European Championships; in the event, the merger came before they were due to meet that November. The anonymous author of the article in the Hampden programme grasped a more fundamental point about the free market, 'The net is tightening on a number of top GDR players who are wanted by West German clubs... No doubt there will be some prospective buyers sitting in the Hampden stand tonight, and not necessarily from West Germany.'

Uwe Rösler was in the East German squad listed in the programme for that 1990 visit to Scotland, though he was not one of the players spotlighted as likely to move to a West German club. It was not until 1992 that he joined FC Nürnberg, where he flopped and was loaned back to Dynamo Dresden, before forging a successful career with Manchester City. Some years later, he was quoted as saying of his experience in the former West Germany, 'I suddenly saw more individualistic thinking, cliques, a powerful press and personal politics around team selection. The Wall was still there in some people's heads and in many ways I was naive.' Decades later, the fracture lines within the reunified Germany still exist.

As the Iron Curtain was torn down, people moved west and money moved east. The USSR transitioned first to the Commonwealth of Independent States, and then, by the time they came to play a European Championship qualifying match in Glasgow in November 1994, to Russia. Just a month after the value of the rouble on international markets had fallen by 27 per cent in a single day, the programme that night noted, 'A relatively recent development has been the departure of top Russian players to Germany, Italy, Spain, Portugal, and, of course, England.' The line-up in the centre page listed them – Kanchelskis with Manchester United, Kiriakov with Karlsruher SC, Kulkov of Porto, Karpin at Real Sociedad, Gorlukovich (Bayer Uerdingen), Shalimov (Duisburg), Dobrovolski (Atletico Madrid) and Radchenko (Real Racing Santander).

On 3 October 1990, Manchester United played Pécsi Munkás in the Hungarian city of Pécs, a settlement with Roman origins and close to the then Yugoslavian border, and a place I had visited the previous year. The programme for the European Cup Winners' Cup tie included a 'hearty welcome' in English from the Pécs Workers' Sports Club Soccer Section to the visitors, though advertisements took up seven of the 16 pages. Some of these were for the definitive cars of the fraternal states of the USSR, Trabants, Ladas and Wartburgs, but these shared a page with an advertisement for IBM computers and one that asked in Hungarian, 'Do you love rock and roll? Do you like reggae music? Come and try Pécs' latest nightclub – Pepita.' Again this evokes memories of that period of transition, as what was proclaimed to be 'actually existing Socialism' gave way to the pervasive market economy.

The fumes of the Trabbies still hung in the air. I was driven around in a Lada by the driver of the research institute I was visiting (he always free-wheeled downhill to save on fuel). Before the days of GPS, unregulated taxi drivers, newly arrived from the countryside, provided an erratic service to addresses they did not know. Ambitious young entrepreneurs set up stalls in subway concourses to sell all sorts of goods. I remember watching a young couple set up camping chairs and a display rack to sell picture postcards in a square in Pest alongside the Danube.

One regret is that it was not always possible to get a programme when attending a game in eastern Europe. One such occasion was while I was working on a project in Bulgaria, and managed to grab an opportunity to see a CSKA Sofia home game. Like Dukla in Prague, CSKA were the army club, and their ground was known as the Stadium of the Bulgarian Army. So it was that on a raw December afternoon, with the light already fading, I arrived about ten minutes before kick-off, and managed to find a spare seat on a wooden bench as the teams emerged, then lined up without the formality of a toss. Within a minute or two of the kick-off, a large man made his way along the row to my seat and addressed me in fluent and animated Bulgarian. While his words were lost on me, it was very easy to understand that I had upset him, most probably by taking a seat he had assumed was his. Lacking both the vocabulary and courage to spark an international incident, diplomatically I surrendered the seat and sought one elsewhere, albeit one offering a less central view of the pitch. Everything became clear 45 minutes later when the referee blew his whistle and the stadium began to empty: I had arrived during the half-time interval, the game having started at 2pm, an hour earlier than I had expected.

Another regret is that I missed seeing Maradona play for Napoli at his peak. In early September 1986, I had participated in an international planning theory conference in Turin, which was my first exposure to Italian academics, and my first visit to the country since a package holiday to Lido di Jessolo in 1972. Participants were put up in student accommodation belonging to the Politecnio di Torino, and we had been given vouchers to get breakfast in a nearby café. I did not know then that breakfast is a non-event in Italy, but the café had been coached about the expectations of the international visitors who would descend upon them. So when you handed over the voucher, you were given an espresso, a Weetabix, and one of those little pots of milk with a tear-off top that you pour into a cup of coffee. It is hard to say who was most bemused by this unusual meal, the recipients or the cafe owners.

When the conference finished I went to Milan, to see the city, and from there, on the Sunday I decided to go to Verona to see the famous Roman amphitheatre. So I went to the huge Milano Centrale Stazioni, got a day return ticket to Verona and boarded the train. My carriage was full of three-generational groups of men, decked out in blue and white scarves. I realised they were going to a match, but knew that Milan's colours were red and black and Inter's were blue and black. Gradually, it dawned on me that they were Napoli fans, part of the diaspora that had moved to the northern cities in search of a better life, but, like migrants everywhere proudly clinging to their roots of which their football team was a vital part. The train stopped at Brescia and emptied, and in those few minutes I made the wrong decision to stay on (I had checked the times of return trains from Verona, would they all stop at Brescia? Would a ticket from Verona be valid?).

It was the first game of the season. Napoli had a long history, but few trophies: like Naples itself they were behind the big-city teams from the north. Maradona had joined from Barcelona in 1984. They finished eighth in his first season and third in his second. I did not know it, but the greatest player of his generation was about to embark on a campaign that would see underdogs Napoli win the Scudetto. Predictably, he scored that afternoon, giving Napoli a 1-0 win at newly promoted Brescia. More than that, it was a typical Maradona goal. A pass was fizzed to him from central midfield, not a good pass for he was closely marked and had to jump to collect it on his chest, just outside the D. Controlling and moving at the same time, he instantly went left, dribbled past a clutch of defenders and hit a powerful left-footed shot across the goalkeeper. Instead, I saw the Roman arena at Verona. It was impressive too, but if I could time-travel back to that train, I would have got off at Brescia.

Programmes cited in Chapter 12 that are in the collection:

- 13 November 1957, Manchester United 3 Dukla Prague 0, European Cup first round first leg
- 13 October 1976, Czechoslovakia 2 Scotland 0, World Cup qualifying group
- 14 September 1983, Manchester United 1 Dukla Prague 1, European Cup Winners' Cup first round first leg
- 27 September 1983, Dukla Prague 2 Manchester United 2, European Cup Winners' Cup first round second leg
- 19 October 1983, Spartak Varna 1 Manchester United 2, European Cup Winners' Cup second round first leg
- 15 June 1985, Lech Poznań 0 Bałtyk Gdynia 2, Polish League First Division

- 1 October 1986, Dukla Prague 1 Heart of Midlothian 0, UEFA Cup first round second leg
- 11 March 1987, Sparta Rotterdam 0 Ajax Amsterdam 0 (Ajax won 4-3 on penalties), KNVB Cup third round
- 20 April 1988, Ajax Amsterdam 1 Olympique Marseille 2, European Cup Winners' Cup semi-final second leg
- 19 July 1988, Silkeborg Idrætsforening (SIK) 1 Vejle 1, Danish First Division
- 24 July 1988, Brønshøj Boldklub v. Brøndby IF, Danish First Division (result unknown)
- 27 July1988, Aarhus Gymnastik Forening v. Boldklub 1903, Danish First Division (result unknown)
- 9 September 1989, Újpest Dózsa v. M.T.K., Hungarian League First Division (result unknown)
- 25 April 1990, Scotland 0 East Germany 1, friendly
- 30 September 1992, Heart of Midlothian 4 Slavia Prague 2, UEFA Cup first round second leg
- 20 March 1994, Dukla Prague v. Banik Ostrava, Czech First League (result unknown)
- 16 November 1994, Scotland 1 Russia 1, European Championship qualifying group
- 24 November 1996, Slavia Prague 2 FK Jablonec 1, Czech First League

Chapter 13

From the Terraces to the World-Wide Sofa

MONEY WAS always central to professional football, by definition and by practice. However, for most of the 20th century and across all of the world, its hold on the game was constrained by a variety of factors. From their origins, clubs had been rooted in places and this reality circumscribed the revenue they could generate: even at the biggest of clubs, the gate money came predominantly from people travelling just a few miles from their home to watch their local team. Similarly, as shown in previous chapters, it was local businesses that provided much of the money for advertising in a programme. There were also rules and regulations that had to be complied with, which would have deterred those seeking to get rich by investing in a club. Owners again tended to be local businessmen. There were egalitarian systems in place for sharing match receipts, including income from the two providers of TV coverage in the UK, BBC and ITV.

All of this was about to change, and with it my own relationship to the game was also restructured. The Scottish Football Association ceased to be able to dictate what football I would or would not be allowed to watch on TV. From 1983 some live English First Division games had been transmitted on ITV in England, though the Scottish FA were able to ensure that was 'except for viewers in Scotland', and Scottish ITV would instead show an old movie, hoping that nobody would notice. Shouting at the TV or phoning in my complaints proved surprisingly ineffective. However, Borders TV, the ITV franchise for the area on either side of the England-Scotland border, took their feed from England, so did show the English games live. I first realised this at the time of the 1979 FA Cup Final.

For the previous 1970s finals involving United (1975 v. Southampton and 1976 v. Liverpool) we had made a pilgrimage to Manchester, to soak up the special atmosphere in the city that was always a feature of a cup final day with United or City involved, and to watch on TV with my parents. For what would prove to be a dramatic 1979 final against Arsenal, I buckled our year-old twins in to the child seats in the boot area of an old, rusting but newly acquired red Ford Cortina estate, let their older siblings squabble in the back seat about whether the windows should be up or down, and alongside my patient wife, I drove us down to impose our numerous selves on friends in Newtown St Boswells, the heart of the Scottish Borders, there to endure the nerve-shredding last-minute 3-2 Arsenal triumph on their TV. In later years, a 40-mile round trip to a pub in the attractive Borders small town of Peebles, was my bolt hole for must-see matches.

Like the advent of floodlights in the 1950s, and the abolition of the maximum wage in the 1960s, satellite and cable television restructured football in the 1990s. It changed the way the sport was positioned within the leisure and entertainment sector. Like millions of others I became a consumer, and thanks to the depth of analysis now provided, I also became more aware of the way that tactics during a game, and the way teams set up, could influence matches. Football became a part of the globalisation that followed the opening up of China in the 1980s and the collapse of the Soviet empire in their bitter war in Afghanistan at the end of that decade.

As my own career became globalised, in the guest house on the campus of the University of Witwatersrand, on my first visit to Africa, I was able to watch live as United drew 1-1 at Nottingham Forest on a (southern hemisphere) summer evening in late November 1995. In a Beijing hotel, on what would become the first of many visits to China, late one Saturday night in the spring of 1997 I watched, bemused and perplexed, as Paulo Wanchope picked up the ball on the halfway line and ran with it through the Manchester United defence to put Derby County 2-0 ahead in front of Old Trafford's Stretford End and on the way to a 3-2 victory. That surprise result was an omen: it soon became clear that my being abroad somehow seemed to have an adverse effect on United's performances, though it was not easy to pin down why that should be the case. To cite just a couple of more recent examples, in Kuala Lumpur for the 2018 World Urban Forum I witnessed a miserable 1-0 defeat at Newcastle, while in Guangzhou in August 2018 I watched Brighton sail to a 3-0 half-time lead and finally win 3-2. Even Sir Alex Ferguson was powerless in the face of my jinx. There were Champions League exits: in the group stage after losing 2-1 to Basel when I was in Robertsfors in the north of Sweden; Arjen Robben putting them out on away goals in the 2010 quarter-final (I was in Cesis, Latvia, running a workshop); and the 2011 final when I was in USA, though I grant that Messi may also have influenced Barcelona's victory.

As Chapter 11 showed, the football industry in Britain had suffered during the 1980s. Even when the Premier League started in 1992, with the Stretford End closed while the terracing was being replaced by seating, the highest attendance in Manchester United's first four home league games was

31,901, and that was for the visit of Everton. Getting in to see a match had become more difficult, with many Premier League fixtures now all-ticket in the wake of the Hillsborough disaster. A glance at the league tables in various programmes reveals how, by the late 1980s, clubs with proud histories, like the industries which had given their fans a living, were in perilous positions. For example, Wolverhampton Wanderers, titans of the late 1950s, were the visitors to Scarborough in the Fourth Division on the opening day of the 1987/88 season. This was Scarborough's first appearance in the Football League, and, thanks to Euan's diligent collecting of such mementos, we have the programme. I had seen Burnley clinch the 1959/60 First Division title by beating Manchester City 2-1 at Maine Road (my programme has some sugary stains of unknown origin on the back, but probably related to some nourishment provided by my mother to sustain her 15-year-old son until his safe return home). In 1986/87, it was only a win by that same score over Orient in the last game of the season that prevented 1960's champions from being relegated from the Fourth Division to the Conference.

English clubs could not compete with Europe's elite. They had been banned from the European competitions after the 1985 Heysel Stadium disaster (see Chapter 12), and were only readmitted in 1991. Nor could they compete financially. An article by Keir Radnedge in the Tottenham Hotspur v. Manchester United programme on 19 September 1992, a game where I saw a young Ryan Giggs score an outstanding goal, explained. Successful lobbying by the big clubs had led to a change in rules in Italy, which allowed Italian teams to sign as many foreigners as they wanted. That summer, they had spent £56m. Juventus had bought Brazilian centre-back Júlio César from Montpellier, German defender Jürgen Kohler from Bayern Munich, and Kohler's countryman Andreas Möller from Eintracht Frankfurt. Champions AC Milan had been the biggest spenders, paying Torino a then world record £13m for Gianluigi Lentini, a winger whose career was wrecked by a car crash in August 1993. Milan were owned by media tycoon Silvio Berlusconi, who would become Prime Minister in 1994, illustrating again the way football was being taken over by media and big business. Berlusconi's Milan also had Jean-Pierre Papin and Ruud Gullit (both mentioned in Chapter 12), and the talented Yugoslavian internationals Zvonimir Boban and Dejan Savicevic. The article continued by noting that Real Madrid had paid £3m for Chilean centre-forward Ivano Zamorano, while Barcelona had the outstanding Bulgarian Hristo Stoichkov. Of course the cruellest part for the Spurs fans thumbing through the programme that sunny September afternoon was the advertisement for a trip to see their team's friendly in Rome with Lazio, who had captured White Hart Lane and England idol Paul Gascoigne for £5.5m that summer.

ITV's screening of live games on a Sunday afternoon had made them a big player in the football industry where many were struggling financially, but some were potential cash cows. By the autumn of 1990, ITV were actively exploring the chances of buying the TV rights for the then 'Big Five' (Arsenal, Everton, Liverpool, Manchester United and Tottenham Hotspur) separately from all the other First Division clubs. The Football League blocked this by agreeing a four-year deal with ITV, which allowed the clubs to keep 75 per cent of the money, rather than sharing half of it with the lower-league clubs as had been the case previously.

Enriched, but wanting more, the Big Five came to an agreement with the FA who commissioned a study to plot out the Premier League. The task was contracted to advertisers Saatchi & Saatchi and accountants Ernst & Young, businesses whose ascendency epitomised the 1980s as much as did the closure of coal mines and steel works. The Football League had unknowingly shot themselves in the foot, vis a vis the

FA, by extending the number of clubs in the First Division from 20 to 22 for the 1991/92 season, thus squeezing the availability of players and dates to the FA's England team. Just as important to the FA, it would get a cut of revenues brought in by broadcasting of the Premier League. However, the clubs were soon able to divest themselves of any obligations to the FA and to split the money between themselves: 50 per cent was to be split equally between all the Premier League clubs, 25 per cent to be distributed based on league position, and the remainder was to be paid dependent on the number of times a club was shown on TV.

In short, football was to become a commodity in the entertainment industry, consumed primarily on TV. At this point enter Rupert Murdoch, who, with a bit of inside help, and a partnership with the BBC, was able from New York to gazump ITV's bid for the TV rights to the new league. In those early days of square satellite dishes and paying for TV channels, Murdoch's Sky was losing money. Its deal with the new Premier League, which began in August 1992, meant all that was about to change.

The audience for advertisers, once local, became not just national but global. Advertisements spliced within and between the build-up, the live coverage, the post-match interviews and analysis, and the re-runs could reach many more people in many more places than was previously possible. Along with the perimeter advertising and shirt sponsorship, all of this was being beamed globally. It also meant that now only a tiny minority of those watching a Premier League match had bought the programme. As the game became a worldwide commodity, global companies acquired a local presence. McDonald's, the icon of the early 1990s era and sponsors of the 1994 World Cup, began to advertise in places far from their American heartlands, such as Falkirk (v. Hearts, 28 September 1991) and Dundee United (v. Hearts, 28 August 1993).

Some fans were unenthusiastic about the make-over and its associated razzmatazz. Journalist Tony Millard, writing in the Brighton and Hove Albion v. Swansea City programme on 27 March 1993, observed, 'Dancing girls and fireworks have upset some traditionalists, but the self-same people, or at least their predecessors of 50 years or so ago, probably disapproved of short sleeved shirts, low cut boots and synthetic balls.' He floated the idea of 'playing in four quarters with timeout for all breaks in play', noting that this would create commercial breaks that would benefit the game financially.

Programme Spotlights 56: Reach for the Sky
6 September 1992, Manchester United 2 Leeds United 0, Premier League

This Premier League meeting with the final First Division champions was the first home Manchester United match shown live on Sky. Sky's slogan to promote the new product was 'It's a whole new ball game', hinting at the kind of marketing of sport in the USA that would shape their approach. Thus, in the Monday night matches, there was half-time entertainment from the Sky Strikers, a group of cheerleaders.

This programme includes a one-page article titled 'Quality is the key to TV coverage of the Premier League.' It went on to describe BSkyB's two live games a week (Sunday afternoon and Monday night) as 'a football fan's dream'. It also acknowledged that the new regime might disrupt traditional match times, while assuring readers that 'fans' convenience is a priority', an assertion widely negated by subsequent realities. The sponsors shown on the shirts in the cover page picture of the Nottingham Forest v. United match the previous weekend reflect the dominance of breweries and electronics companies in the game at that time.

Looking through the photos in programmes in the early period of the Premier League gives an insight into the wider transition that was taking place. Breweries, traditional advertisers in football programmes, remained prominent though now the brands were mainly international. Spurs had carried the name of the German brewery Holsten across their shirts from 1983 and continued to do so until 1999, when IT firm Hewlett Packard from Palo Alto, California, replaced them, before Holsten were back from 1999 to 2002. From 1982 to 1988, Liverpool's shirts had been emblazoned with Crown Paints, based not far away in Darwen, Lancashire. A four-year spell with Italian manufacturers Candy followed, but from 1992 until 2010 the famous red shirts advertised Carlsberg, who were also the first Premier League sponsors. From 1993, Nottingham Forest carried the name of the Canadian brewers Labatts for away matches and the more traditional Shipstone's for their home kit (see Programme Spotlights 56). The Glasgow-based McEwan's were sponsoring Blackburn Rovers, and also, outside the Premier League, Newcastle United, Notts County and Glasgow Rangers.

Those early years of the Premier League in England coincided with the interlude between the boom in home computing and the advent of e-business. Britain was off the pace as a new industrial revolution began, driven from the USA and Japan. For a while some low-stream assembly work came to factories in new towns or in more traditional settings. Sharp, for example, were in Miles Platting, near the old Newton Health Loco ground (see Chapter 3) in the north of Manchester, but the upstream work on design and innovation was being done elsewhere.

The history of this pivotal period of economic and technological transition is written in the football programmes, which reveal the significant presence of international companies involved in information technology, particularly with traditionally bigger clubs. In 1992/93, the first year of the Premier League, Sharp electronics (headquarters Osaka, Japan) were the Manchester United sponsor; Arsenal's shirts advertised JVC electronics (Yokohama, Japan); Mita Copiers, another leading Japanese company at the time, were on Aston Villa's kit; NEC (Nippon Electric Company) were with Everton; and Brother, from New Jersey, were on Manchester City's sky blue shirts. The soon-to-fold Commodore were Chelsea's backers, and another doomed IT company, Tulip, sponsored Cristal Palace.

Two exceptions stand out. Queens Park Rangers were sponsored by a radio station, but not just any old station, rather Classic FM. In contrast, 'Laver' was written across the red and white stripes of Sheffield United players, being the company of Arnold Laver, a Sheffield-based timber merchant, founded in 1920. The company's full-page advert in their programmes struck a discordant note with the townscape of Sheffield – it depicted a Manhattan skyline against a starry sky and the simple line, 'Cities built the Laver way.'

Merchandise became a further income stream for clubs, and was umbilically tied to globalising their brand. Not surprisingly, Liverpool and Manchester United were the market leaders but many others followed their path. In the 1993/94 season, the Manchester United programmes carried adverts for club consumer goods. Against West Ham on 1 September, there were promotional pictures of club tracksuits, T-shirts and a fleece top, and another of the full-colour pages was given over to Club Call, a phone line offering commentary and post-match analysis of United's European Cup games: the cost (48p per minute or 36p off peak) was in small print across the bottom of the page.

The 24 November game against Ipswich Town had Mark Hughes holding his MUFC Visa Card, 'Exclusively for Manchester United Supporters', then a couple of pages later there was an advert for the club's museum and stadium tour. For 1 January 1994 against Leeds United, it was Lee Sharpe with the Visa card and there was a page promoting volume two number one of the bumper new year issue of 'Britain's biggest selling football monthly', the club's in-house glossy magazine.

Finally, for the visit of Southampton in May, which became a title-winning celebration, the programme had a page seeking to lure fans to book a 'bargain break fly cruise' to Stockholm and Helsinki, organised through the commercial department, while there was also a 12-page stapled insert for United-branded leisure wear and knick-knacks. United had opened English football's first megastore, though it was no more than a 5,000sq ft warehouse behind the Stretford End, in time for Christmas 1994. The previous club souvenir shop had been an unprepossessing shed on the car park near the bridge over the railway leading to the ground.

We have two Liverpool programmes from that 1993/94 season, for trips Euan made to Anfield while a postgraduate at Lancaster University. They are for their games against Aston Villa (a televised Sunday fixture on 28 November 1993) and Coventry City (26 February 1994). They carried adverts for the club's 'Official Colour Merchandise Catalogue', offering training gear, replica strips, leisure wear, gifts, hats and scarves, Adidas nostalgia and lifestyle ranges, 'and much more'. These could be accessed by mail from the UK, Ireland and Europe or the rest of the world. While space in club programmes had traditionally been given over to news from supporters' clubs, Liverpool's had a page for their international branches, reflecting their success the previous decade and the live TV coverage across Scandinavia of top English matches.

Taxpayers also were contributing to clubs' sudden largesse. The final Taylor Report into the Hillsborough disaster was published in 1990. It recommended that stadiums should become all-seated or be refused a safety licence. Fans buying a ticket would be allocated a specific seat. The thinking was made explicit, 'To achieve a new ethos for football... There will also be an improvement in behaviour, making crowd control easier.' The Conservative government under John Major was much more sympathetic to sport than its predecessor when Margaret Thatcher was Prime Minister, though that particular bar was set very low. Faced with pleas from clubs that they could not afford to upgrade their stadia, Major's government provided some £200m of public money to help them. All-seater stadia became compulsory from the start of the 1994/95 season in the Premier League.

While the moves in England did not legally apply north of the border, the Scottish Premier League also made all-seater stadia a condition of membership. The Hearts programme for the Edinburgh derby on 27 August 1994 contained a police message, which made it clear, 'Now that the stadium is all seated, you are reminded that it is club policy to ensure that all persons remain seated during the match.' There was also a reminder that it was an offence under the Public Order Act 1986, Section 18, to make racist comments, and that 'consuming or carrying an alcoholic drink within the stadium' or 'being in possession of a controlled container' were also offences. With Hibs ending a 22-game sequence of failing to beat their city rivals, thanks to a rare goal by defender Gordon Hunter, it is no surprise to find that video highlights online reveal that not 'all persons' did 'remain seated'.

Several clubs sought to relocate to new stadiums, typically moving from inner-urban locations to edge-of-city sites. Such changes were often controversial with fans because of their emotional attachment to the traditional grounds, but they were also problematic for local council planners since they were often speculative ventures that fell foul of planning policies. A classic example was the saga of Heart of Midlothian, whose chairman at the time, Wallace Mercer, just happened to be a property developer. In the summer of 1990, Mercer had been thwarted in a £6.2m attempt to buy out Hibernian, merge the club with rivals Hearts, and relocate 'Edinburgh United' to a new site to be built on green belt land in the west of Edinburgh owned by then-Rangers chairman David Murray. Hibs' biggest shareholder, Monaco-based businessman David Rowland, was prepared to sell. However, angry fan reactions and a majority vote by other shareholders saw the proposed deal fall through.

Months later, in his column in the Hearts programme for the game with St. Johnstone on 6 March 1991 (see Programme Spotlights 57), Mr Mercer drew attention to the planning application that had been submitted to Midlothian District Council for a site at Millerhill on the south-east of Edinburgh (the opposite side of the city from the club's long-established home ground). He advised fans to buy the *Hearts Newspaper* to get more details. However, there was also a one-page article in the same programme, about the 'ambitious plan for a new 30,000 seater stadium on a site adjacent to the City By-pass'.

This announcement was followed by a single-sheet insert a few weeks later addressed to 'Dear Supporter'. In this letter, Mercer mentioned the Taylor Report and the 'growing demands of an increasingly sophisticated football public'. This open letter said that lack of parking and 'enormous' traffic problems made it necessary to move from Tynecastle. Tynecastle is in an area of 19th-century tenement housing, about a mile and a half from the city centre and well served by buses. The sheet summarised the planning application: there would be a 'multisport leisure area covering 50 acres and ten acres of interactive landscaping', though just what interactive landscaping meant was not explained. The all-seated stadium would eventually hold 30,000. The scale of the project had quadrupled: in the 6 March 1991 programme, it was just 15 acres.

The development was described as a 'seven day a week active leisure complex'. In a resonant closing appeal, Mercer asserted, 'This is not the time for narrow minded and short sighted local ambitions,' and urged readers to send letters supporting the application to the Convenor of the Regional

----

Programme Spotlights 57: The stadium that never was

6 March 1991, Heart of Midlothian 2 St Johnstone 1, Scottish Premier Division

The stadium that never was. 'No-one really wants to leave Tynecastle, that is where our heart is but we must look to the future,' said the accompanying article. No one, except possibly an ardent Thatcherite property developer. As the article mentioned in passing, the development would also include 'hotels, retail and industrial units, a children's farm, etc.'. In other words, the speculative stadium was to be just one part of a much larger development. It would occupy six acres, but 'the ground in the immediate surroundings of the stadium planned will be much larger – 15 acres'. Weeks later, the proposal was for a 60-acre development.

The article explained that two new companies had been set up 'to manage the task'. A 'Stadium company' would do the construction of the stadium, while a 'Development Company' would 'supervise the whole area plan'. Was the difference between lower and upper cases, company/Company, an unconscious indication of where priorities lay? Profits from the Development Company would 'fund the stadium'. Indeed they would – and more! No indication was given of the ownership of either company or where either would be registered for tax purposes.

What was addressed was transport. There would be space for 5,000 cars and 350 coaches. 'For those fans who use public transport, our intention is to run subsidised transport from Gorgie,' i.e. from the Tynecastle area, it continued. The Intergovernmental Panel on Climate Change had been set up in late 1988, more than two years earlier.

Council. The fact that the site was in the designated green belt was not mentioned: this blind spot is an occupational hazard for developers.

Some 18 months later, at the start of the 1992/93 season against Falkirk, the Hearts chairman's column in the programme mentioned in passing that the club had decided not to pursue the Millerhill proposal, 'for a variety of reasons', without saying that refusal of planning permission had been one of them. They were now looking at a site on the west of the city that would have lots of parking. Mercer now explained that it was 'common sense' to locate a new stadium on the west side of town, as most fans travelled from that direction; the attempt to develop at Millerhill presumably lacked such 'common sense'! Mercer again talked up the traffic problems, and again urged supporters to lobby the council to support the scheme, while again forgetting to mention the fact that this new site also would be in the green belt. This proposal again fell through and to this day Hearts remain at an upgraded Tynecastle.

All-seater stadia flew in the face of traditional fans whose views were ignored. Liverpool's programme for their match against Coventry City at the end of February 1994 included a short item about the high demand for tickets for the final home game of the season against Norwich City, which would be the last day of the traditional Kop. Along with the programme we have a handbill, printed in red and white, that was distributed by disgruntled fans that day. On one side it says, 'NO SEATS. We are the famous Kopites. We shall not, we shall not sit down, We shall not, we shall not sit down, We are the KOP, We are the famous Spion Kop and we shall not sit down.'

The reverse side announced a flag day for the forthcoming derby with Everton. The text said, 'The pictures from SKY TV's coverage of the Man Utd game on 4 January went all around the world. Anyone who saw them have been impressed

[sic] by the Kop that night.' Rightly, it rhapsodised about the spectacle and the noise, as 'truly awe inspiring', before quoting from the *Manchester Evening News*, 'Once the Kop has become all-seater, I doubt whether we will ever witness such passion and commitment from a crowd again.' Below in bold capitals it says 'NO SEATS … NO SPONSORS… NO SEATS… NO SPONSORS'. Fans had no say in the matter. Rather they became a kind of screensaver or backdrop to the global marketing of the Premier League brand, as their absence during the lockdown and empty stadia in 2020 would demonstrate.

A similarly dissonant tone was expressed in a letter from a fan that was published in the Manchester United v. Coventry City programme on 3 January 1995. It asked, 'Is Old Trafford, with its private boxes, executive members, limited capacity and increased ticket prices, becoming elitist and out of bounds to the working class?' Hindsight suggests the answer should have been 'yes', but the chairman, Martin Edwards, who would 'earn' a reported £94m by selling his stake in the club that he inherited from his father, replied 'no'. However, he went on to explain that although 94 per cent of those attending matches were non-executives, the remaining six per cent produced 29 per cent of the gate money. It does not take much imagination to extrapolate the logic of those figures to the commercially minded. Lest there be any doubt that Edwards was so minded, it should be remembered that he had tried to sell his interest in the club for £10m in 1989, and then had floated United on the London Stock Exchange in 1991. That game against Coventry, on a cold January night, sticks in my mind because United had a small ginger-haired kid playing at centre-forward, Paul Scholes, who opened the scoring. Other youngsters in that line-up were Gary Neville, Nicky Butt and Keith Gillespie, alongside the relative veteran, Ryan Giggs.

Displacement of traditional fans, and a takeover of the spaces that they and generations before them had seen as almost sacred, was not just a physical thing. Global companies were able to appropriate the competitions, the trophies and even the associated memories and legends. The 1999 FA Cup Final programme for the meeting of the Uniteds of Manchester and Newcastle exemplifies this. The Paris-headquartered multinational finance company AXA had provided £25m sponsorship of the cup for a four-year period, and for that time the grand old competition became the FA Cup Sponsored by AXA.

There were three full-page AXA advertisements in the programme, including one on the back cover. Each proclaimed in bold letters, 'The F.A. Cup. Brought to you by AXA.' In each case there was a photo of fans holding the cup, which was festooned with AXA ribbons. This reflected the fact that AXA had allowed fans to get a photo of themselves with the trophy, but the words and the ribbons also established whose cup it now was. So, literally, AXA were bringing the hallowed trophy to the fans, and so building a bond of gratitude with them. But metaphorically, the FA Cup had always belonged to the fans: its calendar and routines marked every year of our lives without the need for it to be 'brought to you by AXA'. The history of the competition, the great moments and memories, were mine, yours and everyone else's ... things we carried with us, not something brought to us and badged by a finance company's logo.

Since the 1990s, the lustre of the FA Cup has been considerably diminished. Premier League clubs in particular have often fielded under-strength sides. Crowds have dwindled for all but the big games. Quite simply, Premier League achievement, and particularly Champions League involvement, bring much greater financial rewards, while the chance of glory for lower-league sides has been reduced as the financial gap between the elite and the rest has widened. Whichever TV company has the broadcast rights does its best to invoke 'the magic of the cup' and scrabbles to find the occasional 'shock' and to lionise the 'giant-killers', but for many fans the sparkle has been lost, along with the replays and mud-bath pitches that made the competition such an integral part of our winters. There can still be thrilling encounters, just as there were dross games in the past, but the zeitgeist of the competition has been irrevocably changed.

Programme Spotlights 58: Whose heritage is it?
22 May 1999, Manchester United 2 Newcastle United 0, FA Cup Final

This lavishly illustrated, full-colour programme extensively repackaged the history of the FA Cup for its readers in order to associate AXA's range of financial services products with the competition. Eight pages celebrated 'Cup Final Heroes': 1951 Jackie Milburn; 1953 Stan Matthews; 1958 Nat Lofthouse; 1971 Charlie George; 1973 Jim Montgomery; 1981 Ricky Villa; 1986 Ian Rush; 1996 Eric Cantona.

There was another two-page historical feature recalling 'FA Cup Final History Makers'. In addition, another four pages were devoted to the 1898/99 season's competition with engaging sepia photos, including ones of winners Sheffield United in horse-drawn carriages following their 4-1 victory over Derby County at Crystal Palace. In all these pages, and others, AXA's logo was displayed.

The game saw United win 2-0 with goals from Sheringham (an early substitute for Roy Keane) and Scholes. It was the second leg of the Premier League, FA Cup and Champions League treble that Alex Ferguson's team won that season.

The satellite television-driven internationalisation of football in the 1990s and beyond widened not only the gaps between the importance attached to the FA Cup and the Premier League, but also the gaps between and within national leagues. The reach of the English Premier League became global in every sense, and not least in player recruitment. The Arsenal team that lined up at Old Trafford on 24 January 2000 had four French players (Grimandi, Vieira, Petit and Henry) plus the Brazilian defender Sylvinho and Swede Freddie Ljungberg. Five years earlier, Martin Edwards, in Manchester United's programme v. Coventry, had shown foresight in writing, 'Further expansion of our merchandising operation will be an important area of our funding. At the moment we are only really selling into the UK market and there is tremendous potential for us in the Far East and in Scandinavia.'

Fast forward to 24 July 1999 and United were playing in Hong Kong. Victor Apps, president and CEO of Manulife (International), was providing the message of welcome in Chinese and English for the match with the South China Athletic Association (see Programme Spotlights 59). Manulife are not, as cynics might imagine, another tentacle of Manchester United's commercial machine. They are a long-established finance house, the Manufacturers' Life Insurance Company, headquartered in Toronto, but operating in the USA as John Hancock. They launched a bank in 1993, and went public in 1999 with the largest initial public offering (IPO) in Canadian history.

Another fund manager advertising in that programme was Paribas, with these words, 'A leading player in the primary and secondary equity markets worldwide, with strong teams in Europe, Asia and the Americas, Paribas offers institutional investors a truly global research and trading capability.' There was another full-page advertisement from Pegasus Fund Managers, again offering corporate portfolio management, but also financial services to individuals. The

similar advertisement placed by The Sovereign Group drew
the eye with the words printed in gold, 'Save Tax Legally'.
They offered 'confidentiality of dealing direct with one of
the largest offshore service providers in the world'. Contact
phones and e-mail addresses were provided in well-known
tax havens: British Virgin Islands, Turks and Caicos Islands,
Gibraltar, and of course, London. While the products of other
advertisers such as Coca-Cola, Kent cigarettes, and Kentucky
Fried Chicken were targeted at a more general audience of
fans, it seems possible that the finance companies were seeking
reputational enhancement as much as new clients by being
associated with the match.

Programme Spotlights 59: Hong Kong's finest
**24 July 1999, South China Athletic Association 0
Manchester United 2, friendly**

This large, glossy and colourful 32-page programme is in Chinese
and English. One of the full-page adverts inside is for ProEvents,
who had organised Manchester United's pre-season tour, which
also took in a game in Shanghai, as well as this one in Hong Kong.
They had organised Asian excursions for United in 1995 (to Kuala
Lumpur) and 1997 (to Bangkok, Hong Kong and Tokyo), as well
as similar trips for Chelsea in 1997 and Arsenal in 1999, as English
clubs sought to market their brand in the East Asia.

Predictably, most of the articles and photos focused on United
and their recent treble. Their opponents, known as the Sweet
Caroliners, had formed in 1908 and were the best supported team
in Hong Kong.

In 2003 the governor of Chukotka in the far north-east
of Russia, a former street trader and mechanic who had
reportedly had been arrested in 1992 for theft of state
property, bought Chelsea. Roman Abramovich was able to
do this because, still in his 30s, he happened to have become

one of the owners of a company that owned much of Russia's oil wealth. The transformation of Chelsea to champions on the pitch, and to 'Chelski' off it, was a landmark change in ownership of leading British clubs.

The Wolverhampton Wanderers v. Manchester United programme from the start of the 2019/20 season (see Programme Spotlights 60) shows just how comprehensively the Premier League clubs became entwined in global circuits of capital. Wolves' executive chairman, Jeff Shi, wrote an introductory column in the programme, as chairmen often do. Mr Shi is the senior assistant president of Fosun and chairman of Fosun Sports Group. Fosun is a leading Chinese conglomerate, founded in 1992 and headquartered in Shanghai. It bought Wolves in 2016 for £45m, small change for a company of Fosun's size.

By 2020, owning a football club had become a way to globalise assets and move money around for giant corporations, hedge funds, the super-rich and sovereign states with nasty human rights records. 'Sportswashing', a term coined by Amnesty International in December 2018 to describe Abu Dhabi's ownership of Manchester City, had arrived. Behind the programmes now were people wanting to make a lot of money without paying much tax on it in the UK, or those wanting to rebrand their reputations globally. Football, and in particular the Premier League, was just one part of the UK's offer, along with a laid-back attitude to sale of national assets, a lax regulatory regime and exceptional connections to tax havens.

Yet, as that programme shows, nostalgia can be part of the commodity that is sold to the fans. 'The Archives' included a feature on Wolves legend Steve Bull (see Chapter 11), another on Billy Wright (see Chapters 2, 4 and 7) who captained the title-winning sides of the 1950s, and also recalled some past meetings with Manchester United from

1967 onwards. On the other side of the coin, as it were, from the past, the programme also included a page advertising a cryptocurrency exchange platform, Coindeal, one of the club's 'global partners'.

- -

Programme Spotlights 60: New York, Portugal, Wolverhampton and China

19 August 2019, Wolverhampton Wanderers 1 Manchester United 1, Premier League

This compact, thick, colourful and information-packed programme from the start of the 2019/20 season typifies the state of club publications at the time. It includes a page explaining when the Video Assistant Referee can be used: this was the first season VAR had operated in the Premier League. There are lots of photos and player profiles, and even a tear-out poster. The squads are listed on the back cover, including the inevitable sponsors' logos. Seven of the 21-man Wolves group are Portuguese, reflecting the club's close ties with super-agent Jorge Mendes. There is also a report on the club's pre-season tour to China, and a couple of pages on Wolves Women, who were playing in the FA National League First Division Midlands. Another page covers the New York supporters' club formed the previous year.

There is also a section on the new Wolves Fantasy Premier League competition, played online and on mobile phones, that allows 'Wolves fans from across the globe' to compete with each other. There is also plenty of nostalgia in 'The Archives', including a couple of pages on past meetings, complete with programme covers.

- -

However, as the Covid pandemic and lockdown approached it was not so much cryptocurrencies that defined the Premier League as the global online gambling industry. The front cover of that programme shows not just a player, Diogo Jota, but also ManBetX as Wolves' shirt sponsor for 2019/20. They are a gambling firm from the Philippines and best known in Asia, but with a European headquarters in Malta.

The fixture list for the season has been an enduring feature of football programmes. In that schedule, which would be disrupted in March 2020 by the pandemic, were forthcoming meetings with nine other Premier League clubs whose shirt sponsors were gambling businesses based offshore. The clubs, the companies and their headquarters were Aston Villa (W88, The Philippines); Bournemouth (M88, The Philippines and Gibraltar); Burnley (LoveBet, Malta); Crystal Palace (ManBetX, Malta); Everton (SportPesa, Kenya and Isle of Man); Newcastle United (Fun88, Isle of Man); Norwich City (Dafabet, The Philippines); Watford (Sportsbet.io, Curaçao); West Ham United (Betway, Malta). During the 2020 lockdown, Bournemouth ended their shirt sponsorship with M88 after UK gambling regulators investigated the company.

Yet as the world's super-rich were embracing English football, traditional fans were feeling excluded. Admittedly, ground improvements at Old Trafford had reduced capacity temporarily in 1995, but then and in the years that followed just getting into the stadium for a game was challenging. The 3 January 1995 programme v. Coventry explained what you needed to do to watch the home game with Aston Villa on 4 February. First of all you had to purchase membership; in effect you paid an annual fee for the right to try to buy a ticket, or rather to enter a lottery in which you might win the chance to buy a ticket. Members could apply five weeks in advance, so for the 4 February game this meant 31 December, i.e. four days before the Coventry game. 'Applications must include all relevant membership documentation,' came the advice, plus an open cheque, stamped and addressed envelope and letter of application. 'If oversubscribed on the first day of sale,' as it always was, 'a postal ballot will be held to determine the successful applicants.' Those responding to the notice in the

3 January programme would actually have had no realistic chance of getting a ticket for the visit of Villa. The programme did warn that 'any member who requests additional tickets for non-members should be aware that it is highly unlikely that their application will be successful'.

For the 2002 World Cup Finals in Japan and Korea, the first time the finals were held in Asia, the process of getting to a game was even more complicated and restrictive. The spectator guide produced for the tournament explained what to do. Fans should arrive at the stadium as early as possible: gates would open three hours before kick-off. 'You cannot enter a stadium using a Smartcard. Also Smartcard users cannot collect their tickets at the stadium.' Rather, Smartcard users had to collect their tickets the day before the match from a FIFA World Cup Ticketing Centre (though there were no such centres in two of the host cities). 'Please bring identification when you go to a match.' Those with the stamina to get that far then had to pass through three rings of stadium security. First was a ticket check and body and bag search. Then, at the stadium entrance, the ticket stub would be collected. Finally, at the third gate, stewards would check the ticket and conduct the spectator to the assigned seat. 'You cannot re-enter the first and second gates.'

All of this reflected the nervous world after the 11 September 2001 atrocity in the USA, and the fear that terrorists besotted by global spectacle would target the World Cup. There was a list of prohibited items that included swords, 'sealed paper cartons', non-foldable umbrellas, confetti, and a catch-all, 'Other items that security personnel judge could inhibit the smooth running of the tournament or endanger other spectators.' The guide had an equally extensive list of 'Forbidden Acts inside the Stadiums', which included 'damaging, soiling or misusing facilities or equipment', 'insulting, provoking other people', 'setting up tents', 'speeches, group gatherings or preaching'. Loitering just about anywhere was also forbidden, as was starting fires or hiding one's face or littering, to name just a few.

Another page informed readers that surveillance cameras were installed in all the stadiums, each of which also had a security command centre. A further page was given over to a welcome from the National Police Agency and Ministry of Justice (Japan) on its security policy. It included 13 bullet points of acts illegal in Japan, which included 'loitering in groups in public places', a time-honoured activity of football fans. The centre pages warned against another danger identified by FIFA, 'ambushes' by companies trying to associate their product with the World Cup without paying into the bloated FIFA coffers for the privilege. 'Do not bring commercially branded material (company names, logos etc.) into the stadium, such as flags, banners, hats, balloons, scarves. Please be aware that Stadium Security will be removing all such items at the stadium entrances.'

Nearer to home, the stricter security measures complicated my mother's attempt to ensure that when going to game, her grandchildren and I were well stocked with sufficient sweets, tangerines, fizzy drinks and sundry other preparations to survive a siege. Bag searches at the gates meant such dangerous items had to be consumed before admission was granted. It could be a tall order, and Mum took some persuading that more meagre rations were appropriate. In summary, by the new millennium the once simple act of going to watch a game, while still possible below the top level, had been engulfed by surveillance and a range of restrictions. In part that was a response to crowd trouble, and in part to international terrorism. But it was also entwined with corporate privilege and protectionism, whether through the banning of competitors' logos, or the purchase of executive boxes in stadia in which to lubricate relations with potential clients or simply provide another perk for well-paid staff or owners.

The 2002 World Cup was characterised by a series of scandals within FIFA. In particular, Spain and Italy were eliminated by hosts South Korea after being on the wrong end of some contentious refereeing decisions. The Ecuadorean referee who wrongly sent off Italy's Francesco Totti was jailed in 2010 for drug trafficking in New York. The Italian newspaper *Corriere dello Sport* alleged that the Egyptian referee and Trinidadian linesman who presided over Spain's quarter-final defeat were chosen by Jack Warner, whose fiefdom was in the Caribbean and who was indicted subsequently by an investigation into FIFA corruption. Football had become a way to get very, very rich, and the rich and powerful took a firm grip on the game.

While football in England was detaching itself from its traditional base, it was establishing new footholds in the USA. Euan was there doing a PhD, and so programmes – or rather 'programs' – from Major League Soccer began to enter our collection. MLS was a relaunch of football in the USA. The North American Soccer League had been set up in 1968 and was best known for the ageing stars that it signed up, including luminaries Pelé, George Best and Franz Beckenbauer. However, it folded in 1984, having always struggled to compete for media attention with the nation-building domestic sports, notably baseball and American football, but also basketball and ice hockey. Despite this setback, 'soccer' was growing in popularity at school level, with many suburban 'moms' seeing it as less of a risk to youngsters' bodies than American football. In addition, ethnic groups, and particularly the large Mexican-American community, retained their love of 'proper' football. In 1988, FIFA awarded the USA the 1994 World Cup finals, on condition that a new professional league was created.

Euan's programmes from the games he went to at New England Revolution and at Washington DC United in 1996, the inaugural season of MLS, were basically the same, with the same cover name, *Freekick*, and many of the same big US company advertisements, for Kellogg's and Budweiser, for example. While professional football in its European and Latin American heartlands had grown bottom up, in the USA it has been a top-down, corporate-driven project, with recognition of its appeal to the growing market represented by Latin-Americans. The advertisement in the programmes for the telecom company AT&T was in Spanish, and the welcome to Major League Soccer from the Commissioner was presented in English and Spanish. Presumably in the franchised world of US soccer, programmes of other clubs were also following this template.

In best USA style, the early MSL programmes were large. They came with the compliments of the club, and covered four matches (including away games), with a smaller, single-sheet insert for the particular match. Terminology showed obvious influences from and appeals to followers of the gridiron form of football: between the team 'matchups' (line-ups) and 'roster' (list of the playing staff) was a box headed 'What to watch for' which covered 'Offense' and 'Defense'. Another page provided an explanation of what happens if there was a 'tie' at the end of 'regulation'. The game would go directly to a shoot-out, with 'players on each team challenging the opposing goalkeeper in a one-on-one situation'. The player would start with the ball 35 yards from goal and have five seconds in which to shoot, while the keeper had to start on the goal line but could move. Initially each team would have five players attempting to beat the goalkeeper, and if still level, the process would continue until there was a winner.

Each program contained a Fan's Corner column, which explained a 'Buzz Word'. For the DC United issue for their home games with Los Angeles Galaxy, Dallas Burn, NY/NJ Metrostars and Columbus Crew in April-May 1996, that word was 'Nutmeg'. 'You just got "nutmegged" if you got caught standing still and your opponent dribbled the ball between your legs. Ouch!' You can almost hear new converts sounding it out, 'Nut-megged'. In that same month's issue, New England Revolution fans had 'Magic Sponge' explained in the same slot, 'A quick rubdown with the sponge and water can miraculously heal players who only moments before appeared to be in great pain… the sponge is most often used late in a game when a player is very tired.'

In short, these programmes from the start of the MLS have a missionary aura, grafting a new religion on to cherished pagan traditions. But one thing more than any other connected MLS with the English Premier League. It was that football had become a commodity in search of new customers. As the MLS commissioner wrote in those programs for the opening round of matches, what was being offered was a 'sports entertainment experience'. Importantly, the programmes carried news that ESPN, 'the world's largest cable network', would be televising games. In addition, 'Univision, which has broadcast the past seven World Cups to America's Spanish-speaking audience' would also screen matches. It made reference to Univision commentator Andres Cantor's 'trademark "goal" call', which I can easily imagine as a high decibel, extended explosion of excitement.

Scotland played the USA in New Britain, Connecticut on 26 May 1996, as part of their preparation for the Euro '96 finals in England. It was still the early weeks of MLS. The programme did not include a team sheet, and only four Scots were profiled as 'Players to Watch': skipper Gary McAllister; Celtic midfielder John Collins ('the only player to play in all of Scotland's qualifying matches for Euro '96'); 'one of the best young players' in Eoin Jess, then with Coventry City; and Scott Booth of Aberdeen who had scored five times in his ten international appearances. Scotland lined up with Leighton; Boyd, Hendry, Calderwood and Whyte; Jess, Burley, Gemmill and Jackson; Booth and Durie. McAllister, Collins, Spencer and McCall came on as subs along with Nicky Walker, who replaced Leighton. It was not a vintage Scottish squad, but it would be the last to reach a Euros finals for a generation.

Programme Spotlights 61: Star-spangled banner
26 May 1996, USA 2 Scotland 1, friendly

This is one game that Euan went to, naturally, while doing his PhD at Syracuse University. He was part of a crowd of just over 8,000, which meant the Willow Brook Park stadium was almost full. Glossy and colourful, the programme has no local content. The image on the front shows the most recognisable USA player of his era, defender Alexi Lalas, who looked like he was a member of a heavy metal band.

Unusually for the time, the short text from the president of US Soccer made reference to the nation's women's team, who had won the FIFA Women's World Championship in 1991 and finished third in 1995. In most European countries, women's participation in football was ignored.

The photos of the members of the US squad include several who would forge careers in Europe. Goalkeeper Brad Friedel was already with Galatasaray in Turkey, then between 1997 and 2015 he would play for Liverpool, Blackburn Rovers, Aston Villa and Tottenham Hotspur. Midfielder Tom Dooley was already playing in Germany for FC Schalke 04. Striker Jovan Kirovski's club was given as Manchester United Reserves: the UK would not grant him a work permit and he moved to Borussia Dortmund, appearing for them in the Champions League. Joe-Max Moore was with Nuremberg; goalkeeper Jurgen Sommer was with Queens Park Rangers, having been at Luton Town from 1991 to '95, during which time he had a spell on loan at Torquay United; Claudio Reyna was at Bayer Leverkusen, and from 1999 to 2007 he played in midfield for Rangers, Sunderland and Manchester City. Striker Ernie Stewart was at NEC Breda: he had grown up in The Netherlands as the son of an African American air force

man. John Harkes, then with DC United, had returned to the
USA after six years in England with Sheffield Wednesday, Derby
County then West Ham. Winger Cobi Jones had had a brief spell
at Coventry City. Forward Eric Wynalda had played in Germany
for 1 FC Saarbrücken and for VfL Bochum. This was the first
time that the USA beat Scotland.

For the American squad, the programme included their photo,
height, weight, date and place of birth, home town, college
and finally club. These basic details give a sketch of how
and by whom professional football was being created in the
USA in the early 1990s. Twenty players were illustrated. Five
had been born outside the USA: Jeff Agoos in Geneva; Tom
Dooley in Bechofen, Germany; Tab Ramos in Montevideo,
Uruguay; Ernie Stewart in Veghel, the Netherlands; and
Martin Vasquez in Jalisco, Mexico. Others, though US-born,
were from recent immigrant families: Jovan Kirovski, for
example, was born and grew up in Escondido, California,
of Macedonian parents; Claudio Reyna's father had played
professionally in his native Argentina before migrating to
the US in 1968. The father of Alexi Lalas was Greek; Eric
Wynalda's ancestry was Dutch.

Within the USA, there was also a geography of where the
players grew up. Nine of them had home towns in California.
Dooley was among them: his home town, Mission Viejo, is
included in an Open University video I used to show students
in which geographer Ed Soja highlighted Mission Viejo as
an example of post-modern urbanism, a masterplanned
Orange County commuter city marketed by its developers
as an incubator for sporting excellence. California is by far
America's most populous state, so that might partly explain
the scale of its representation in the national squad. Also it
has large numbers of Hispanics and Latinos, which helped to
seed a football culture.

The home states of the rest of that 1996 squad were scattered – three from New Jersey, two from North Carolina, and one each from Texas, Florida, Ohio, Massachusetts, Michigan and Missouri. It is also worth noting that only Dooley, Kirovski, Stewart and Steve Pittman had no college listed. As in other US sport, and in contrast to the UK, college scholarships were a route into the professional game.

Recalling that match, Euan says 'The Scotland v. USA game in Connecticut was weird. It was in a high school stadium, I think, and we sat on the metal bleachers, like they have at all parks here. I remember being very close to the players and was stunned that the crowd could get so close to these people who had played in/would play in World Cups, that they could chat to them as if they were standing on either side of a garden fence. It was all very suburban and middle-class.'

In contrast to the rise of the game in the USA, the satellite and cable TV-driven era witnessed a sad decline in the status of Scotland's clubs and national team. A whole book could be written about that story. The agency of clubs and the Scottish FA would be part of it, not least in explaining the steady diminution in the production and promotion of players of the highest quality. Yet there are structural factors too, with the small size of the Scottish market a deterrent to accessing the largesse of the broadcasters, and hence pricing even Rangers and Celtic out of the market for top players. Before the 2020 lockdown shut out spectators, the Old Firm clubs had average home attendances of over 49,000, putting them in the top 20 globally, and well in excess of what many Premier League clubs manage in England.

The lack of domestic competition, which has charact-erised the Scottish game since the brief rise of Aberdeen and Dundee United in the 1980s, is not a sufficient explanation for the slump. Dominance by one or two clubs is now common across major European leagues as the rich have got richer. However, the Scottish experience, alongside other smaller nations such as some in eastern Europe, deserves more analysis, just as does the success of Iceland, a very small country that invested in the physical and human infrastructure to develop the sport. It is equally notable that the anticipated breakthrough in the World Cup by African countries has not happened, despite the steady flow of players to top European leagues. Even China, India and the Asian Tiger Cub Economies have struggled to make an impact, except in online gambling. Globalisation has reinforced the dominance of the traditionally big clubs, while geographically diversifying their ownership and where they choose to pay taxes. For fans, it meant a move from the terraces and a pre-match sweepstake on the first goalscorer, to a seat on the world-wide sofa in front of a multi-channel TV and the chance to bet in-play on whether the Albanian wing-back will get a yellow card.

Programmes cited in Chapter 13 that are in the collection:

- 2 May 1960, Manchester City 1 Burnley 2, Football League First Division
- 1 May 1976, Manchester United 0 Southampton 1, FA Cup Final
- 21 May 1977, Liverpool 1 Manchester United 2, FA Cup Final
- 12 May 1979, Arsenal 3 Manchester United 2, FA Cup Final
- 15 August 1987, Scarborough 2 Wolverhampton Wanderers 2, Football League Fourth Division
- 6 March 1991, Heart of Midlothian 2 St Johnstone 1, Scottish Premier Division
- 28 September 1991, Falkirk 1 Heart of Midlothian 2, Scottish Premier Division

- 5 August 1992, Heart of Midlothian 3 Falkirk 0, Scottish Premier Division
- 6 September 1992, Manchester United 2 Leeds United 0, Premier League
- 19 September 1992, Tottenham Hotspur 1 Manchester United 1, Premier League
- 27 March 1993, Brighton & Hove Albion 0 Swansea City 2, Football League Second Division
- 28 August 1993, Dundee United 0 Heart of Midlothian 0, Scottish Premier Division
- 1 September 1993, Manchester United 3 West Ham United 0, Premier League
- 24 November 1993, Manchester United 0 Ipswich Town 0, Premier League
- 28 November 1993, Liverpool 2 Aston Villa 1, Premier League
- 7 December 1993, Sheffield United 0 Manchester United 3, Premier League
- I January 1994, Manchester United 0 Leeds United 0, Premier League
- 26 February 1994, Liverpool 1 Coventry City 0, Premier League
- 27 August 1994, Heart of Midlothian 0 Hibernian 1, Scottish Premier Division
- 4 May 1994, Manchester United 2 Southampton 0, Premier League
- 3 January 1995, Manchester United 2 Coventry City 0, Premier League
- 20 April 1996, D.C. United 1 Los Angeles Galaxy 2, Major League Soccer
- 27 April 1996, New England Revolution 1 DC United 1 (after extra time, Revolution won 3-2 in a shoot-out)
- 1 May 1996, D.C. United 3 Dallas Burn 1, Major League Soccer

- 4 May 1996, New England Revolution 1 San Jose Clash 2, Major League Soccer
- 12 May 1996, NY/NJ MetroStars 1 DC United 1 (after extra time, MetroStars won 2-1 in a shoot-out), Major League Soccer
- 15 May 1996, Columbus Crew 2 DC United 5, Major League Soccer
- 19 May 1996, New England Revolution 2 NY/NJ MetroStars 0, Major League Soccer
- 25 May 1996, New England Revolution 2 Colorado Rapids 2 (Revolution won 1-0 in a shoot-out), Major League Soccer
- 26 May 1996, USA 2 Scotland 1, friendly
- 24 July 1999, South China Athletic Association 0 Manchester United 2, friendly
- 24 January 2000, Manchester United 1 Arsenal 1, Premier League
- 19 August 2019, Wolverhampton Wanderers 1 Manchester United 1, Premier League

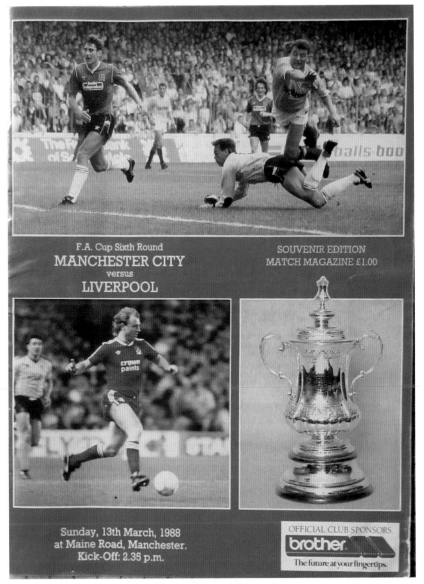

F.A. Cup Sixth Round
MANCHESTER CITY
versus
LIVERPOOL

SOUVENIR EDITION
MATCH MAGAZINE £1.00

Sunday, 13th March, 1988
at Maine Road, Manchester.
Kick-Off: 2.35 p.m.

Programme Spotlights 47: The highest forklift truck in Europe

Programme Spotlights 48: The Wakes

Programme Spotlights 49: Did AC Milan train on Bovril?

Programme Spotlights 50: Scottish Torquay United Supporters' Club away day

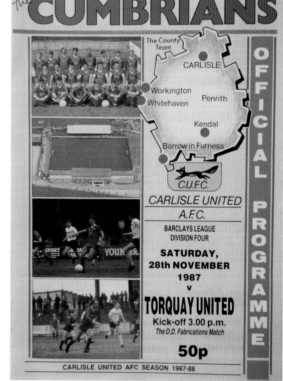

015690 **PRIS: kr. 7,-**

PROGRAM
BRØNSHØJ - BRØNDBY
24. juli kl. 19.00

Brønshøj gør det sværere og sværere for sig selv ...

På baggrund af BB's sidste kamp i foråret, hvor vi slog Silkeborg med 4-1 og endda måtte undvære karantæneramte Leif Sørensen og Lars E. Jensen, skrev jeg i medlemsbladet, at nu måtte optimismen lav ethvert om at være det og at vi, hvis vi fortsætter de takter, ville blive etableret hold i 1. division.

Gode træningsresultater

Optakten til turneringsstarten i Herfølge har da også været levende. Ikke en kamp har vi tabt, og vi sluttede med at vinde Hvalsø CUP med 6-4 over Næstved efter forlænget spilletid og straffesparkskonkurrence. Den ordinære kamp endte 1-1. Sejren indbragte 5.000 kr.

God kamp, men nederlag i Herfølge

Optimismen var da også stor,

da vi i søndags lagde ud mod Herfølge. Nu skulle de gode takter fortsættes og vort kompleks på udebane overtales. Desværre gik det anderledes. Endnu engang måtte vi konstatere, at trods overvægt i spil og chancer, så løb Herfølge med begge points i kraft af en 1-0 sejr.

Ikke særlig, at vi alle hang med hovederne efter kampen og følte os rædt snydt. Men lad os glemme resultatet og konstatere, at vi trods alt spillede bedst og ind i mellem viste flot bold. Vi har bare gjort det sværere for os selv.

Hver kamp på hjemmebane skal vindes

Vi vil ikke overtræt vort udebanekompleks i Herfølge, på den anden side skal det presset på vore spillere, når de spiller her i Vanløse, idet hver kamp skal vindes uanset modstander.

I dag gælder det så montene fra Brøndby, en tilsyneladende uoverkommelig opgave. Men lad os nu se.

Brøndby fik da den ventede puljesejr i Toto-turneringen, og hjemvendte spillere fra feriet samt indspilning af nye folk, efter salget af John »Faxe« Jensen og Claus Nielsen kan betyde sand i maskineriet.

Lad os udnytte det i dag, og lad os se det BB-spil, vi kender og holder til meget af. Så vinder vi også i dag. Rigtig god fornøjelse.

Walde

En sejr her kunne have givet Brøndby »The double«, men det glippede altså.

I den hjemlige turnering er Brøndby's øjeblikket placeret som nr. 2. Kun Silkeborg har været i stand til at besejre Brøndby i foråret. Med modtagesejren over OB, har Brøndby tilbageerobret 1. pladsen, som enhver anser som en naturlig placering.

Salget af John »Faxe« Jensen og Claus Nielsen kan dog midlertidigt slå rytmen i stykker, indtil Per Bartram, købt af Glasgow Rangers for 4 mill. kr., Rene Hansen, hentet hjem fra Helsingør og Ole Østergaard (udlagte fra Sion) m.fl. bliver spillet ind på holdet.

I den nys afviklede Toto-turnering har den unge angriber Torben Frank virkelig fyret s. Claus Nielsen favnet. 5 gange har han scoret. Brøndby sluttede på 3. pladsen i sin gruppe, ldt skuffende for dem selv måske, men det er dog værd at bemærke, at flere stamspillere var på ferie.

Til kampen i dag stiller Brøndby op i stærkeste opstilling, og det bliver interessant at se, om de fra ferie hjemvendte spillere, sammen med de nye på holdet, med det samme finder sammen i den altindtrentende stil, som normalt kendetegner holdet. Gør Brøndbys det, venter der BB en særdeles varm aften og måske ubehagelig overraskelse.

Der er ét sted, du ikke behøver slås for en god placering.

sds *sds*

Brøndby, en magtfaktor i dansk fodbold...

I dag har vi fornøjelsen af at byde velkommen til Brøndby, danmarksmestrene fra 1987. Brøndbys betrifter de seneste år er vel efterhånden alle bekendt og også, at klubben har udviklet sig til en magtfaktor i

dansk fodbold. Kort og godt, en suveræn fodboldklub med økonomi og spillertrup helt i top.

Denne stjernestatus har selvsagt medført krav om resultater ikke kun i DM, men også

ved deltagelse i de store europæiske cup-turneringer. Indtil nu har spillerne opfyldt de spillemæssige forventninger, omend det var en skuffelse, at landspokalfinalen blev tabt til AGF med 2-1.

V

Vær på tæerne for at skaffe dine penge den bedst mulige placering. Ispørget om din indtening ligger i pulinge- eller unionseblten.

SPAREKASSEN *sds*
— til svede for dig

Sun Shipping

& THORNS ApS

WORLDWIDE TRANSPORT

SUN SHIPPING ApS
»MÆGLERGAARDEN«
GL. LYNGEVEJ 18, 3450 ALLERØD

02 27 51 51

Programme Spotlights 51: A Danish detour

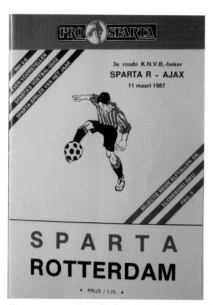

Programme Spotlights 52: A great Ajax side

Programme Spotlights 53: Thoughts of Josef Münzberger

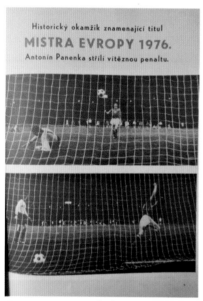

Programme Spotlights 54: The first 'Panenka'

Programme Spotlights 55: It's a gas

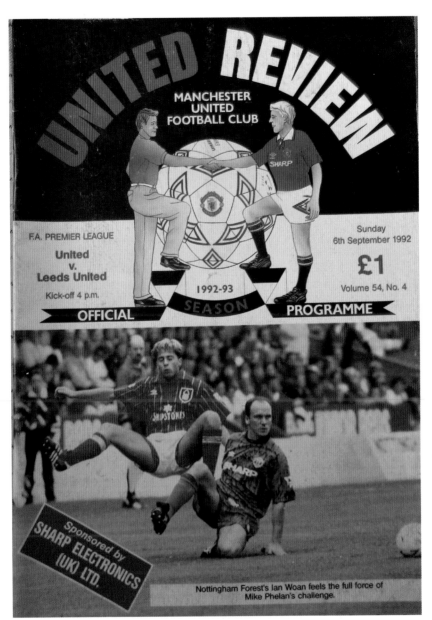

MANCHESTER
UNITED
FOOTBALL CLUB

F.A. PREMIER LEAGUE

United
v.
Leeds United

Kick-off 4 p.m.

Sunday
6th September 1992

£1

Volume 54, No. 4

1992-93

SEASON

OFFICIAL   **PROGRAMME**

Sponsored by
SHARP ELECTRONICS
(UK) LTD.

Nottingham Forest's Ian Woan feels the full force of
Mike Phelan's challenge.

Programme Spotlights 56: Reach for the Sky

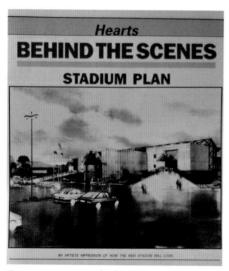

Programme Spotlights 57: The stadium that never was

Programme Spotlights 58: Whose heritage is it?

Programme Spotlights 59: Hong Kong's finest

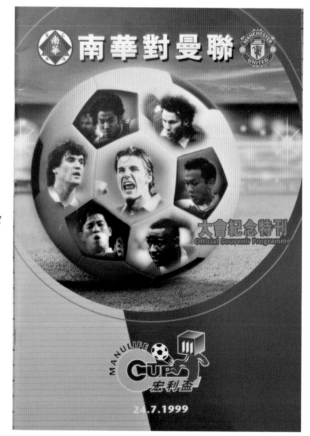

*Programme Spotlights
60: New York, Portugal,
Wolverhampton and China*

*Programme Spotlights
61: Star-spangled banner*

Programme Spotlights 62:
Behind closed doors

Programme Spotlights 63:
Big coat day

Manchester United centre-forward Jack Rowley, having lobbed Blackpool keeper Joe Robinson, taps in to equalise in the 1948 FA Cup Final.

Jack Crompton in action for Manchester United. In the last league game of 1948/49 he had saved a penalty securing a second place finish. In the early 1950s he was running a sweets and tobacco corner shop.

Bert Trautmann, Manchester City's outstanding goalkeeper, makes a save against West Ham United at Upton Park, 7 November 1959.

The picture of the Busby Babes that I had on my bedroom wall. Back row (left to right): Duncan Edwards, Bill Foulkes, Mark Jones, Ray Wood, Eddie Colman and David Pegg. Front row: John Berry, Bill Whelan, Roger Byrne, Tommy Taylor and Dennis Viollet.

Nandor Hidegkuti completes his hat-trick by driving home Hungary's sixth goal in their 6-3 victory over England at Wembley. Others in the picture (left to right) are Jimmy Dickinson, Zlatan Czibor, Billy Wright, Sandor Kocsis and Harry Johnson, with Stanley Matthews watching on in the distance.

Martin Peters, a star from his days as a schoolboy, scores England's second goal in the 1966 World Cup Final, with Roger Hunt, whose career began in non-league football, close by.

Two of Scotland's all-time greats, Denis Law (left) and Kenny Dalglish, on the attack against Czechoslovakia, 23 September 1973, on a delirious night at Hampden when Scotland qualified for the 1974 World Cup Finals.

Laurie Cunningham, the second black player to win a full England cap, takes on Ashley Grimes, England v. Republic of Ireland, Wembley, 6 February 1980.

Argentinian star Ossie Ardiles and his Spurs team-mates Mickey Hazard and number six Steve Perryman chase Leicester City's Andy Peake in the 1982 FA Cup semi-final, 3 April 1982, the day after Argentina invaded the Falkland Islands.

Michel Platini sends Liverpool keeper Bruce Grobbelaar the wrong way to fire home the penalty that won the 1985 European Cup for Juventus, in the game overshadowed by crowd violence and the deaths of 39 people, mostly Italians.

Dave Bennett
scores Coventry
City's 99th-
minute winner
against Leeds
United in the FA
Cup semi-final,
12 April 1987,
in front of the
fearsome fencing
at the Leppings
Lane end of
Hillsborough.

Midfielders John
Collins and Valeri
Karpin challenge
for a header in
the 1-1 European
Championship
qualifier at
Hampden in
November 1994.
Karpin was born
in Estonia, which
had been part of
the USSR.

The 1999 FA Cup Final 'Brought to you by AXA': Paul Scholes scores Manchester United's decisive second goal, despite the pressure from Newcastle's Laurent Charvet.

Jay Lynch of Salford makes a save during the National League North match between FC United of Manchester and Salford City at FC's Broadhurst Park ground on 28 January 2017.

The changing face of football: Kirsty Hanson of Manchester United is challenged by Maz Pacheco of West Ham United during the Barclays FA Women's Super League match between Manchester United Women and West Ham United Women played behind closed doors at Old Trafford during lockdown.

Programmes!
Programmes!

Chapter 14

Wartime to Lockdown

LIKE MANY everyday objects, but perhaps more than most, football programmes embody entangled histories. They are products of their time and their place, but also the bearers of personal experiences and memories. The paper they are printed on, the images and words they contain are mundane and fleeting: usually they are produced for once-only consumption, for a few inconsequential minutes on one afternoon or evening, while the reader is waiting for the teams to appear or is travelling home after a game. They are ephemeral, disposable within the day, forgettable in their banality. Even when promoted as souvenirs of once special occasions such as a cup final, most will soon fade from care and consciousness. Yet they have been an intrinsic part of football and its history. From the mid-20th century they had an allure for kids like me who became collectors. Despite the instant availability of information on our phones, and the lockdown that required games to be played without fans, clubs still produce printed programmes, and fans still collect them.

I would never have thought in those days of short trousers and scabby knees so long ago that programmes could be proxy for state-of-the-nation documents, or even milestones marking my life, though that is what they have become. Ember-like, programmes keep memories warm even as memory fades. Manchester United 1 Everton 2 in March 1955 was the first game I was allowed to go to without an adult, a new freedom at a time when my life was lived very locally. I went with my school pal David Dawson: today, would parents let a couple of ten year-olds travel by themselves on buses across a big city to watch a Premier League game? We stood at the front of the Stretford End, and all I can remember is Everton's rumbustious centre-forward Dave Hickson scooping mud on to his knee to claim a foul.

The cartoon page of that programme (see Programme Spotlights 62) offered 'a shocking peep into the future', which anticipated the way football was being staged as I was finishing this book. The cartoonist depicted football in an empty stadium with the 'crowd' watching at home on their television. The sketches imagined incidents in the match being appropriated by advertisements which would be interspersed with the action. It bears an uncanny resemblance to what happened in the coronavirus pandemic of 2020, when the domestic season was suspended in March, and resumed in June behind closed doors, with clubs desperate not to lose revenue from the contract with TV companies. However, fans in 2020/21 watching on TV or streaming on their computers or mobile phones were wearing replica club shirts, not a mackintosh and rosette as they were in the 1955 cartoon.

The action photo on the front cover of that same 1955 programme shows Bobby Charlton's opening goal in the 9-0 FA Youth Cup quarter-final win over Plymouth Argyle the previous Saturday. According to the report, the tie had drawn a crowd of 5,322 to Old Trafford: the word was out about the talent coming through. As well as Charlton (who got a hat-trick), United's Under-18s that day included others mentioned in earlier chapters – Eddie Colman, Duncan Edwards, Wilf

WARTIME TO LOCKDOWN

McGuinness, Ken Morgans, Terry Beckett and Shay Brennan. Edwards played inside-left in the First Division match with Everton.

Programme Spotlights 62: Behind closed doors
19 March 1955, Manchester United 1 Everton 2, Football League First Division

The cartoon by Butterworth was a regular feature in Manchester United's programme. This one is fascinating for two reasons. Firstly, it illustrates how television and advertising might come to dictate the way football was packaged and consumed. The cheque from TV would replace pay at the gate fans for club secretary (there was no treasurer) Walter Crickmer. Then in 2019/20 the season was halted in March due to the coronavirus pandemic, and restarted in June in closed stadia, mainly because of the risk of losing money from the TV contracts. Fans watched on, with options to have recorded crowd noise accompanying the live game to replicate the experience of a match.

Thus this simple, creased programme tells multiple stories. One is about my own roots and boyhood. It speaks of my life in a three-generational family household, with close relations living in quite a small area across north and east Manchester, and visiting each other regularly. I lost contact with David Dawson, and other school friends, just months later as I went to grammar school but they did not. I wonder what life he had? I remain grateful to him for helping me get the autographs of many of that United team, which remain a treasured possession. The programme cost me four pence, a reminder of pre-decimal coinage and the education that went with it, multiplying and dividing numbers by 12 (there were 12 pennies in a shilling), inkwells, blackboards, maps with the British Empire coloured in pink, the walk to school, the simple game of football in the playground and in the street. The programme affirmed, and reaffirms, the pride I had in coming from Manchester, and the football that was a manifestation of my individual and collective identity, which was a prop when I moved to the alien world of a Cambridge college.

The second, and most obvious, story is about the game that day and the world in which it was set. There were the names of the players set out across the centre pages. United: Wood; Foulkes, Byrne; Gibson, Jones, Whitefoot; Berry, Taylor, Webster, Edwards, Scanlon. Everton ('Shirts Royal Blue, Knickers White'): O'Neill; Moore, Donovan; Farrell, Jones, Lello; McNamara, Fielding, Hickson, Parker, Eglington. I had marked in the goalscorers: Scanlon, Parker and Eglington. Eglington was part of Everton's strong connection across the Irish Sea and with the Irish diaspora in Liverpool, a reminder of the poverty that drove so many people out of Ireland. O'Neill, Donovan and skipper Peter Farrell all hailed from Ireland too.

The fixture list, league table and half-time scoreboard show where football power lay in 1955. Wolverhampton Wanderers were two points clear at the top, with a game in hand. Having played 31 of the 42 games in the season, they had lost seven. Sunderland were second. Arsenal and Tottenham Hotspur languished in the lower half of the table, Chelsea were third, Charlton Athletic sixth. Portsmouth were fourth, Manchester City fifth, United seventh and about to slip below Everton. Meanwhile at Anfield, Liverpool were entertaining Lincoln City in a Second Division match.

That day at Old Trafford, entertainment was being presented by the Butlin's Young Ladies' Display Team, performing 'Youth in Rhythm', and by the Beswick Prize Band who were playing six tunes, concluding with the march 'Colonel Bogey', to which, in popular culture, words deriding Nazi leaders had been added during the still-recent world war.

In the black and white photograph on the programme cover, the pitch is muddy and the chimneys and warehouses of the Trafford Park industrial estate rise above the roofing covering the low terrace (which we used to call 'the Cowshed') where people are standing to watch the FA Youth Cup match: a crowd of workers in a Lowry townscape. It is difficult to compress these diverse ephemera into a single 'state-of-the-nation' summary, but it might be something like this: an old industrial country, proudly but slowly recovering from a devastating war, had its simple entertainments, working-class heroes and hopes for a better future for the next generation, mine.

The third story woven across the 12 pages of the programme is of a future that was soon to come. Directly, that is the story of the Busby Babes, who would become league champions in 1956 and 1957, and would have gone to further success but for the Munich air crash. Their names are scattered through the pages, in the listings for the first team, reserves, 'A' team and youth team. As well as those already mentioned in this chapter, there were Viollet, Blanchflower, Pegg, Whelan, and reserve left-back Geoff Bent, who would be another victim of the Munich crash.

Local journalist Tom Jackson's column in the programme discussed the forthcoming close-season 'junior "World Cup"'. It related how a United youth squad had won an international competition in Switzerland the previous year, the FC Blue Stars Tournament, and would return to defend their trophy, as well as playing in Denmark and in another competition in Munich. In Eamon Dunphy's 1991 book, *Sir Matt Busby and Manchester United: A Strange Kind of Glory*, Bobby Charlton recounted the significance of these European games, 'The tournament was a vital part of our education. We played against Italians, Germans and Yugoslavs and learned about their different ways of playing.' Opponents played with a sweeper, something no team in Britain was doing at that time.

The development of young players became a trademark of Manchester United because of that first golden generation, and had an influence across the game much more widely. So the programme also points to a much longer-term future.

So this 1955 programme, like every other one, has multiple stories to tell, each one construed through the reader's own subjectivity. As will be clear by now, I was a child of the welfare state, with my world view shaped by class, gender and place, and any objectivity I had in respect of following football was lost by the age of eight. When I was 13, my heroes, whose pictures I had carefully cut out from the *Manchester Evening News* and *Manchester Evening Chronicle* and pinned to my bedroom wall, died in Munich on their way home from their European Cup tie with Red Star Belgrade. It was my first encounter with grief, made all the deeper because the shock hung over the whole city in those bleak February days, despite the fact that so many households must have suffered the loss of loved ones in the war not so long before. For me, and friends from that place and time, our bond with those wearing the red Manchester United shirts became profound beyond even the normal irrational passion of football fans: it was as if there was a moral imperative for remembrance through reaffirmation.

So when concluding this book by fusing my life and times with football, I hope readers will forgive me if I focus on just a couple of Manchester United programmes that bookend the span of the previous chapters. My education and subsequent career as an academic means that for programmes, as for any other objects, instinctively I ask some critical questions: who has the power and authority to make these objects, how was that power obtained and for whom are the objects made? What do they tell us about times and places, from wartime to the second decade of the 21st century?

Improbable as it may seem today, Manchester United's first home game once national league football resumed again after the war was against Grimsby Town on 31 August 1946. Goals by Jack Rowley and debutant Charlie Mitten gave the home team a 2-1 win. The programme had 16 pages, a surprisingly large number given paper rationing. The front cover, the only place where colour was used, depicts a well-dressed fan, with suit, trilby and red rosette, facing and shaking hands with a player in his United strip, while behind them is a brown leather football that was the norm of the day. I remember how such balls seemed to weigh a ton when wet. The image conveys a sense of equality and common purpose between the players and supporters. Manager Matt Busby, writing his first column, expressed the hope that his regular articles in subsequent programmes 'will bring us even closer together'. You sense the solidarity necessarily forged during the war.

The front-cover fan's attire looks more posh than the flat caps and fags that would have been the norm on the terraces. The photo on page two of Busby addressing the 18 members of the playing staff shows them wearing sports jackets and flannels, and all but captain Johnny Carey wearing a tie, while at the bottom of page three is an advertisement for John Macdonald 'Men's Complete Outfitters' with the eye-catching line, 'Personality! That so coveted possession is greatly added to by apparel of distinction with all its correct accessories.' The same jacket, shirt and tie dress code is evident in the eight other portraits of individual players, officials and journalists on other pages. Every haircut is a short back and sides. It all hints at a continuity of pre-war class, formality, conformity and military discipline.

This same combination was made explicit in the page written by another local journalist, Tom Jackson, who opined, 'Discipline is just as essential in football as on the barrack square.'

Jackson, like Clarke, would lose his life in the Munich crash. In this article he went on to describe an anecdote from when a United team had played in Hamburg a few months before in a friendly against the British Army of the Rhine. For the return rail trip to Calais, 'a special coach normally reserved for high-ranking officers (nothing less than Colonels)' was made available to the club. Jackson continued, 'Imagine the surprise next morning for the brigadiers, major-generals and "what-have-yous" when the United players walked into the dining coach for breakfast.' There they mingled with the top brass, an arrangement repeated at subsequent meals. As they boarded the boat to cross to England, 'a rather aloof type of Army officer' asked who the gatecrashers were. On receiving the answer, Jackson reported that the military man looked 'a trifle astonished', and said, 'Well, if they can play as well as they behave, then, by jingo, they must be pretty good footballers.'

This story told by Jackson feels like a parable for the desired post-war transition as an accommodation between the classes. The footballers would generally be men who had received only an elementary school education, ending at 14 when they had to find a job as best they could in coal mines or factories. They would have spoken with strong regional accents in stark contrast to the way the officers spoke, by jingo! Yet, contradicting expectations, they had behaved impeccably, winning new respect from their traditional 'betters', who therefore did not resent sharing their privileges with them.

In his 'Chairman's Greetings', Mr J.W. Gibson referred to the bombing in March 1941 that had left the club's Old Trafford ground 'damaged beyond repair'. It remained in that state 'owing to the Government policy of issuing only limited licences for building materials while the housing problem is so manifest'. He went on to thank Manchester City for providing a temporary home. There was also a nostalgic pre-war photo of 'the old ground'. Elsewhere in the programme there were references to the players training at the Manchester University facilities at Fallowfield. Reminders of the privations of the time are evident in a couple of the advertisements. Razor blades made in Sheffield were claimed to 'Knock H out of S(H)aving', while Victory V gums and lozenges (2oz for 6d including tax) required no (rationing) points.

On page ten there was a short article about Walter Crickmer, 'our genial secretary'. It told how he was on police duty during the Blitz, when his station received a direct hit by an enemy bomb. 'Walter was a lucky one who escaped alive,' and went on to do important work including storage of government supplies. In fact Crickmer had been buried under rubble for several hours, and sustained injuries to both arms and legs, while a number of his colleagues were killed in the blast. Crickmer was another who died in the Munich crash.

Another Munich victim was Alf Clarke, from the *Manchester Evening Chronicle*. His article recollected the last pre-war game at Charlton Athletic, with searchlights in the night sky on the Friday night, 1 September 1939, the day Germany invaded Poland, and barrage balloons around the Charlton ground the next day. War was declared two days later, on Sunday, 3 September. Clarke went on to honour three young players whose lives were claimed by that war. George Curless had been 'a young full back, of rich promise', who became an RAF pilot, and one day never returned from a bombing mission over Germany. Inside-forward Ben Carpenter had signed from Burton early in 1939; he was lost in the retreat from Dunkirk. Bert Redwood had established himself as the first-choice right-back, but was invalided out of the army. 'I saw him in the dressing room at Maine Road. He was ill and a dying man. I never saw him alive after that.' Finally, George Gladwin, the 'diminutive inside right from Doncaster whose nimble feet had defenders guessing... will never play football again. The Japs slashed his legs to ribbons'.

The 'Editor's Note Book' page also lamented that 'many a man who used to yell "Goal" at Old Trafford will never come back'. It went on to offer a specially warm welcome 'to you ex-servicemen who gather again to cheer Manchester United', noting, 'It's not easy to settle down again after all that. And things are not too easy for anybody.'

It is still painful to read of these tragedies, which doubtless had their equivalents in other programmes that day. However, the cartoon page is also distressing. It portrays other clubs on the '1st Division Ship' in the form of their monikers – including Chelsea (the pensioner), the Bolton Trotter (a pig), and the Derby ram. Above them like a bright sun with a smiley, emoji-like face, is 'United', dropped by a fan with aeroplane wings exhorting 'Atomise 'em'. Below is the line, 'Our own little atom bomb drops today.' This was little more than a year after the devastation wreaked on Hiroshima and Nagasaki. The trivialisation of that human catastrophe says something about attitudes at that time. There was sexist humour too on page six: a man compliments a woman who is 'a bit thoughtless in her speech' on her new shoes, saying that they look comfortable. She replies, 'I like their comfort – they make street walking so easy.' There was also a joke about Stalinism, with a Russian soldier claiming he had the freedom to go to the Kremlin, see Stalin, wave a fist in his face, 'and tell him exactly what he thinks – about the British Foreign Secretary' (the staunchly anti-Soviet Ernest Bevin).

There were 27 names on the list of 'M.U.F.C Professional Playing Staff'. Only three of them were six feet tall. For ten of them, their last club was stated simply as 'Local', a definition that must have been tightly drawn as others were listed as from Radcliffe, Stalybridge, Winsford and St Helens, all places no great distance from the city. Inside-forward Edward Buckle was listed as 'London boy', while Charles Mitten was 'From Scotland as boy.' Again we need to remember that these were men who left school at 14 years of age; 'boy' was an accurate description for many.

The pen portraits of 14 Grimsby players included several who had been with the club before the war. Five players hailed from the north-east of England, including brothers J.V. and S. Hodgson, and there was one Scot. No player from either club was from beyond the British Isles. Below the line-ups in the centre pages was the information that team changes would be indicated by notice board; presumably there was no public address system in operation.

The club was a limited company. The board were listed in the programme. Chairman J.W. Gibson was a businessman, born in Salford, whose company, Briggs, Jones and Gibson, manufactured military uniforms and had prospered in World War I. In 1931 he had loaned £2,000 to United to save them from bankruptcy and enable them to pay players' wages over Christmas. The man who had taken the begging bowl to Gibson was club secretary Walter Crickmer, who was also acting manager at the time. Wigan-born Crickmer had joined the club as a junior clerk just after World War I. He had managed the club through World War II, while also carrying out his police work mentioned above.

H.P. Hardman was another director. A Manchester-born solicitor, he had had a career as a professional footballer with northern clubs (including United) before World War I and also won England caps. Other directors, who I have not been able to track down, were Dr W. Maclean and Mr G.E. Whittaker. The editor of the programme was Sidney F. Wicks, who had been born in Epsom where his father was a blacksmith. He became a Minister in the Congregational Church, which took him to Liverpool. He had worked in the advertising department of the *Manchester Guardian* in the 1920s before founding his own Manchester-based firm that gave advertising and business consultancy.

These then were the people with the power and authority to make the programme, with Wicks as editor the most direct influence. He had stood unsuccessfully as a Liberal candidate in the 1928 Manchester City Council elections and, as well as editing the *Manchester Weekly News*, appears to have given time and support to several voluntary organisations in and around Manchester, though he had moved to Buxton to protect his health from the city's endemic smogs.

Reviewing the backgrounds and records of these leaders of the club in 1946, it is no surprise to find that they were generally middle-class, but what is also clear is that they had deep roots in Manchester and to the club in particular, and that they were not driven by self-interest. In producing the programme, their aim was to reach out to men from in and around Manchester, many of whom had experienced recent active service in the armed forces, and for whom life was still hard after demobilisation. They wanted to reconnect with these people after the hiatus of the war, and to build a new confidence and pride in the club.

Some 70 years later, on 27 November 2016, United hosted West Ham United in a Premier League game that kicked off at 4.30pm on a Sunday, for live TV. It is the most recent United home programme that I have, and was given to me by a friend. The publication is still called *United Review*, one constant over that long period. The image that was traditionally on the cover page of the fan and player shaking hands in front of a football can also still be found, though now on page 66 in 'The United Family – The Section dedicated to you, the fans'. It is no surprise that this modern programme, like its predecessors, seeks to nurture a connection between the club and its fans; programmes always have that aim. However, compared with 1946, the fans have become consumers.

The 84-page, full-colour glossy programme is visually much more appealing than the 1946 version, but it did cost £3.50 rather than the 1946 price of three pence, which would have been equivalent to about 60 pence in 2016, allowing for inflation. Several 2016 pages are used to sell club products: subscriptions to *United Review* and the monthly club magazine, season tickets, the 2016/17 United third shirt (inevitably), and a 'Matchday VIP experience' features on three different pages, costing from £179 (including VAT). Then there is the museum tour (from £12) and official membership (from £22); an asterisk and small print indicates that these lowest prices are for juniors. One page sells the club's TV channel, and another promotes United's presence on various social media outlets, while there is also a page for the club's free fixtures calendar which can be scanned into Apple, Android and Outlook devices. There is another full page for the official free-to-download Premier League app, and one for the *FIFA 17* computer game. These multiple channels of electronic communication and marketing contrast with the only media adverts in the 1946 programme, which were for print media, the *Evening News* and three local weekly newspapers that focused not on the stars of the day but on 'news of the soccer stars of the future'.

As well as those for club merchandise, there are 15 other pages of advertising. One, in colour on a white background, under a heading 'Supporting Manchester United', has the logos of the following global companies: Adidas, AON, Chevrolet, Abengoa, Aeroflot, Aperol Spritz, Apollo, Casillero del Diablo, DHL, EA Sports, Epson, HCL, Marathon Bet, MLILY, Nissin, Swissquote, Tag Heuer, Toshiba Medical and Yanmar. Several of them have full-page advertisements of their own as well: Adidas, Chevrolet (the shirt sponsor), Aeroflot (the club's 'official carrier'), AON (promoting their expertise in Defined Contribution Pensions, Tag Heuer ('proudly keeping the time for Manchester United'), Virgin Money Lounges ('exclusively for Virgin Money customers' and offering 'a range of Man Utd products'), Swissquote ('CFDs and Forex are leveraged products; trading on margin carries a high degree of risk'), EPSON (for their high end printers), Casillero del Diablo wine, and the 'Official Global Noodle Partner of Manchester United Nissin Pot Noodle.' There is also a full page for Heroes, the club's 'Official Formal Footwear Partner'. There are many more advertisements than in 1946, and they are global rather than local, but also the products are directly connected visually, as well as in words, to the club and its star players. In this artful blurring of brands we see a hydra-headed global business that would have been unimaginable 70 years previously, when a 'hero' meant something more profound than an expensive shoe.

Players and coaches had also become globalised. Nationalities of the West Ham players featured included New Zealand, Spain (three), Italy (two), Norway, Argentina (two), Algeria, Senegal, France, Turkey, Switzerland, and Ghana, as well as eight from the British Isles. The Croatian Slaven Bilić was their manager, while José Mourinho of Portugal was in his first season in charge at Old Trafford. Ownership of the business had also changed in a fundamental way. Co-owners were listed as Joel Glazer and Avram Glazer, with Bryan Glazer, Kevin Glazer, Edward Glazer, and Darcie Glazer Kassewitz listed along with Ed Woodward, Richard Arnold, Michael Edelson, and David Gill, along with club legends Sir Bobby Charlton and Sir Alex Ferguson as directors. Manchester United were no strangers to debt before World War II, but J.W. Gibson had loaned his own money to save the club. In contrast, the Glazer family loaded debt on to the club, so that they could own it. Such a leveraged buy-out of other shareholders would have been inconceivable to those directors listed in the 1946 programme. They would have been even more bemused to hear that the new owners of Manchester United were the owners of Tampa Bay Buccaneers, a team playing American 'football'. The Glazers appear to have had no particular interest in 'soccer'; acquisition of Manchester

United was above all a way of securing and expanding their business interests.

Seventy years earlier, fans would have been equally shocked to find a page in the programme proclaiming the club's support for a lesbian, gay, bisexual and transsexual charity. The 2016 programme described how Stonewall FC, 'the UK's first gay football team', had been welcomed to the 'AON Training Complex' for a game against a United XI. In 1946, homosexuality was punishable by imprisonment. The 2016 programme also had a two-page spread given over to junior fans, another group who were invisible in the older editions, and there are women and girls in the photo of fans walking to the game. Similarly, there was a colour photo of West Ham fans heading towards their 'shiny new stadium', which again showed women and children among the crowd. However, nothing in the programme explained the fact that West Ham had been able to acquire the rights to that stadium through a very favourable deal with the London Legacy Development Corporation, which in essence was bankrolled by taxpayers to the benefit of the owners of West Ham, a private company.

Comparing the two programmes, it is clear that football had become a money-making exercise for some very rich people. However, it had also become more explicitly inclusive in terms of race, gender, nationality and sexuality; though it was significantly more exclusive towards young, working-class men, as again the photo of fans going to the game in the 2016 programme confirms. Society and places changed, football changed, and those with power and authority to produce football programmes changed too, and one thing they changed was the relation between the football club and its fans. As one of those fans, I too changed: I went from a boy standing on the terraces to a septuagenarian watching games on TV anywhere in the world, and without buying a programme. The ghosts of my past linger in those fragile pages of programmes from long ago.

The last time I saw a live Premier League game at Old Trafford was on 26 February 2005, sitting high in the stand at the Scoreboard End, as part of a then-record Premier League crowd of 67,989. Two goals by a young Wayne Rooney secured a 2-1 victory over Portsmouth. More than the match, what I remember is the persistent chants of 'United, United, not for sale. United! Not for sale!' The Glazers were circling. Just weeks later, in May, they owned the club. The fans had no say in the matter. In response, some fans set up FC United of Manchester.

Until lockdown, on trips down to Manchester I would go to an FC United game. They began in 2005 in the Second Division of the North West Counties League. In those days, they had no ground, and played home fixtures at Bury's Gigg Lane. By 2015 they had reached the National League North, only to be relegated in 2019 back to the Northern Premier League, where they were well placed when the coronavirus pandemic ended the season prematurely in March 2020. By 2015, fundraising by fans, helped by grants from government and charities, raised the capital needed to build a 4,400-capacity home ground at Broadhurst Park in Moston. It stands on a site where I used to play football and cricket with other lads when I was a teenager, and is not far from the railway lines of Newton Heath where Manchester United were born. Going to home games feels like going home.

The programme for the game against Grantham Town on the Saturday before Christmas in 2019 gives a good indication of what FC United is about, and shows that football can still be enjoyed away from the product offered by plutocrats. The inside cover page has a narrow column down the left-hand side, giving the kind of information most clubs provide about their board and staff. The first line, directly beneath the club badge, reads 'Owners: The Fans'. That same column also spells out the FC United manifesto. Democratically agreed by the club members and owners, it reads:

- The board will be democratically elected by its members
- Decisions taken by the membership will be decided on a one-member, one-vote basis
- The club will develop strong links with the local community and strive to be accessible to all, discriminating against none
- The club will endeavour to make admission prices as affordable as possible, to as wide a constituency as possible
- The club encourage young and local participation, playing and supporting, wherever possible
- The board will strive to avoid outright commercialism
- The club will remain a non-profit organisation

The FC United programme also had two pages on 'the new and extended deal' with Manchester City Council. It included use of the 3G pitch beside the ground for matches in a local junior league and for training by local teams; an academy delivering a BTEC in Sport; a weekly pan-disability football session; FC United community coaches working in local schools and after-school clubs; a weekly football session with asylum seekers who had suffered torture; two weekly walking football sessions for people aged 50 to 75; a weekly football session for adults with mental health conditions; Big Coats Day clothing collections for homeless people; a Christmas dinner event for homeless and vulnerable people; a weekly Sporting Memories Group to help older people overcome social isolation; an annual free entry visit to a home game for youngsters locally and from across Manchester – 'for many this is the first time they have been to a live sporting event'; a programme for local young unemployed people; and, of course, the club pays the Living Wage to its employees. There is a reserve team, youth team, academy teams and women's team. In the 2015 Index of Multiple Deprivation, Moston was ranked 3,686 out of 32,844 areas in England, where the most deprived area is ranked 'one'. Just down the road, Harpurhey was one of the 100 most deprived places. Lockdown threatens the future existence of clubs like this, whose income depends much more on gate receipts than on TV companies.

Programme Spotlights 63: Big coat day

21 December 2019, FC United of Manchester 4 Grantham Town 0, Northern Premier League

This pocket-sized, 20-page programme is in full colour throughout, making extensive use of red, reflecting the team's shirt colours and those of Manchester United. This issue includes information about FC's annual Big Coat Day, when they ask fans to donate warm clothing to support the homeless and vulnerable through the cold winter months. One of the few full-page adverts is for Andys Man Club, a peer to peer support group that addresses the high suicide rates of men under 45. Another page is about raising awareness of the risks of cardiac arrest in young people.

In the game, FC stormed into a 3-0 lead within 15 minutes, with star man Tunde Owolabi bagging a couple in a prolific season, at the end of which he moved to Hamilton Academical in the Scottish Premier League.

In June 2016, far from where I started collecting football programmes, and far from Edinburgh where he was born, I sat next to my son at Soldier Field in Chicago. We were able to enjoy the skills of Lionel Messi, who scored a hat-trick after coming on as a substitute, helping Argentina beat

Panama 5-0 in the Copa America. The game was carried by satellites to a global audience, who would know Messi and his colleagues as household names, even if Panama's best remained unknowns. We bought the 'programme', but it wasn't really a programme at all. It was a magazine covering the whole Copa America finals in the USA, across all the venues. It had been printed before the squads were named, so it did not list the expected line-ups for Argentina v. Panama. It didn't even have the numbers on the shirts. It was big and glossy, and in colour and branded by the logos of the various global corporations acting as sponsors. We gave it away to a young boy who lives across the road from Euan and his family. I wonder if he will still be treasuring it decades from now. How might lockdown change football itself? Will there even still be football programmes? I hope so, for as I have tried to show, 'Programmes! Programmes!' tell the stories of football and life.

Programmes cited in Chapter 14 that are in the collection:

- 31 August 1946, Manchester United 2 Grimsby Town 1, Football League First Division
- 19 March 1955, Manchester United 1 Everton 2, Football League First Division
- 26 February 2005, Manchester United 2 Portsmouth 1, Premier League
- 27 November 2016, Manchester United 1 West Ham United 1, Premier League
- 21 December 2019, FC United of Manchester 4 Grantham Town 0, Northern Premier League

Bibliography

Adamson, R., *Bogota Bandit: The Outlaw Life of Charlie Mitten: Manchester United's Penalty King* (Edinburgh: Mainstream Publishing, 1996).

Best, C., *The Acid Test,* (Liverpool: deCoubertin Books, 2006).

Charlton, R., *The Autobiography: My Manchester United Years,* (London: Headline Book Publishing, 2008).

Connor, J., *Lost Babes: Manchester United and the Forgotten Victims of Munich* (London: Harper Collins, 2010).

Dunphy, E., *Sir Matt Busby and Manchester United: A Strange Kind of Glory* (London: Heinemann, 1991).

Earwaker, J., *The Definitive Guide to Football Programmes* (Ipswich: Chapter 6 Publishing, 1987).

Engels, F., *The Condition of the Working Class in England* (St Albans: Panther,1969).

Eyre, F., *Kicked into Touch – Plus Extra Time* (Keighley: Pomona Books, 2005).

Finn, R., *Champions Again: Manchester United 1957 and 1965* (London: Robert Hale, 1965).

Gardiner, S., *The Wanderer: The Story of Frank Soo* (Stowmarket: Electric Blue Publishing, 2016).

Green, G., *There's Only One United* (London: Hodder and Stoughton, 1978).

Gregg, H. with Anderson, R., *Harry's Game* (Edinburgh and London: Mainstream, 2002).

Larkin, P., *High Windows* (London: Faber and Faber, 1974).

Leighton, J., *Duncan Edwards – The Greatest* (London: Simon and Schuster, 2012).

Magris, C., *Danube* (London: Penguin Random House, 2016).

Packard, V., *The Hidden Persuaders* (London: Longmans, Green & Co, 1957).

Rowlands, A., *Trautmann: The Biography* (Derby: Breedon Books Publishing Company, 2005 edition).

Rybarr, C., *Prague: Guide, Information, Facts* (Prague: Olympia, 1979).

Shaw, P., *Collecting Football Programmes* (St. Albans: Granada Publishing, 1980).

Stiles, N. with Lawton, J., *After the Ball: My Autobiography* (London: Hodder and Stoughton, 2003).

Taylor, R. and Jamrich, K. (eds.), *Puskas on Puskas: The Life and Times of a Footballing Legend* (London: Robson Books, 1998).

Welsh, I., *Trainspotting* (London: Secker and Warburg, 1992).

Whelan, T., *The Birth of the Babes: Manchester United Youth Policy 1950/57* (Manchester: Empire Publications, 2005).

Whittell, P., *Alick Jeffrey – The Original Boy Wonder* (Chronicle Publishing, 2003).

Index of Clubs, Managers and Players

Also available at all good book stores

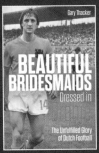

9781785318467

9781785318399

9781785317699

9781785316449

9781785316708

9781785316463

9781785316791

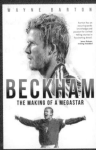

9781785316760

9781785316814